T0330768

ROUTLEDGE LIBRARY EDITIONS: ACCOUNTING HISTORY

Volume 37

A SCOTTISH CONTRIBUTION TO ACCOUNTING HISTORY

A SCOTTISH CONTRIBUTION TO ACCOUNTING HISTORY

Edited by
T. A. LEE

Routledge
Taylor & Francis Group

LONDON AND NEW YORK

First published in 1986 by Garland Publishing, Inc.

This edition first published in 2021
by Routledge
2 Park Square, Milton Park, Abingdon, Oxon OX14 4RN

and by Routledge
52 Vanderbilt Avenue, New York, NY 10017

Routledge is an imprint of the Taylor & Francis Group, an informa business

British Library Cataloguing in Publication Data
A catalogue record for this book is available from the British Library

ISBN: 978-0-367-33564-9 (Set)
ISBN: 978-1-00-304636-3 (Set) (ebk)
ISBN: 978-0-367-50369-7 (Volume 37) (hbk)
ISBN: 978-1-00-304973-9 (Volume 37) (ebk)

Publisher's Note
The publisher has gone to great lengths to ensure the quality of this reprint but points out that some imperfections in the original copies may be apparent.

Disclaimer
The publisher has made every effort to trace copyright holders and would welcome correspondence from those they have been unable to trace.

A SCOTTISH CONTRIBUTION TO ACCOUNTING HISTORY

T. A. Lee, editor

Garland Publishing, Inc.
New York and London
1986

For a complete list of Garland's publications in accounting,
please see the final pages of this volume.

The articles in this book are reprinted with the permission of the following:

Abacus, 'Bibliographical Notes on Five Examples of Pacioli's Summa (1494) in
Scotland'. *The Accountant's Magazine*, 'The First Scottish Book on
Accounting: Robert Colinson's *Idea Rationaria* (1683)', 'A Scottish Farmer
and His Accounts: 1822–3', 'A "Careful and Most Ingenious Fabrication of
Imaginary Accounts": Scottish Railway Company Accounts Before 1868', 'The
Emergent Professionals', 'Accountants in Old Aberdeen', 'Qualification for
Membership a Hundred Years Ago', 'Accounting at Heriot Watt College 1885–1920'.
Journal of Accounting Research , 'The Historical Development of Internal
Control From the Earliest Times to the End of the Seventeenth Century'.
Frank Graham, 'A Pitman's Notebook'. *Accounting Historians Journal*,
'Whether Malcom's is Best or Old Charge and Discharge', 'Early Debates on
Financial and Physical Capital'. *Accounting and Business Research*, 'Early
Canal Company Accounts: Financial and Accounting Aspects of the Forth and
Clyde Navigation, 1768–1816', 'The Evolution and Revolution of Financial
Accounting: A Review Article'.

Library of Congress Cataloging-in-Publication Data

A Scottish contribution to accounting history.

(Accounting thought and practice through the years)
Includes index.
1. Accounting—Scotland—History. I. Lee, T. A.
(Thomas Alexander) II. Series.
HF5616.G72S377 1986   657'.09411   86-9950
ISBN 0-8240-7867-5

Design by Bonnie Goldsmith

The volumes in this series are printed on acid-free, 250-year-life paper.

Printed in the United States of America

*This book has been published on behalf of
the Scottish Committee on Accounting History
of the Institute of Chartered Accountants of Scotland.*

CONTENTS

Introduction

Preprofessionalism

Professionalism

Overview

INTRODUCTION

The Scottish contribution to the history and development of modern accounting has been considerable despite Scotland's small population and relative lack of economic resources. Prior to the formation of professional accountancy bodies in the nineteenth century, there was a Scottish tradition of businessmen who were involved in the practice and, on occasion, teaching of accounting. Men such as Alexander Herreot, George Watson, and Alexander Farquharson helped provide an eighteenth-century basis for the emergence of professional bodies in the nineteenth century.[1] The forerunner of all such bodies was founded by Royal Charter in 1854 as the Society of Accountants in Edinburgh.[2] Several of the society's members at the beginning of the twentieth century were responsible for the formation of practicing firms that were the beginning of today's worldwide accounting organizations—for example, George Touche and James Marwick.[3]

This anthology is a small celebration of that Scottish influence and tradition. The writings are relatively recent contributions to the study of accounting history and have been written mainly by Scots about predominantly Scottish matters. In particular, the collection is a reminder of the work of the Scottish Committee on Accounting History of The Institute of Chartered Accountants of Scotland. It is dedicated to the memory of two of the founding members of the committee.

The Scottish Committee on Accounting History

In October 1970 the first International Symposium of Accounting Historians was held in Brussels. It was resolved that each participating country should form an accounting history committee with the objectives of bringing together accountants interested in the history of the subject; improving research facilities for accounting history; helping to provide material for research in accounting history; and collaborating with other accounting history bodies. Professor Bob Parker, then of the University of Dundee and now of the University of Exeter, approached

The Institute of Chartered Accountants of Scotland with the suggestion of forming an accounting history committee in Scotland. In April 1971 the institute's council approved the formation of its Scottish Committee on Accounting History (SCAH) with a remit to promote the study of accounting history and to establish and maintain contact with accounting historians and with other committees of accounting history throughout the world.

The first convener of SCAH was Professor Parker, and its original membership included leading practitioners and nonaccounting historians and antiquarians. The total membership has numbered usually between six or seven persons, at all times maintaining a balance of accountants and nonaccountants.

During the 1970s SCAH undertook a number of projects including the formation of a collection of corporate financial reports for use by researchers into the history of reporting (under the direction of Professor Tom Lee); a bibliography of books and writings located in Scotland and of interest to accounting historians (undertaken by Professor Bob Parker and Janet Pryce-Jones); and a study of the original members of the Institute (the earliest members being researched by James Stewart, and later members by Moyra Kedslie). Two major publications resulted from this research. [4] Both these publications were published originally by the Institute, with Garland Publishing reprinting the first in 1984 and the second in 1985. Further work supervised by SCAH includes an anthology of items from *The Accountant's Magazine* by Colin Storrar, which is published in this Garland Series, as well as this collection of writings. It should be noted that *The Accountant's Magazine* is the official journal of The Institute of Chartered Accountants of Scotland and, when founded in 1897, was one of the first such journals.

Founding Members

Two of the founding members of SCAH died recently, and this collection is dedicated to them. In their different ways they represented the diversity that exists amongst accounting historians.

Tom Robertson was a senior lecturer in accounting at the University of Edinburgh and a member of The Institute of Chartered Accountants in England and Wales. Born in South Shields in the North-East of England, he spent the majority of his working life as a university lecturer in Scotland. During that time he developed his interest in history, concentrating largely on that of the coal-mining industry. His major publication in this area is reproduced in part in this collection.[5] He was responsible also for the reproduction of a nineteenth-century glossary of coal-mining terms.[6]

James Stewart, on the other hand, was a leading practitioner member of The Institute of Chartered Accountants of Scotland. He was a member of its council from 1956 to 1961 and president from 1962 to 1963. He wrote occasionally on accounting matters, and his best-known contribution was his work on the earliest members of the institute mentioned above.

Contents

The contents of this anthology can be divided into two main sections. The first deals specifically with the development of accounting thought and practice prior to the emergence of a regulated accountancy profession in the mid-nineteenth century. It reveals the considerable activity that took place over the centuries and that provided a platform for the professional developments of the last hundred and thirty years.

The second section relates to the first sixty or seventy years of the accountancy profession and portrays some of the problems that had to be faced and the people involved in resolving them. As with the first section, the accent of the writings is predominantly Scottish. The writers, too, are mainly Scottish. The choice of writers and writings has been conditioned by this link to Scotland—first to SCAH (Dunlop, Lee, Mepham, Parker, Robertson, Stewart, and Vamplew have been or are members of SCAH, and Kedslie has worked on a project initiated by SCAH) and, second, in relation to the small community of Scottish writers on accounting history matters in recent times (Forrester is the only such writer who has not been associated with SCAH).

One further comment is appropriate in relation to the choice of writers. Apart from Lee, two other writers are or have been members of SCAH and produced historical writings on a fairly regular basis during its history. Bob Parker, the first convener of SCAH, recently produced an anthology of his writings on accounting history for Garland,[7] and it was felt inappropriate to reproduce these further in this collection other than one item on Colinson that has a distinctly Scottish flavor and was written during his convenership. Likewise, Professor Chris Nobes of the University of Strathclyde has reproduced his historical work recently with Garland.[8] Such necessary exclusions in no way reflect the valuable contributions made by both men to the work of SCAH.

Preprofessionalism

Modern accounting could not exist in its present form without the generations of accountants, businessmen, and teachers who developed its principles and practices over many centuries. Dunlop (Paper 1) examines one of the earliest and most important contributors in this evolutionary process—that is, Luca Pacioli and his seminal work on double-entry bookkeeping published in 1494. She examines several copies of the book that exist in Scotland and analyzes differences in layout, presentation, and typeface. In doing so, she helps to remind the reader of the importance of the written word in accounting development and how difficulties of publishing in these early times were a severe constraint on the spread of such development.

In Paper 2 Parker reveals the extent of Pacioli's influence in terms of accounting texts. Colinson's text represents evidence of the spread of knowledge of double-entry bookkeeping procedures in written form from Italy to Scotland via the Netherlands. However, it had taken nearly two hundred years for this to happen, and Colinson's text should be regarded as one of the first to appear in the UK. This is not to suggest that double-entry bookkeeping had not appeared in the UK before Colinson's book.[9] But Parker's paper does reveal the relatively primitive form of accounting of the times—the procedures being directed mainly at recording transactions.

The growing sophistication of accounting procedures over the centuries is highlighted in the wider context of internal control systems by Lee (Paper 3). Providing evidence from the earliest of times up to the beginning of the eighteenth century, his paper shows the consistent awareness of businessmen and others for internal control procedures. This growing sophistication of business and businessmen is portrayed in Robertson's account of a coal-mining manager's diary in the middle of the eighteenth century (Paper 4). The relative complexity of the management tasks are evidenced in the extracts reproduced—that is, the estimating of costs and profit, the forecasting of the life of the colliery, and the need for a rudimentary management information system. But there is little evidence of the existence of sophisticated accounting systems with which to aid such a manager.

This lack of accounting sophistication is the focus of Forrester's paper (5) relating to the eighteenth-century controversy in Glasgow College concerning the then need to improve the professionalism of its management—particularly by the introduction of an adequate accounting system. Because of the lack of professional accountants at the time, it is interesting to note the (unsuccessful) attempts of bankers and lawyers to introduce such a system.

The rudimentary form of accounting systems in the late eighteenth and early nineteenth centuries is a theme continued by Forrester in a further paper (6). In this case, a canal company is examined, and the analysis portrays the steady improvement in reporting systems, auditing difficulties faced by nonaccounting auditors, problems caused by the accounting system being in the hands of one individual, and the complex relationships that existed (and still exist) between the public and private sectors of the economy.

Robertson (Paper 7) provides an insight into the considerable intelligence applied to the problems of a business "start-up" situation—in this case, a Scottish farm in the early nineteenth century. In particular, the accounting system of Trotter was constructed specifically to aid his management decisions, and he placed considerable importance on accounting cost allocations for this purpose. He also regarded net realizable values to be important information for a businessman. Whereas Trotter perceived accounting allocations as a useful information support for management, the worst side of this process is seen in Vamplew (Paper 8), in which deliberate manipulations of allocated accounting data were made in financial reports in order to justify the payment of dividends to shareholders of a railway company. This is an example of the type of problem that arose and gave need for company legislation requiring compulsory audits. The financial reports were unintelligible and in a very primitive form—the method of manipulation concerning the classification of expenditure as either revenue or capital.

Professionalism

Vamplew's example of mid-nineteenth century manipulation in financial statements is an appropriate point at which to examine the gradual emergence of a regulated accountancy profession in Scotland and elsewhere. Stewart's review (Paper 9) is a summary of his larger work.[10] It describes the setting up of the Edinburgh and Glasgow Societies of Accountants within the context of railway scandals, insolvencies, and industrialization. Businessmen and lawyers were not admitted to membership, and the earliest members were not examined on their knowledge of accounting. Kedslie (Paper 10) provides a picture of the situation in the other remaining Scottish society in Aberdeen. Her findings reveal that situation being influenced by the then banking crisis, the earliest members of the society apparently having, on average, a better educational background than their Edinburgh and Glasgow counterparts.

The transitional and relatively loose arrangements for membership to these professional bodies on their formation were soon to be overtaken by necessary formalization of educational and training requirements. Stewart (Paper 11) examines these in detail and discovers certain features that continue to this day (a preliminary examination) and others that have long since disappeared (bursary and fellowship awards to encourage good examination performances). He also evidences a reluctance for would-be chartered accountants to take the prescribed examinations.

The Scottish tradition in high-quality education very much affected the formation of a regulated accountancy profession, and Mitchell and Mepham's paper (12) describes the existence of accounting in Heriot-Watt College (now University) at the end of the nineteenth and beginning of the twentieth centuries. The lecturers concerned were chartered accountants and, as well as teaching, were well-known contributors to the then accountancy literature. In fact, George Lisle (a lecturer from 1896 to 1903) was a fairly prolific writer.[11]

This academic flavor is continued by Lee (Paper 13) in his detailed exploration of a complex debate on capital maintenance that took place at the beginning of the twentieth century; it is included in this volume as evidence of the growing maturity of the accountancy profession and the links that then existed between academics and practitioners—in some instances, the two roles being conducted by the same person. The paper also reveals that the issues concerned continue to be debated today, and this is the somewhat depressing theme of the last overview paper (Paper 14)—that a study of the history of accounting evidences the propensity for accountants not to resolve issues despite the maturity of the profession and the inevitable re-cycling of these issues. It is hoped, however, that there is also sufficient evidence in this volume that the part that Scottish accountants have played in accounting history and the maturity of the accountancy profession has more than outweighed the resolution of its problems.

NOTES

1. Institute of Chartered Accountants of Scotland, *A History of the Chartered Accountants of Scotland From the Earliest Times to 1954*, Garland Publishing, 1984, pp. 1–19.

2. Ibid, pp. 20–31.

3. T. A. Wise, *Peat, Marwick, Mitchell and Co.: 85 Years*, Peat, Marwick, Mitchell and Co., 1982, pp. 1–7 and 29.

4. R. H. Parker and J. Pryce-Jones, *Accounting in Scotland: A Historical Bibliography*, First Edition, 1974, and Second Edition, 1976; and J. Stewart, *Pioneers of a Profession: Chartered Accountants to 1879*, 1977.

5. T. Robertson, *A Pitman's Notebook*, Frank Graham, 1970.

6. G. C. Greenwell, *A Glossary of Terms Used in the Coal Trade of Northumberland and Durham*, Bemrose and Sons, 1849.

7. R. H. Parker, *Papers on Accounting History*, Garland Publishing, 1984.

8. C. W. Nobes, *The Development of Double Entry*, Garland Publishing, 1984.

9 See C. W. Nobes, "The Gallerani Account Book of 1305–1308," *The Accounting Review*, April 1982, pp. 303–10.

10. Stewart, *op cit*.

11. For example, G. Lisle, *Accounting in Theory and Practice*, reprinted by Arno Press, 1976.

Preprofessionalism

ABACUS, Vol. 21, No. 2, 1985

ANNA B. G. DUNLOP

Bibliographical Notes on Five Examples of Pacioli's *Summa* (1494) in Scotland

Among five examples of the '*Summa*' (1494), all in Scotland, four show minor bibliographical variations, but the fifth is a major variant.

Typography, standard of printing, misprints and correction‹ aberrations of woodcut initial letters, paper and watermarks, collation, bindings and manuscript annotations are all examined, and relevant works of reference noted.

Some possible inferences are drawn.

Illustrations of the typesettings and drawings of the watermarks are provided, as is an appendix classifying the main variations found.

The aim is to provide a methodological guide to the bibliographical comparisons which underlie textual comparisons.

Key words: Bookkeeping; Books; History.

3

Of the five *Summas* examined, two are the property of The Institute of Chartered Accountants of Scotland, Edinburgh. In 1982 they were deposited on long-term loan, along with the rest of the Institute's Antiquarian Book Collection, in the National Library of Scotland, Edinburgh. The other three copies[1] are respectively in the libraries of the University of Glasgow, University of Edinburgh and Royal Observatory, Edinburgh (Crawford Library).

Four of the *Summas* are examples of what is generally agreed to be the first state of the first edition (editito princeps). (See Antinori, 1980; Dunlop, 1961).

The fifth, the 'Edinburgh' *Summa* of the Scottish Institute, is a variant of the first edition. The Scottish Institute's other copy is referred to as the 'Aberdeen' *Summa*, because it was sent to the Institute's headquarters from its then Aberdeen Library.

All five *Summas* are in good condition. All are set in romano-gothic type and have some manuscript notes in various hands, some of which, to judge by their style, were added early in the life of the volume. The book consists of two works by Pacioli, 'Arithmetica' and 'Geometria', bound together in that order.

---

[1] In English, 'copies' may mean 'replicas', but equally may mean 'examples', especially of a book, in which case it means 'originals', as it is used here.

ANNA DUNLOP now retired, was the Keeper of the Antiquarian Book Collection of the Institute of Chartered Accountants of Scotland and is a member of the Scottish Committee on Accounting History.

The paper was presented at the Fourth International Congress of Accounting Historians, at Pisa in 1984. The author is indebted to Mr J. Baldwin (Glasgow University Library); Dr J. T. D. Hall (Edinburgh University Library); Dr. B. P. Hillyard (National Library of Scotland); Mr A. Macdonald (Royal Observatory Library, Edinburgh); and the Hon. Mrs Jane Roberts (Curator of the Print Room, Royal Library, Windsor) for giving their time to help and for sharing their expertise. She also thanks Professor C. Antinori (Parma University); Professor T. A. Lee (University of Edinburgh); and Dr G. A. Lee (University of Nottingham), for their encouragement.

The following notes were compiled in response to a request from Professor Antinori for comparisons among these copies of the *Summa*. The aim has been to provide a sufficiently detailed bibliographical framework to help others to identify other variants of the *Summa* (1494) and to lay a base for other researchers who may wish to carry out textual comparisons. It may also act as a methodological guide to research on other old books.

'Aberdeen' Summa (Aber.)

This was taken as the most easily accessible basis of the bibliographical comparison and therefore the standard against which the other four *Summas* were compared. Later evidence confirmed the likelihood that it was, in fact, probably the earliest printed of the five *Summas* examined.

Its provenance shows that it had belonged previously to The Institute of Chartered Accountants in England & Wales, in London. While in the possession of the English Institute, it had been fully bound in red morocco by Zaehnsdorff (signed), with that Institute's insignia stamped in gold on the front cover, and with the pages gilt-edged on three sides. In 1933 the English Institute, lacking a second edition of the *Summa* (1523) and having more than one copy of the first edition, offered one of their first edition *Summas* to the Scottish Institute's then Aberdeen library, in exchange for the second edition *Summa* which was there.

The type face used in the *Summa* (Aber.) is consistent throughout and accords with typesetting A, described by B. Boncompagni (1862-63), as quoted by Clarke (1974) but includes on the first page of the Arithmetica, folio 1 *recto* (A), the seven lines printed in red noted in Boncompagni's setting C.

The decorative initials, though roman, are consistent in their style, except for one or two slight variations introduced from other founts.

The first page of text of the Arithmetica includes a woodcut border of a white interlaced design, Celtic in style, on a black background. The text begins with the letter L, which is ornamented, in a large square, with a line drawing, against a 'snowstorm' background, of a monk holding a pair of compasses, with an open book in front of him. Presumably it was intended to represent Pacioli, who became a Franciscan friar while still a professor of mathematics.

This woodcut block letter L appears four more times in the book, one place being the beginning of the text of Distinctio nona (9) Tractatus xi (De computis & de scripturis), the treatise on double-entry book-keeping, at f. 198 *verso* (A). The other positions are ff. 111 *verso* (A), 150 *recto* (A) 182 *verso* (A) and 198 *verso* (A).

The following pecularities appear only in the *Summa* (Aber.): f. 23 *recto* (A) folio number is printed as 24, f. 57 *recto* (A) folio number is printed as 64, f. 71 *recto* (A) folio number is not printed, and f. 223 *verso* (A) decorative initial A is the right way up. The folio number mistakes, corrected in all four other *Summas*, are typical of early printings, though f. 223 *verso* (A) may have been printed later in the run. Two watermarks, a duck and a set of scales (a hanging weighing balance) have been identified in this *Summa*. These are the most easily found identifying features of the *editio princeps Summa*, compared with the other four *Summas* studied.

Glasgow University Library Summa *(GUL)*

The University of Glasgow acquired this *Summa* in 1928, when it was bequeathed, along with the rest of his book collection, by David Murray, a Glasgow lawyer who was a noted historian and bibliophile (Stevelinck, 1972). He mentions Pacioli's *Summa* in his posthumously published book on the history of accounting (Murray, 1930).

This *Summa* is half bound in leather, with pages gilt-edged on three sides. Someone has inserted, throughout, manuscript paragraph signs in red ink.

Typographically it agrees with the description of the *Summa* (Aber.), although there are a few minor differences (some of which have been detailed above, by implication, in the list of distinctions peculiar to that *Summa*).

In addition, in the *Summa* (GUL): f. 209 *recto* (A) 'questi' (last word) is printed as 'quest'; f. 25 *recto* (G) 'Modus' (in a subheading) is correctly aligned. The watermarks are the same as in the *Summa* (Aber.)

5

Edinburgh University Library Summa *(EUL)*

Another distinguished donor was responsible for the presentation of this *Summa*. This was Philip Kelland, Professor of Mathematics at the University of Edinburgh from 1838 to 1879, whose signature appears on the fly-leaf. The book is quarter-bound in vellum, on marbled boards. The edges of the printed pages are coloured red.

Again, it is typographically similar to the *Summa* (Aber.), though not entirely, e.g. f. 25 *recto* (G) 'Modus' is correctly aligned.

A particularly interesting manuscript note on the first page (Contents) adds '& fuorj' ('and elsewhere') after 'del quaderno in vinegia' ('on the ledger in Venice'), referring to the double-entry treatise.

Additional manuscript pages, whose watermark differs from those of the printed pages, are bound in at the end of the printed pages. Here the fore-edges are left untrimmed and uncoloured. The MS consists of 29 folios, together with the *verso* of the last printed folio, making 59 pages.

The manuscript begins on the *verso* (blank of printing) of f. 76 (Geometria). Some of the MS pages, a few of which are in Latin, though most are in Italian, bear the dates 1497, 1501, 1502 etc. The MS must therefore have been added to the *Summa* (EUL) by its first, or a very early, owner.

Most of the pages are in the same hand, a fast, cursive, pre-italic script, different from the writing in marginal notes in the printed part of the book, though similar to the '& fuorj' noted above. It is a small, assured handwriting. The only material breaks in it are on ff. 19 *verso* and 20 *recto*, which are blank, and on ff. 20 *verso* and 21 *recto*, where the handwriting changes to a larger, more irregular style, but still in Italian. Thereafter it reverts to the original hand.

Folio 3 *verso* has the name 'philippi callandrj' at the top, and the first line contains the word 'denaro' ('money'). Many pages have the sign of the cross (+) at the top. There are many geometrical diagrams in the earlier pages. The pages in a different hand contain a mysterious circular diagram with an inscription, and a dagger in the centre.

No reference to this MS has been found in Kelland's published pamphlets in

Edinburgh University Library. However, Dr J. T. D. Hall has identified the presumed writer of the main MS as Filippo Calandri, a Florentine, whose 'Aritmetica', now extremely rare, was printed in Florence by Lorenzo de Morgiani and Giovanni Thedesco da Maganza ('the German from Mainz') and issued on 1 January 1491.

As a Florentine, it would be natural for Calandri — presumably an early, or the first, owner of the *Summa* (EUL) — to dispute Pacioli's description of double-entry as 'the method of Venice', by adding '& fuorj' ('and elsewhere'), since Florence may well have preceded Venice in its use!

Acting on further information from Dr Hall, an excellent copy of Calandri's book was examined, by courtesy of Mr A. Macdonald, in the Crawford Library of the Royal Observatory, Edinburgh. It is a small volume, very well set and printed by the Italian/German partnership, in both roman and romano-gothic types, but with more primitive arabic numerals than those in any of the *Summas*. Calandri does not include money calculations, although he has a ready-reckoner.

It would seem that the manuscript by Filippo Calandri (?) might repay study by a researcher with the ability to read the script in its entirety.

The watermarks in the *Summa* (EUL) are the duck and the scales, as in the two previous copies, and, for the MS pages, a serpent twined around a tall cross growing out of the top of a bull's head.

Royal Observatory, Edinburgh (Crawford Library) Summa *(RO)*

The Crawford Library is the greatest antiquarian library in the world on astronomy and related subjects. It was presented to the Observatory by the 26th Earl of Crawford (who was also the 9th Earl of Balcarres). The offer of his book collection was made by the Earl in 1888, on condition that the Government built a new observatory in Scotland. (The closure of the previous Royal Observatory in Edinburgh, in the centre of the city, was under consideration). A new Royal Observatory was begun, on the outskirts of the city, and Lord Crawford's books were deposited there during the 1890s.

He was a notable astronomer himself, with a private observatory at Dunecht, in Aberdeenshire. He also donated his instruments to the new Observatory. His library was mainly based on the catalogue of the Pulkovo Library in what is now Leningrad, and he had agents throughout Continental Europe helping him to collect the books he needed.

Among these books was a copy of Pacioli's *Summa* (1494). The *Summa* (RO) was bought for the Earl in 1879, along with other items, from the library of a French Professor of Mathematics, Michael Chasles. Its price was 60 francs. This has been computed as equivalent to £2. 10s. (£2.50) sterling!

The *Summa* (RO) is fully bound in tree calf, which is in good condition, although the joints and spine have been refurbished. The fore-edges of the pages have been slightly cropped, so that one or two marginal printings have been damaged.

This copy resembles the *Summa* (Aber.) closely, though as usual, not in all respects. Two peculiarities noticed are: f. 2 *recto* (G) 'f' in the last diagram is correct, and f. 65 *recto* (G) paragraph 85 is correctly numbered.

There are a few manuscript annotations, but it is clear that one owner, writing

6

in a classic italic hand in Italian, did not entirely agree with Pacioli: in the margin opposite the last paragraph of f. 160 *recto* (A) is written, tersely, 'falsa'!

The watermarks in the *Summa* (RO) are even more difficult to see than in the other four *Summas* studied. However, it has been possible to identify the duck watermark in the preliminary pages, and the scales can be partially seen in f. 74 (G).

'Edinburgh' Summa *(Edin. ICAS)*

This *Summa* has been designated the 'Edin. ICAS' copy because it was presented, around 1900, to The Institute of Chartered Accountants of Scotland (then known as the Society of Accountants in Edinburgh) by an Edinburgh member, Richard Brown, C.A., who was, in his spare time, an accounting historian and bibliophile (Brown, 1905). He was the founder of the Institute's Antiquarian Book Collection, of which the nucleus was his own collection. He bought this *Summa* shortly before presenting it, probably on one of his journeys to Continental Europe. It is recorded that he paid £2. 10s. (£2.50) for it, the same price as Lord Crawford paid for his! According to a manuscript note on the first page of the book, it was at one time in the Biblioteca Fontaninia. It is plainly bound in paper-covered boards.

As already indicated, this is a variant example of the first edition, distinguished in particular by the omission, on the first page of text (f. 1 *recto* (A)), of the white on black interlaced woodcut border and by the replacement, on the same page, of the Pacioli portrait capital L by an even larger square floriated roman L, in white on a black background.

Moreover, the text type for the first 52 pages (ff. 1 *recto*-26 *verso* (A)) is different from Type A, as shown in Boncompagni (1862-63). Type B appears again at ff. 31 *recto*-33 *verso* (A); f. 40 *recto* & *verso* (A); and ff. 1 *recto* & *verso* and 8 *recto* & *verso* (G). In the Arithmetica ff. 1 *recto*-24 *verso* make three complete sections (a, b, c); ff. 25 *recto*-26 *verso* and 31 *recto*-32 *verso* form the two outer sheets of section (d); ff. 33 *recto* & *verso* and 40 *recto* & *verso* the outer sheet of section (e); and ff. 1 *recto* & *verso* and 8 *recto* & *verso* the outer sheet of the first section (A) of the Geometria. Thus, in no case do type A and type B appear on the same sheet of paper. In all, there are 64 pages set in type B. The rest of the book is set in type A.

The decorative initials in Type B are consistent, but they differ from the initials used with type A.

As might be expected, there are three watermarks, the duck and the scales as before, but for the pages in type B, a hat.

Manuscript notes in the margins are unremarkable, except for three short notes, on ff. 1 *recto* and 168 *verso* (A), in a very small, apparently reversed, handwriting. It was tempting to ascribe these to Leonardo da Vinci who habitually used mirror-writing (partly because he was left-handed) and who is known to have bought a copy of Pacioli's *Summa* (1494) for 119 soldi soon after it was published. Although Pacioli and Leonardo were close friends, Pacioli does not seem to have given Leonardo a complimentary copy! However, this hypothesis on the notes has been discounted by Professor Carlo Pedretti, the expert on Leonardo da Vinci, who was shown a photograph of them when he visited the Royal Library, Windsor. Another mystery!

7

In type B, some mistakes of type A have been perpetuated, others have been corrected, and some new mistakes have been made. These are listed in Appendix 1.

Peculiarities of the *Summa* (Edin. ICAS) only, in type A, include: f. 52 *recto* (A) the folio number is not printed; f. 92 *verso* (A) 'trovare' (last word) is correctly printed (instead of 'trovar', with 'e' in the line above); f. 146 *verso* (A) the first two or three letters of the first eight lines are not printed; f. 209 *verso* (A) 'simili' (first word) is correctly aligned; f. 6 *recto* (G) 'e' in marginal diagram correctly printed; and f. 58 *recto* (G) signature 'Hij' is correct (instead of 'ij').

It is difficult to draw firm inferences from these peculiarities. Assuming that the type A folios used for the *Summa* (Edin. ICAS) were printed at the same time as the type A folios for the other *Summas* (because of the unlikelihood of type being kept standing) but were not collated until much later when they were needed to produce extra copies of the *Summa* and had to be supplemented by type B folios, it is possible that the type A folios in the *Summa* (Edin. ICAS) had been rejected earlier, or were proofs taken before the original printing run was begun. This might account for ff. 52 *recto* (A) and 146 *verso* (A), but the rest, being correct in this *Summa* only, seem to have been printed early in the original run. On the other hand, the differences are all in vulnerable positions, and the deficiencies of the other versions could have occurred and been noticed during the run, and a pause made to correct them in folios towards the end of the run.

However, the presswork of the *Summa* (Edin. ICAS) seems on the whole better than that of the *Summa* (Aber.) for the type A pages as well as for the later printed type B pages. Time and again, if a letter at a corner of the type area, or a fraction, were indistinct in the *Summa* (Aber.), it was possible to identify it in the *Summa* (Edin. ICAS), especially in the Geometria. On several pages the decorative initials are over-inked in all but the *Summa* (Edin. ICAS), in the type A pages.

This would argue that some type A folios in the *Summa* (Edin. ICAS) may have been among the earliest of the first printing run and, being possibly at the bottom of the pile, were not used until the last.

Collation of the Summa *(1494)*

The *Summa* is a large book, both in the page size and in the number of pages. The table of contents of the Arithmetica appears at the beginning, that of the Geometria at the end.

It was printed in folios, that is, sheets of paper folded once, to make two leaves or folios (four pages). It consists mostly of eight-folio (16-page) sections (stitched gatherings). The folio numbers appear on folio *recto* (right-hand page) only, so that left-hand pages are referred to as folio *verso* of the same number. The register of the printed signature numbers of sheets, showing the collation for binding, has been written by a comparatively recent hand, at the beginning of the *Summa* (Aber.) thus:

[1] a – z ɩ ᴄ ^{8}ʮ^{10}AA^{14}|A – H^8 I K^6 = 308 leaves (616 pages).

(I have inserted a vertical division between the Arithmetica and Geometria.)

The letters 'j' and 'u' are omitted from the signature letters, in favour of 'i' and 'v', and 'w' is omitted altogether. The signatures are normally shown on consecutive

9

Pacioli, *Summa de Arithmetica*, 1494. First page of text of Arithmetica (f.1 *recto* (A)), showing the dedication, set in type A, with L initial portrait block of the author, and interlaced border (reduced in size).

155

10

Aquantita Magnanimo Duca: e si nobile z excellēte cosa che molti phylosophi per questo lhano giudicata ala substantia para: ecōessa coeterna. Peroche hano cognosciuto per verū modo alcuna cosa in rerū natura sença lei nō potere existere. Per la qual cosa de lei itēdo (cō laiuto de colui che li nostri sensi reggi) tractarne: nonche per altri priscbi e antichi phylosophi nonne sia copiosamente tractato: e in theorica e pratica. Ma per che lor vieti gia ali tempi nostri sonno molto obscuri: e damolti male aprese: ale pratiche vulgari ma le applicati: diche i loro operationi molto variano: e con grandi elaboriosi affanni mettano in opera: si de numeri cōmo de misure: unde di lei parlando non intendo se non quāto che ala pratica e operare sia mestiero: mescolandoci secōdo lluogbi opportuni ancora la theorica: caula de tale operare: si de numeri cōmo de geometria. Ma prima accio meglio ̄qllo che sequita se habia apprehendere: essa quantita vniversiremo secōdo el nostro proposito: ediuidendola aciascun suo membro assegnaremo sua propria e vera diffinitione e descriptione. E alora poi sequira quello che Arist. vici in secondo poster. Uc enim maxime scitur aliquid cum habetur suum quid est zc.

Summa (Aber.) *editio princeps*, 1494; initial L portrait block (text type A).

Aquātita Magnanimo Duca e si nobile z excelléte cosa che molti pbilosophi p ̄qsto lhano giudicata ala substātia para: e comessa coeterna. Perocbe hano cognosciuto p verū modo alcuna cosa in rep natura senza lei nō potere existere. Per la qual cosa de lei itēdo (cō laiuto de colui che li nostri sensi reggi) tractarne: nōcbe p altri priscbi e antichi pbylosopbi nōne sia copiosaméte tractato: e l theorica e pratica. Ma p che lor vieti gia ali tēpi nostri sono molto obscuri: e da molti male apresi: eale praticbe vulgari male applicati: vicbe in loro opationi molto variano: e cō grādi elaboriosi affanni mettano in opa: si de nūeri cōmo de misure: vnde di lei parlādo nō intēdo se nō quāto che ala pratica e opare sia mestiero: me scolādoci secōdo iluogbi opportuni ancora la theorica: e causa de tale opare: si de nu meri cōmo de geometria. Ma pria acio meglio ̄qllo che sequita se habia apphende re: essa quātita diuideremo secōdo el nfo ppofito: ediuidēdola aciascun suo mēbro assegnaremo sua ppria e vera diffinitiōe e descriptiōe. AE alora poi sequira ̄qllo che Arist. vici in secōdo poster. Uc eni maxime scif aligd cū babet suuz ̄qd est zc.

Summa (Edin. ICAS) variant, partly 1494, partly later; roman floriated initial L (text type B).

11

Summa (2nd edn), 1523; new initial L portrait block copied from *editio princeps* (text type entirely reset).

PLATE 2

Three versions of part of the first text page of the *Summa*.

ⅅⅈſtinctio quinta .Ʈractatus primus.　ſ7

ⅅⅈſtinctio.ſ.ⱬ tractatus primus eiuſdcȝ.ꝺe modo opȝndi qſtionū.articulus p̄mus.

Ⱥpꝑdiri li modi ꝺe ſant e roria ſapere cōmo fra loⱬo ſe babino e ineſtiero ꝺouer ꝺire ꝺe loro operare neli caſi:e ragioni occurrēti.Ꝑe li quali ō neceſſita ſe bȝo a itromettere.Ⱥ po qui ſeq̄n te comēcaremo a pócre caſi e ꝺo nȝde poſſibili occurrēti.Ⱡō li modi: vie:regole:a farli e ſolucrli.ma prima moſtraremo la re⁊ gola ꝺitta ꝺl.⁊.ouer ꝺe le.ȝ coſe ſecondo groſſi. Ꝑer laq̄l ogni mercanteſca ragione ſe ba abſoluere.Ⱥmoſtrȝrcino' ꝺonde la forⱬa ꝺi tal regola proceda. Ꙅicbe fa bene la nori.Ⱥ poi ſucce⁊ ſiuamente a ciⱬſcuno propoſito e materia ȝdaremo mettēdo ca ſi oucr ꝺomande acio melgio apⱬebenda.

Ⅾe regula trium rerum qua mediante omnes mercatoⱬie queſtiones ſoluuntur.

Gothic Floriated Initial,
f.57 *recto* (Arithmetica). This initial was also used upside-down as D.(text type A)

Ꝓrobemium ac ſecu

ꝶdo eſt pȝ
teſte Ⱥugi
te ꝺe ꝺiuer
lo cbe ſeqt:
ꝺare opa a
tolene ꝺe i
ꝺe miſure.
ꝺe miſure.Ⱡaq̄le pēſando ꝺiⱡ

Large Lombardic Initial,
f.19 *recto* (Arithmetica).
(text type B)

Lombardic Initials in Arithmetica (three on the same page). This D was also used upside-down as Q. (test type B) (reduction of original size)

P

E

D

.Ⅰe figure cbe tȝto vira:e faſſe ir Ⱥlius modus

ⅮȺr laltro modo la ,pu ȝȝdo ꝺa lultia(moⱬe ai ꝺirai coſi 7.e4.fa 11 .⁊ ra ſequête ſēpⱬe cōmo 11 .trato.9.reſta 2.Ⱍual 2.gⱡ to alaltra figura cbe ſeque.ſ.ⱡ ala figura cbe ſeque 6.cbe ē 8 ſeque 8.cbe e 1 .e ꝺira 4.e piu qⱡeſto vltio cōgiūto q̄le e 4.ſⱡ cbe tȝto ꝺe proua baueſti p lo idē.Ⱥ ſe tu nō voleſſe coſi aco⁊ arⱡiſtarerſunmarerutteq̄li quella ſumma gettarai li 9.cⱡ cbe pur tȝto fara.Ⱥnde in q̄ſⱡ ſo per ſummarle 7.e4 11 .e ⱡ ua e 4.ſi cōmo prima e lun ino Ⱍō idē ē ⱡ

ⱷSe tu voi ſape ꝺōde q̄to p la coⱬare ꝺe le t guardi q̄do in q̄ſto nⱡ proua e 2.aloⱬa tu parti 74.p la ſumma prēdere la ,pua quȝ ꝺi laltro ſe a ꝺi proua 2.e coſi cbe ſia vno medeſimo modo fⱡ proprieta ꝺe q̄ſto nūero noue nūero prtito i 9.cioe cb̄ tȝto te pur partita i 9.ſi cōmo ꝺiſopⱬ Ⅾe ,pⱡ

ⅬⰁⱥinoſtrata la ,pua ꝺe q̄la ꝺel 7.laq̄le facilⱡ Ⱥnde la ,pua ꝺe alcū cbe auȝȝa ſia ,pua.Ⱥ q̄do paⱡ

PLATE 3
158

.ı ı.multiplica in se fa.ı 2ı.per la f
Se tu voleffe hauer l
começando va.ı.fine
ciamo va.ı.fin al qdr
.ı.Dico che sempre p
erari che facino qllo:el ql termic

no belle e bone in qsta materia z
memoria.ideo 7C.
E tu voleffe fuccintan
mero voli vifparo lo ı
ri fe excedano eqlmei
eİ p'e vlzio termio:cioe.ı.ı9.fa.2

De terrio modo ı
Z terço modo evetti
plurimum quando z
to picolo che con lar
fi fa cl menore tutto
fa.65.pon.5.erien.6.£poi.ı3.vıa.

mero che.ı0.bauzffe terminato ı
E tu uoleffe hauere l
rı fin che qdrato vi(
nouenario iclufiue:(
li nüeri vifpari p o2(
da el fequzte nücro vifparo ō lu

13

.ȷ.vı.9.fa.ı5.E qsto poi multipl
.ı 65.vt pruıa che an
E tu voleffe hauere ı
li numeri pari:fin qı
Poni.ı0.che e lnlrin

De.4°.mō multiplicandi vıa
Z quarto modo fi vıı
ve qsre figure fi vogli
ōdialtrı p lı molti in
cure efaffı ı qsto mod
vogliano:poi faremo p tre figur

Roman Initial E.
Three versions,
(Arithmetica):
(1) (top) normal,
(2) (centre) variant,
(3) (bottom) another variant, on same
    page as (2).
(text type A)

Roman Initial S.
Three versions, on the same page
(Arithmetica):
(1) (top) variant,
(2) (centre) right fount, but upside-down
(3) (bottom) right fount,
normal.
(text type A)

c.a d.e cofi in fimili fempre vfare
fAcora quando foffe
ro e in vna torre.£ ıı
capo.Jn quefto exeıı
fona e fienno inful pı

Roman Initial A.
This the broken A which appears once in the Arithmetica and repeatedly in the Geometria (here from
f.52 *recto* (G). (text type A) (reduction of original size)

PLATE 4

159

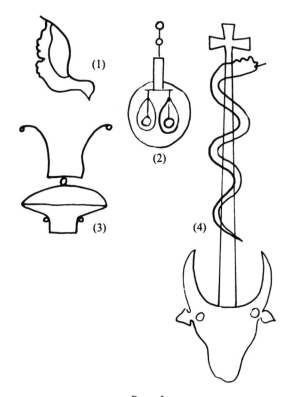

14

P<small>LATE</small> 5

WATERMARKS

(1) *Duck*, in preliminary pages and early and last pages of text (both Arithmetica and Geometria); text type A.

(2) *Scales*, in most of text pages (A) and (G); text type A.

(3) *Hat*, in variant pages of both (A) and (G); *Summa* (Edin. ICAS), variant, only; text type B.

(4) *Bull's head, cross and serpent*, in manuscript pages bound in at end of text; *Summa* (EUL) only.

Reproductions are reduced in size.

folios (re*cto*) as, for example, a,aij,aiij,aiiij, in the bottom right-hand corner of the type area. (In the first folio of a section, the number 'i' was omitted, and it was customary in roman numerals at this time for the last of a series of 'i' to be written as 'j'.) The four subsequent folios of a section are without signatures, since they are the other halves of the relevant sheets.

The first eight folios of the book (the 16 preliminary pages) have no signatures and are therefore given above the signature [1] *et seq.* As often today, the printing of the preliminary pages was the last to be completed, at least in the *editio princeps* printing run. They show, on f.[1] *verso*, the date 20 November 1494, as shown also on the last page of the Arithmetica, f. 224 *verso*. The date on the last printed page of the book, f. 76 *recto* (G), is 10 November 1494, the date on which the Geometria's printing was completed. In addition, f. [1] *verso* shows the complete register of collation signature letters for the Arithmetica, just as f. 76 *recto* (G) does for the Geometria, the latter adding the first words of each folio bearing a signature mark, plus the folio immediately following. The list of Arithmetica signatures is accompanied by an instruction: 'quere in ultima carta totius operis' ('seek on the last page of the whole work') the register of signatures for the Geometria, thus further proving that the Preliminary pages were completed last of the original run.

Incidentally, in a specimen business letter in the text on f. 167 *verso* (A) the date is 9 August 1494; and on f. 199 *recto* (A) an example is dated 8 November 1493, perhaps the dates on which they were written or set in type. The later date for the earlier page may be due to the fact that the letter on f. 167 *verso* is set in the margin, perhaps added by Pacioli when he was proof-correcting.

The treatise, De computis & de scripturis, Pacioli's fundamental exposition of double-entry bookkeeping, appears in Distinctio nona (9), Tractatus xi, from ff. 198 *verso* to 210 *verso* (A) (26 pages). It is preceded by its own one and a half pages detailed contents list.

Methods of Comparison

With a work as large as the *Summa*, the most practical way of comparing the five volumes had to be determined. Ideally, a *portable* Hinman collator[2] might have been the solution, but no such machine exists: this machine is both large and scarce, and none was conveniently available.

Preliminary examinations of the five *Summas* showed that, although all but the *Summa* (Edin. ICAS) were probably entirely from the same printing run as the *editio princeps*, there were minor differences among them. A complete photocopy of the *Summa* (Edin. ICAS), commissioned from the Scottish Institute by Professor Antinori (before the original was transferred to the National Library of Scotland), and kindly left on loan to the present writer until these comparisons were virtually completed, was of great assistance.

---

[2] This ingenious machine was devised by Dr C. Hinman in the United States. By first superimposing on a screen the images of two versions of the same page of text, and then quickly and repeatedly flashing each image on and off, alternating with the other, it makes discrepancies in the pages appear to jump to the eye. However, with a large number of pages to be compared, progress would be likely to be slowed down by eye fatigue.

Since it was impracticable to read the whole text in detail, two specimen pages from the *Summa* (Aber.) and (Edin. ICAS) were selected for more detailed comparison. These were ff. 26 *verso* and 27 *recto* (A), chosen because they showed in the *Summas* (Edin. ICAS) type faces A and B on facing pages. This comparison is summarized in Appendix 2.

In addition, the main features of the rest of the pages were compared as follows. The *Summa* (Aber.) with the photocopy of the *Summa* (Edin. ICAS), page by page, and then the resulting notes with the *Summas* (EUL), (GUL) and (RO), the photocopy being available for reference with all but the last.

The features compared on each page were, where applicable, the printed folio numbers, collation signatures, text type face, decorative initials, running headlines, subheadings, marginal typesetting (text and/or diagrams), other illustrations, and watermarks where discernible. In the course of this comparison, some misprints on other parts of pages were noticed.

Bearing in mind that Pacioli went to Venice to see the *Summa* (1494) through the press, one object in recording minor variations in these features was to provide evidence for identifying pages where the type had been 'handled' during printing, or between printings, with the possibility that these observations could be useful to researchers on textual comparisons.

Text Typography

While both type A and type B are transitional romano-gothic, type B is larger and, on the whole, printed better and blacker (though the standard of the printed impression is good almost throughout in both types). To accommodate the text set in type B in the same number of pages as for type A, the type area for B was made wider and deeper, though the actual number of words on the pages was not matched. Fortunately the margins of the original setting were large enough to allow for type B. Sometimes, though, marginal settings in type B would not fit into the space in the same way as they had in type A, and therefore in type B they were set in more lines, or even vertically instead of horizontally.

The marginal diagrams on pages set in type B were all reprinted from new wood blocks, from redrawn diagrams (not as good as the originals), copied from those printed with type A. That the original blocks were no longer available suggests that type B pages must have been printed much later. If the change of type had been due merely to the fact that type A had been distributed and reset for another book — as was commonly done without delay — the diagram blocks could well have been still in stock.

Strangely, in spite of the improved appearance of Type B, the arabic numerals associated with it are cruder and smaller than those with type A, especially in the fractions.

Contracted words, using additional letters of the alphabet as in 'p̱' (per) and 'secũda' (secunda) in the labour-saving style of manuscript writing, a practice which soon died out as unnecessary in typesetting, often differ in style between types A and B, with B tending to contain more of them. Perhaps this was to help condense the type B text so as to make sure that it fitted the space available for it, a calculation very finely done.

A capital N from some third type face appears repeatedly in the body of text in type A, for example, f. 207 *recto* (A) in 'ANcora'. Similarly an over-sized capital G, though of the correct type face, appears several times in type A, for example, f. 73 *verso* (G) in 'EGlie'. Both these wrong 'sorts' must have, accidentally and unnoticed, found their way into the case(s) of type A, and the fact that they appear several times confirms that the type used for a page was distributed back to its case not long after printing.

Other imperfections noted include unwanted space between letters of a word, for example, f. 117 *verso* (A) 'Tra ctatus' in the running headline, and conversely no space between words, for example, f. 66 *recto* (G) 'Distinctioottaua' for 'Distinctio ottaua' (running headline).

Sometimes the irregularity is that the type is sloping (where it should be upright) due to pressure during printing, and probably indicating a sheet late in the run.

Many vagaries, although useful as identification points, are no more than stylistic inconsistencies, such as the following collation signatures: f. 28 *recto* (A) d iiii instead of d iiij; f. 67 *recto* (A) i iji instead of i iij; f. 178 *recto* (A) z ii with z (ζ) upside-down, *et seq.*; f. 10 *recto* (G) B 2 instead of B ij; and f. 73 *recto* (G) k instead of K. The divergent style of f. 217 *recto* (A) AA 7 was probably deliberate, as the previous signature was the clumsy AA iiiiij!

17

Although spelling and contractions vary, even on the same page, as was not unusual in the 15th century, some irregularities are obvious misprints, for example, f. 201 *recto* (A) 'Capttolo' for 'Capitolo'.

A particularly gross error in folio numbers occurs at ff. 211 and 212 *recto* (A), which are both numbered 918. This is puzzling, but as the material on these pages is tabular, rather than consecutive text, it is possible that they were 'lifted' from some other book.

It is probable that pages which repeat exactly typesetting or printing divergences from the norm in more than one copy of the *Summa* have not been altered during the printing run or between printings. Those which do show typographical discrepancies may be more likely to contain textual differences. Those which display no superficial abnormality may also, of course, be worth checking for textual changes, but these would be less likely. In all, some 370 pages out of 616 were recorded as showing, in some or all five copies, identifiable departures from the norm.

Decorative Initials

The decorative initials with which the *Summa* is liberally sprinkled (at the beginning of each paragraph) are themselves a factor in typographical evidence. At ff. [2] and [3] *recto* of the preliminary pages, the very large decorative initials are missing, though a small lower-case 'q' is set in the initial space in f. [3] as a guide to a possible future artist-illuminator, as was done in MSS.

For Type A Basically, type A is accompanied by roman floriated initials, in white on a square black background, but there are occasional intrusions from two other similar designs, mainly for E and S. One variant initial E has faces rather than flowers in the background, for example, on f. 27 *verso* (A), which also contains a variant S. Both this series and another variant (floriated) E are cruder than the main series.

A few of the main series are slightly damaged: a particular A square with a recognizable nick in its left side appears repeatedly in the Geometria, on ff. 13 *recto* and *verso*, 14 *verso*, 16 *verso*, 19 *verso*, 20 *recto* and *verso*, 30 *verso*, 32 *verso*, 38 *recto* and *verso*, 39 *verso*, 40 *recto*, 44 *recto* and *verso*, 52 *recto*. The same broken initial A also appears at f. 140 *recto* (A), thus confirming the close times of printing of the two works, Arithmetica and Geometria, contained in the *Summa*, and possibly pointing to a late alteration in that page.

The nearness of the above Geometria pages, even including, three times, pages back to back on the same folio, and even allowing for the drying time of one page before its backing page could be printed, shows that the limited amount of type in a case and still more limited number of decorative initials available necessitated distribution and redistribution of initials and therefore early disturbance and probable distribution of text type shortly after printing.

Other idiosyncrasies include upside-down initials, for example, f. 177 *recto* (A) Ɐ for V, and f. 9 *recto* (G) ∧ for A, and both several times elsewhere. As Pacioli's text can be very repetitive, calling for up to ten of the same initial on the same page, it is possible that some of these were deliberate substitutions due to a shortage of initials. More subtly, H,I,O and S, when upside-down, can be distinguished by their background design being reversed.

The five printing positions of the very large L Pacioli portrait initial, and the fact that it appears only four times in the *Summa* (Edin. ICAS) have already been noted.

The few remaining very large initials in the type A pages are of a gothic floriated design. They appear at f. [4] *verso* of the preliminary pages (D); and in the Arithmetica at ff. 19 *recto* (except in the *Summa* (Edin. ICAS)) (O); 57 *recto* (E); 67 *recto* (O); 98 *verso* (A); 150 *recto* (C); 161 *recto* (E); 167 *recto* (D). In the Geometria there is one in f. 1 *recto* (O) [except in the *Summa* (Edin. ICAS)].

A close look at some of these initials proves that some of them were also used interchangeably: C is A upside-down, E is D upside-down, and A in f. 98 *verso* (Arithmetica) is also D upside-down!

For Type B   Type B's accompanying decorative initials are lombardic, of a style more in keeping with the dominant gothic element in the romano-gothic type face of the text. They are freestanding (without background) and most appear in solid black. Again, some are used interchangeably by reversal, for example, f. 21 *verso* (A) an upside-down Q for D. In lombardic letters this is justifiable, but when D and Q are exchanged in roman initials (as they are twice in f. 149 *recto* (A) in 'Quando') it does not work!

The only very large lombardic initials appear at ff. 19 *recto* (A) and 1 *recto* (G). Both are O.

The largest initial of all in the *Summa* (1494), the roman floriated L on f. 1 *recto* (A), has already been noted in the *Summa* (Edin. ICAS).

Running Headlines

These are set in the same type face as the text type of their page, but in a larger size. They are the cause of a good deal of confusion and not a few mistakes. Less important, inconsistencies of style or spacing occur. Often the mistakes, for example, 'Tracatus'

18

for 'Tractatus', appear on several consecutive or nearby pages. This could imply that the compositor who set the headlines was not the person who set the body of the text. In fact, it may have been that the less skilled workers (apprentices?) were entrusted with setting headlines only, which were then taken, as required, by the skilled compositor employed on the main text.

Confusion arises when the ordinal numbers, usually spelled out in words, but using roman numerals towards the end of the Arithmetica, are wrong. Occasionally a headline appears that is doubly wrong: such a line may have been taken from another part of the book. Several of the incorrect running headlines were corrected in the later setting of type B.

Any criticism of the standard of the headlines, however, must be mitigated by the facts that there are over 600 of them and that the style of text type setting used is 'solid', with no change of type face or size to distinguish the headings of new chapters or their subdivisions. These headings are not highlighted by space lines and in some instances they are severely contracted: they therefore often have to be searched for.

In particular, over Tractatus octavus (8) and nonus (9) of Distinctio nona in the Arithmetica, there seems to have been some condensation in the text, since paragraphs (1) and (2) appear to have been omitted, and (3) to (37) are continuous, covering the transition from one Tractatus to the next.

Apart from all this, the top line of a page of type, a short line, was more vulnerable than text lines, and this accounts for some of the irregularities of spacing, inclined letters and perhaps even missing letters in the running headlines, for example, f. 195 *recto* (A) 'istinctio' for 'Distinctio'.

Minor misprints may have been missed in proofreading, but a gross misprint, f. 220 *recto* (A) 'tiaffa' for 'Tariffa', could only be explained by supposing that the original type actually fell out while the page of type was being printed and was hastily replaced by the printer rather than the compositor—union demarcation lines not yet having been invented!

Watermarks

Paper of the period of the *Summa* was made by hand from linen rags, each sheet being formed by dipping a wire mesh tray into a vat of paper pulp. The marks of the wires can be seen on the paper, especially by holding it up to the light. There are close, fine horizontal lines ('laid' lines), with stronger vertical lines ('chain' lines) at regular intervals. Watermarks were made by twisting wire into patterns peculiar to the papermaker's firm (a form of trade mark) and attaching the design, with fine wire, to the chain lines. The watermarks in the *Summa* (1494) are not easy, indeed sometimes impossible, to identify, since they appear (all but one) in the centre of the page and the printed text is closely set and heavily inked. Five watermarks were identified (heights shown):

(1) Duck (c. 5 cm.)   This was always shown vertically. It appears in every case in the eight preliminary folios and, except for the *Summas* (RO) and (Edin. ICAS), at the beginning of the Arithmetica; at the beginning of the Geometria (except for the (Edin. ICAS)) and on f. 76 (G), the last folio of the book. This is more than just a printer using up some paper left over from a previous book, since it is deliberately

19

using what is probably a better paper for the parts of the book exposed to most wear: the first and last folios. It is also used for the first folios of text, in order to give a good impression to a prospective buyer. In this connection, it is significant to note that the Geometria treatise also uses this paper in early folios, possibly indicating an intention of publishing it separately at some later date.

Briquet (in Stevenson, 1968) shows a very similar watermark in use in 1498 in Italy.[3]

(2) Scales (c. 6 cm.)   This is a balance, enclosed within a circle and hanging from a two-link chain, and it is the commonest watermark in the *Summa*. It appears upside-down as well. In the *Summa* (RO) it is much less visible, but it does appear on f. 74 (G). According to Allan Stevenson (1968), it was also common in Venetian incunables (pre-1500) and indeed up to 1555. A similar design is illustrated in Briquet, dated Venice 1496 (in Stevenson, 1968).

20

(3) Hat (c. 6 cm.)   Always appearing upside-down, and therefore not at first recognizable, this is a broad-brimmed hat with tie strings. It is confined to folios set in type B, not surprisingly, since they must have been printed at a different time from their counterparts set in type A. This watermark therefore appears only in the *Summa* (Edin. ICAS), the variant. A similar mark has been recorded by Briquet, dated 1503.

(4) Letter p (c. 4 cm.)   This lower-case letter 'p' appears at the bottom outside corner of f. 215 (A) in the *Summa* (EUL) only. It may have been accidentally placed on the papermarking tray. Another guess is that it might have been the paper-maker's mark for the customer, the printer of the *Summa*, Paganino de Paganini.

(5) Bull's Head, Cross and Serpent (c. 18 cm.)   A very large watermark, of a front-facing, horned bull's head, with a long-shafted cross growing out of the top of it and a (transparent) snake twined round the shaft, appears in 16 folios of the 29-folio MS bound in at the end of the *Summa* (EUL). As some of these folios are blank in part and none are printed, their opacity is not as great as that of the printed folios, so that this watermark is more clearly visible.

At the period of the *Summa*, watermarks for printing and writing paper were commonly similar, though more glue (sizing) was added to the latter to prevent the water-based writing ink from spreading. This watermark (which hedges its bets by mingling pagan and Christian symbols!) was originally an Italian design but was soon imitated in Germany. An almost identical watermark was listed by Briquet from a MS in Austria dated 1498.

Some General Conclusions

Although all incunables are rare books, the number of copies of the *Summa* (1494) extant today argues that the original number printed was larger than usual for its period, even discounting the variant reprints.

Early printers were also publishers and even booksellers, but they were not usually binders. It was up to the buyer to have the book (sold in the form of collated sections)

---

[3] Pacioli's *Summa* is not listed among the early books studied by Briquet for their watermarks.

bound. No doubt Paganini's sales of the *editio princeps* of the *Summa* continued over several years from its publication date of 1494.

When his stock became depleted, before the demand slackened, he may have consulted Pacioli before resetting and reprinting the sheets which were exhausted. There may therefore be author's corrections in some type B pages. Yet, though some type A misprints are corrected in type B, others are not, in particular the mistake in line 27 of the arithmetical progression in the margin of f. 8 *recto* (A), which affects all further numbers and was probably therefore an author's error (unlike the mistake in line 4, which was a simple misprint).

The facts that the sheets reprinted were all complete sheets and came at the beginning of the two works in the book, and that the preliminary pages (the last to be printed originally) did not require to be reset, may mean that Paganini used some early text sheets to publicize the book in the market place and was so encouraged by the response that, being a 'prudente homo' as he is described in the colophon on f. 76 *recto* (G), he increased the number to be printed from then onwards.

21

The preliminary pages of all five *Summas* examined show, for example, the obvious misprint 'tuttta' for 'tutta' in the prominent position of the first line on f. [4] *verso*, further confirming that these pages all belong to the original printing run.

The demand for the *Summa* continued, so that other variants (e.g. the copy in Piacenza, Italy—Antinori, 1980) appeared, with other replacements of out of stock sheets. Its popularity led to a second edition, entirely reset in a new type face, a smaller and more refined romano-gothic, printed by Paganini in Tuscolano in 1523, probably after the death of the author.

The *Summa* was soon translated and plagiarized widely in Europe.

Although over half of the pages of the *Summa* (1494) show divergences from the norm, one cannot help marvelling at the expertise of Paganino de Paganini (and his employees) in setting such a long and complex textbook, furnished with many subdivisions of various grades, and this in the infancy of the craft of printing with movable type in Europe. Seemingly inexplicable mistakes, for example, in folio numbers and running headlines, are more than balanced by this considerable achievement of setting and printing such a book so amazingly well in the 15th century.

APPENDIX 1

Misprints Perpetuated from Type A Setting (Arithmetica)

f.8 *recto* two arithmetical errors (and some consequent errors) in the progression printed in the margin
f.8 *verso* (Tractatus) 'primus' for 'secundus' in running headline
f.11 *recto* (Tractatus) 'quartus' for 'tertius'
f.21 *verso* (Tractatus) 'secundus' for 'primus'
f.22 *recto*   "   "   "   "
f.22 *verso*   "   "   "   "

Corrections of Misprints in Type A Setting (Arithmetica)

f.6 *recto* folio number corrected from 9
f.10 *recto* (Tractatus) 'tertius' corrected from 'quartus'
f.10 *verso*   "   "   "   "   "
f.11 *verso*   "   "   "   "   "
f.13 *recto* folio number corrected from 14
f.13 *recto* (Tractatus) 'quartus' corrected from 'tertius'
f.14 *recto* folio number corrected from 15
f.14 *recto* (Tractatus) 'quartus' corrected from 'tertius'
f.14 *verso*   "   "   "   "   "
f.15 *recto* folio number corrected from 16
f.15 *recto* (Tractatus) 'quartus' corrected from 'tertius'
f.15 *verso*   "   "   "   "   "
f.19 *verso* (Distinctio) 'secunda' (Tractatus) 'primus' from 'prima', 'quartus'
f.20 *recto* folio number corrected from 10
f.20 *verso* (D) 'secunda' (T) 'primus' corrected from (D) 'prima' (T) 'quartus'
f.21 *recto* (T) 'primus' corrected from 'secundus'
f.22 *verso* 'Articulus' (undecimus) corrected from 'Aticulus'
f.23 *recto* folio number corrected from 24 (as in *Summa* (Aber.) only)
f.23 *recto* (T) 'primus' corrected from 'secundus'

(Geometria)

f.8 *verso* 'Ancora' corrected from 'AAncora' (with decorative initial A)

New misprints in Type B Setting (Arithmetica)

f.6 *verso* 'quarttus' instead of 'quartus' in a subheading
f.7 *verso* (Tractatus) 'primus' instead of 'secundus'
f.16 *verso* 'vuadrato' instead of 'quadrato' in first line (and 'qna' instead of 'vna' in second line)
f.17 *recto* (Distinctio) 'secunda' instead of 'prima'

* For Arithmetica f.26 *verso*, see Appendix 2.

APPENDIX 2

Summa (Aber.)	*Summa* (Edin. ICAS)
	f.26 *verso*
Type A	Type B
line 11 'ela' for 'e la'	'ela' for 'e la'
" 18 'Di' for 'di'	corrected
" 23 'bisogna mo' for 'bisognamo'	'bisogna mo' for 'bisognamo'
" 33 'omale' for 'o male'	corrected
" 36 'adiectoe' for 'adiecto e'	corrected
" 50 'intaola' for 'intauola'	'intaola' for 'intauola'

correct	line	3 'mulliplicatiõe' for 'multiplicatiõe'
correct	"	23 'laltre' for 'altre'
correct	"	32 'trouerai' for 'Trouerai'
correct (quedã)	"	36 'q̃da' for 'q̃dā' or 'q̃dam'
correct	"	43 'Seq xaltera' for 'Sexq altera'
correct	last line	'L,E,E,U' for 'l,e,e,u'

f.27 *recto*

both in Type A

line 3 'numeribassi' for 'numeri bassi'
" 10 'quãtoche' for 'quãto che'
" 26 'arecogliere' for 'a recogliere'
" 37 'casteluccio' for 'castelluccio'
" 39 'moltiplicatione' for 'multiplicatione'
" 40 'dicinevia' for 'dicine via'

From the results in Appendix 1, it will be realized that, even although Type B both repeats some of Type A's mistakes and makes a few of its own, these are outnumbered by the corrections made by the printer in setting Type B. If proofs of the new setting were sent to Pacioli, the author may have had a hand in the corrections too. On the other hand, Appendix 2 shows that, on f.26 *verso* (A) at least, Type B setting had as many mistakes as Type A.

23

APPENDIX 3

SOME MISPRINTS SUMMARIZED AS THEY OCCUR IN THE FIVE *SUMMAS* (1494)

Folio	Aberdeen (Aber.)	Gl Un (GUL)	Ed Un (EUL)	Roy Ob (RO)	Edin (ICAS)	Correct
		(1) Misprints in folio numbers				
(Arithmetica)						
6 *recto*	9	9	9	9	6 ⌉	6
13 "	15	15	15	15	13	13
14 "	15	15	15	15	14 Type	14
15 "	16	16	16	16	15 B	15
20 "	10	10	10	10	20 ⌋	20
23 "	24	23	23	23	23 ⌋	23
35 "	34	34	34	34	34	35
45 "	46	46	46	46	46	45
52 "	52	52	52	52	not printed	52
57 "	64	57	57	57	57	57
71 "	not printed	71	71	71	71	71
167 "	168	168	168	168	168	167
211 "	981	981	981	981	981	211
212 "	981	981	981	981	981	212
(Geometria)						
22 *recto*	19	19	19	19	19	22
33 "	40	40	40	40	40	33
		(2) Signature numbers				
(Arithmetica)						
178-180 *recto*	z upsidedown	same	same	same	same	z
(Geometria)						
33 *recto*	not printed	"	"	"	"	E
58 "	ij	ij	ij	ij	Hij	Hij
72 "	ii	ii	ii	ii	ii	Kij
73 "	kiij	kiij	kiij	kiij	kiij	Kiij

(3) *Subheadings*

(Arithmetica)

6 *verso*	quartus	same	same	same	quarttus (B)	quartus
22 "	Aticulus (11)	"	"	"	Articulus	Articulus
104 "	Petitiooes	"	"	"	same	Petitiones
127 *recto*	bioomij	"	"	"	"	binomij
148 "	Secondum	"	"	"	"	Secundum
148 *verso*	Secundum	"	"	"	"	Tertium
201 *recto*	Capttolo (12)	"	"	"	"	Capitolo
213 *verso*	Qnesti	"	"	"	"	Questi
221 *recto*	Custumi	"	"	"	"	Costumi

(Geometria)

30 *recto*	Capitulnm primum	"	"	"	"	Capitulum secundum
75 *verso*	(La quinta) distintione	"	"	"	"	distinctione

24

(4) *Running headlines*

(Arithmetica)

7 *verso*	(T)secundus	same	same	same	primus	secundus
8r & v	(T)primus	"	"	"	same	secundus
10r & v	(T)quartus	"	"	"	tertius	tertius
11 *recto*	(T)quartus	"	"	"	same	tertius
11 *verso*	(T)quartus	"	"	"	tertius	tertius
13 *recto*	(T)tertius	"	"	"	quartus	quartus
14r-15v	(T)tertius	"	"	"	quartus	quartus
17 *recto*	(D)prima	"	"	"	secûda	prima
19 *verso*	(D)prima(T)quartus	"	"	"	secûda, primus	secunda, primus
20 "	(D)prima(T)quartus	"	"	"	Type B — secunda, primus	secunda, primus
21 *recto*	(T)secundus	"	"	"	primus	primus
21v-22v	(T)secundus	"	"	"	same	primus
23 *recto*	(T)secundus	"	"	"	primus	primus
30 "	(T)tercius	"	"	"	same	tertius
49 "	(D)tercia	"	"	"	"	tertia
50 "	(D)tercia	"	"	"	"	tertia
56 *verso*	(D)secunda	"	"	"	"	quarta
80 "	(T)quintus	"	"	"	"	quartus
101 *recto*	(T)secundus	"	"	"	"	primus
101 *verso*	(T)secundus	"	"	"	"	primus
105 *recto*	(T)primus	"	"	"	"	secundus
119 *verso*	(T)secundus	"	"	"	"	tertius
142 *recto*	(T)tertins	"	"	"	"	tertius
144 "	(T)quartus	"	"	"	"	quintus
145 *verso*	(T)tertius	"	"	"	"	quintus
146 "	(T)tertius	"	"	"	"	quintus
147 "	(T)tertius	"	"	"	"	quintus
148 "	(T)tertius	"	"	"	"	sextus
149 "	(D)nona(T)primus	"	"	"	"	octaua, sextus
153 *recto*	Tracatus	"	"	"	"	Tractatus
154 *verso*	(T)secundus	"	"	"	"	primus
157r-159r	Tracatus	"	"	"	"	Tractatus
161 *verso*	(D)octaua	"	"	"	"	nona
162 "	(D)octaua	"	"	"	"	nona
163 "	(D)octaua	"	"	"	"	nona
164 "	(D)octaua	"	"	"	"	nona
165 *recto*	(T)quarttus (*sic*)	"	"	"	"	tertius

166 "	(T)quarttus	"	"	"	"	tertius
166 *verso*	(T)quartus	"	"	"	"	tertius
167 *recto*	(T)quarttus	"	"	"	"	tertius
168 "	(T)quarttus	"	"	"	"	quartus
173*r*-176*v*	(T)quintus	"	"	"	"	quartus
177*r*-181*v*	Tracatus	"	"	"	"	Tractatus
194 *verso*	(T)xi	"	"	"	"	x
194 "	De scripturis	"	"	"	"	De straordinaris
195 *recto*	istinctio	"	"	"	"	Distinctio
201 "	Tracatus	"	"	"	"	Tractatus
203 "	Distincto	"	"	"	"	Distinctio
210 "	Tracatus	"	"	"	"	Tractatus
220 "	tiaffa	"	"	"	"	Tariffa

(Geometria)

3 *verso*	(C)teritum	"	"	"	"	tertium
5 *recto*	(C)quartnm	"	"	"	"	quartum
5 *verso*	(C)quintnm (*sic*)	"	"	"	"	quartum
6 *verso*	(C)qnintum	"	"	"	"	quintum
7 *recto*	Capitnlum	"	"	"	"	Capitulum
15 "	(D)secunda (C)secundum	"	"	"	"	tertia, primum
20 "	(C)tertium	"	"	"	"	secundum
28 *verso*	(C)secundum	"	"	"	"	primum
29 *recto*	(C)secunum (*sic*)	"	"	"	"	primum
29 *verso*	(C)secundum	"	"	"	"	primum
33 *recto*	(D)quinta	"	"	"	"	quarta
40 *verso*	(D)quarta	"	"	"	"	quinta
41 *recto*	(D)secundum	"	"	"	"	tertium
44 *verso*	(D)secundum	"	"	"	"	tertium
50 "	(C)secudum	"	"	"	"	secundum
65*r* & *v*	(D)quinta (C)secundum	"	"	"	"	(D)octaua
67 *verso*	De corporibus regularibus	"	"	"	"	(prematurely printed)
70 *recto*	not printed	"	"	"	"	(D)octaua
70 *verso*	(D)quarta (C)secundum	"	"	"	"	(D)octaua De Corporibus regularibus
73 *recto*	regulabus	"	"	"	"	regularibus

25

(5) *Decorative initials*

(Preliminary pages)

[2] *recto*	not printed, but C inserted by hand	not printed	same	same	same	C
[3] *recto*	q (in text size type)	same	"	"	"	Q

(Arithmetica)

50 *recto*	∀	"	"	"	"	V
83 "	G	"	"	"	"	C
83 *verso*	G	"	"	"	"	C
89 "	∧	"	"	"	"	A
140 *recto*	A (broken)	"	"	"	"	A

(This particular A, with a break in its left border, appears again, in all five *Summas,* in the Geometria, in ff.13 *recto* & *verso*, 16 *verso*, 19 *verso*, 20 *recto* & *verso*, 30 *verso*, 38 *recto* & *verso*, 40 *recto*, 44 *recto* & *verso*, 52 *recto*.)

148 *verso*	∀	same	same	same	same	A
149 *recto*	D, D	"	"	"	"	Q, Q
159 *verso*	∀	"	"	"	"	V
169 *recto*	"	"	"	"	"	V
177 "	"	"	"	"	"	V
180 *verso*	"	"	"	"	"	V
181 *recto*	"	"	"	"	"	V
223 *verso*	A	∀	∀	∀	∀	A

(Geometria)

1 *recto*	G	same	same	same	C (type B)	C
9 *recto*	∧	"	"	"	same	A
12 *verso*	"	"	"	"	"	A
13 *recto*	"	"	"	"	"	A
16 "	"	"	"	"	"	A
18 *verso*	"	"	"	"	"	A
19 "	"	"	"	"	"	A
44 *recto*	F, ∧	"	"	"	"	E, A
62 "	V	"	"	"	"	E

(6) Marginal typesetting

(Arithmetica)

8 *recto*	2125899898454016 (4th line from top)	same	same	same	same	1125899898454016
	134217727 (and consequent errors) (27th line from top)	"	"	"	Type B "	134217728 (and consequent corrections)
19 *verso*	(set normally)	"	"	"	L-shaped captions set upsidedown (type B)	
55 *recto*	$\dfrac{14}{43}$	"	"	"	same	$\dfrac{14}{33}$

(Geometria)

2 *verso*	f (defective in last diagram)	"	"	f(correct)	f(defective)	f
6 *recto*	e (not printed in last diagram)	"	"	same	e(printed)	e

(7) Miscellaneous

(Preliminary pages)

[4] *verso*	tuttta (top line)	same	same	same	same	tutta

(Arithmetica)

92 *verso*	trovar (last word)	"	"	"	trovare	trovare
194 "	Undic (line 10)	"	"	"	same	Undici
209 *recto*	questi (last word)	quest	questi ·	questi	quest	questi
221 *verso*	(A) Llucca	same	same	same	same	(A) lucca

(Geometria)

25 *recto*	Modus (subtitle misaligned)	correct	correct	correct	misaligned	Modus
58 *recto*	(Paragraph) 75	57	57	57	57	57
65 "	8 (line 2)	8	8	85	85	85

REFERENCES

Antinori, C., 'Un'Edizione Anomala della "Summa" 1494 di Luca Pacioli', presented at the 3rd International Congress of Accounting Historians, London 1980; Palatina Editrice, Parma 1980.

Boncompagni, B., 'Intorno ad un trattato d'aritmetica stampato nel 1478', Atti dell'Accademia Pontificia de'Nuovi Lincei 16, anno 16, 1862-63.

Briquet, C. M. (ed. A. Stevenson), *Les Filigranes*, Jubilee edn, Paper Publications Society, Amsterdam 1968.

Brown, R. (ed.), *A History of Accounting and Accountants*, A. C. Black, Edinburgh 1905; reprinted by Frank Cass & Co., London 1968.

Clarke, D. A., 'The First Edition of Pacioli's "Summa de Arithmetica" (Venice, Paganinus de Paganinis (1494))', Gutenberg Jahrbuch 1974.

Dunlop, A. B. G., 'Pacioli's Summa de Arithmetica', *The Accountant's Magazine*, September 1961.

Murray, D., *Chapters in the History of Book-keeping and Accounting*, Jackson, Glasgow 1930.

Pacioli, Luca, *Summa Arithmetica, Geometria, Propertioni e Proportionalita*, Paganinus de Paganinis, Venice 1494.

Stevelinck, E., 'David Murray: Accounting Historian 1842-1928', *The Accountant's Magazine*, Edinburgh, August 1972.

Stevenson, A. (ed.), *Les Filigranes*, 1968 (see Briquet).

27

The First Scottish Book on Accounting:

Robert Colinson's *Idea Rationaria* (1683)*

R. H. PARKER, B.SC.(ECON.), F.C.A.

28

It was near the end of the 17th century, and the initiative in publishing books on accounting was beginning to pass from the Netherlands (where it had gone from Italy) to Scotland. As the writer of a poem in praise of the author of this book put it in the contemporary style of poetic diction:—

" Let Florence, Venice, Holland no more boast;
The Flag of Traffique's in our Northern Coast:"

The following century brought many Scottish books on accounting, but Robert Colinson blazed the trail. There is a copy of his book in the Antiquarian Collection of The Institute of Chartered Accountants of Scotland.

The 1680s were an important decade in Scottish history. Scots law was presented as a complete and coherent system for the first time in Stair's *Institutes*, published in 1681. The deposition of James VII and II in 1688 marked the effective end of a dynasty which had ruled Scotland since 1371. In the religious settlement which followed presbyterianism was firmly established.

It was during this same decade, in 1683, that the first Scottish book on accounting was published, nearly two centuries after Pacioli's *Summa* of 1494 † and 140 years after the first book on the subject in the English language, Hugh Oldcastle's *A briefe instruction and maner how to keepe bookes of Accompts* . . . of 1543. The long delay reflects the relatively underdeveloped state of the Scottish economy and the ready availability of textbooks from south of the Border.

By 1683 there was, as J. Row Fogo observed, " no particular merit . . . in producing a good work on book-keeping ".[1] Robert Colinson's *Idea Rationaria* is, however, " sensible and reasonably straightforward "[2] and for this reason, as well as for its chronological importance in the

* This article is taken from the Appendix to " Accounting in Scotland: a historical bibliography ", compiled by Janet E. Pryce-Jones; annotated by R. H. Parker; 96 pages; 11 illustrations; author index; title index; £2·50.
The bibliography is the first publication of the Scottish Committee on Accounting History of The Institute of Chartered Accountants of Scotland. It has just been published.
An order form for it appears at page i.

† Summa de Arithmetica etc., Venice, which contains the first printed exposition of double-entry bookkeeping and of which there are two copies in the Antiquarian Collection of The Institute of Chartered Accountants of Scotland.
[1] R. BROWN (ed.): A History of Accounting and Accountants; (Edinburgh: *Jack*, 1905), page 155.
[2] B. S. YAMEY, H. C. EDEY AND H. W. THOMSON: Accounting in England and Scotland; (London: *Sweet & Maxwell*, 1963), page 171.

history of accounting in Scotland, it is worth a short article. The practices recommended in it are typical of their time and show interesting variations from those of the present.

The Book

The title page is reproduced opposite. Note the reference to the " Italian Methode ", as double-entry bookkeeping was still commonly called; the method of teaching by " Queries and Answers " which is characteristic of the period; and the names of the recommended books of account.
The arrangement of Colinson's book is as follows:—

(*a*) Title page (see reproduction).

(*b*) Dedication to the Honourable Mr James Kennedy, " Lord Conservator of the Priviledges of the Scots Nation in the 17. Provinces of the Netherlands, and his Majesties Resident there, for all affaires of his Majesties ancient Kingdom of Scotland, &c ".

(*c*) Two laudatory poems by Mr Ninian Paterson and Mr J. Kniblo. These are of no great literary merit, but Professor Yamey regards them as one of the attractions of the book to present-day readers.[3] Elsewhere[4] he has considered at length the strength of Paterson's claim for double entry, that:—

This was the fam'd, and quick invention, which
Made Venice, Genoa, and Florence rich:

(*d*) Table of Contents.

(*e*) A letter to the " Merchants in Edinburgh, And all other Lovers of this Profitable Science ".

[3] *ibid.*
[4] B. S. YAMEY: " Scientific Bookkeeping and the Rise of Capitalism ", ECONOMIC HISTORY REVIEW, June 1949, reprinted in W. T. BAXTER: Studies in Accounting (London: *Sweet & Maxwell*, 1950).

R. H. Parker was appointed to the Chair of Accountancy in Dundee University in 1970. He has written a number of articles on accounting history and also the book, " Management Accounting: an Historical Perspective " (1969), which contains a valuable bibliography of material on this subject.
Professor Parker's recent published work includes a Penguin book on " Understanding Company Financial Statements " (1972).
He is Convener of the Scottish Committee on Accounting History, a committee of The Institute of Chartered Accountants of Scotland.
With regard to this article, Professor Parker says: " I am indebted to Professor B. S. Yamey, of the London School of Economics, and Professor T. A. Lee, of Liverpool University, for their comments on a previous draft."

IDEA RATIONARIA,

OR

THE PERFECT ACCOMPTANT,

Neceſſary for all Merchants and Trafficquers;

CONTAINING

THE TRUE FORME OF *BOOK-KEEPING*,

According to the *Italian* Methode:

Wherein is Firſt,

The Introduction to the Forme,

244. *Queries* and *Anſwers*, with Inſtructions how to Ballance the *Leger*, two *Waſte-Books* tranſported in two *Journals*, out of which are tranſported 2. *Legers* both Ballanced.

After which followes

A MONETH-BOOK,

INVOYS-BOOK,

FACTOR-BOOK,

SPECIE or CASH-BOOK;

Inſtructions how to keep a Book of Petty-Charges or Pocket-Book.

By ROBERT COLLINSON.

EDINBURGH,

Printed by DAVID LINDSAY, Mr. JAMES KNIBLO, JOSUA van SOLINGEN and JOHN COLMAR, in the Year 1683.

29

(*f*) Thirty-one pages describing the "Convenience" of bookkeeping; the various books of account Colinson deems it necessary to keep: Waste Book, Journal, Ledger, Factor Book ("to place down what is sent you by others, to dispose of the charges and sales"), Invoice Book, Month Book ("which tells you what summes you are to pay every moneth in the year, and day when, and who is to pay you"), Book of Petty Charges, Specie or Cash Book (necessary where more than one currency is dealt in: Row Fogo points out that, in addition to the national coinage, which was very bad, there were large quantities of foreign money in circulation particularly English and Dutch), Copy Book of Letters; and 244 questions and answers to "find out the right Debitor and Creditor upon all the Posts[5] of the Wast-Book, when you transport them to the Journal, and first of placing down the Inventar of the Stock". The questions and answers are interrupted between nos. 138 and 139 for a brief instruction (not in question and answer form) on balancing accounts, transferring them to a new book and on "companies-accompts" (*i.e.* partnership accounts).

(*g*) Two specimen sets of books (waste-book, journal and ledger).

The Author

Who was Colinson? Both Paterson and Kniblo refer to him as "Captain". He tells us that he has been "both a Student and Practitioner [of commerce] now these 25 years". It is clear from several references that, like many Scottish merchants of his time, he had lived and traded in the Low Countries. The title of his book is in Latin; his only quotation in a foreign language is in Dutch.

The Rules

The usual method of expounding the rules of double entry in English language textbooks on bookkeeping up to the 18th century was "to present a great mass of rules applicable to the particular cases of a large variety of transactions",[6] to do so by means of a series of questions and to follow this by a specimen set of books. Some, but not all, authors also included a general rule. Occasionally this was in verse. Dafforne, for

[5] *i.e.* items; the modern French word is "poste".
[6] J. G. C. JACKSON: "The History of Methods of Exposition of Double-entry Book-keeping in England"; in A. C. LITTLETON and B. S. YAMEY: "Studies in the History of Accounting" (London: Sweet & Maxwell, 1956), at page 288.

example, the only English author on bookkeeping to whom Colinson refers, wrote as follows in "The Merchant's Mirrour"[7]:—

> The Ower, or the Owing thing,
> Or what-so-ever comes to thee:
> Upon the Left-hand see thou bring;
> For there the same must placed bee.
>
> But they unto whom thou doest owe,
> Upon the Right let them bee set;
> Or what-so-ere doth from thee goe,
> To place them there doe not forget.

Colinson fortunately does not break into verse, but neither does he, regrettably, include a general rule. Instead, he immediately plunges into detail. Here are the first three questions and answers:—

(1) Q. What make you Debitor for the first branch of your Stock [i.e. Capital], which is ready money?

A. Cash Debitor to my Stock, for so much as I have in it at the beginning. This word Cash is used now generally for money Accompts, it comes from the Italian word Cassa, which is a money Chest, or the like, which keeps it; therefore you Charge it Debitor for what is in't.

(2) Q. What is Debitor for the several Marchandize that you have lying by you unsold?

A. Such goods, naming them in your Journal, or as many of them as you will keep a particular Accompt of, Charging every one by itself Debitor, to Stock for the whole value it cost, with the Charges it hath cost since bought.

(3) Q. What is Debitor for your houses?

A. Such a house called so and so, every one of them what they stand me Debitor to Stock for all Charges, and Reparations to this day.

Specimen Accounts

In connection with this last entry some contemporary writers recommended the inclusion of both private and business assets in the accounts. Colinson is quite clear about the necessity to separate business and private assets:—

Now I say, a man may have a private stock which he will conceal, and a stock in trade [i.e. business assets] also; but then he must bring none of his private stock into his trading stocks Books, lest he confuse himself. Wherein can this private stock consist? it must be in Lands, Houses, Rents, Jewels, and House-furnishing, &c. for

[7] RICHARD DAFFORNE: "The Merchant's Mirrour" (London, 1636); introductory pages to specimen ledger. There is a copy of this book in the Antiquarian Collection of The Institute of Chartered Accountants of Scotland.

30

F.15

Edinburgh, Anno 1682.

PROFITE and LOSS, Debet.

Febr.	14	To *Thomas Trader*				4	4 |—
		To Cash for rebate to *James Truly*			1	4	—
Mar.	29	To *Thomas Factor* my accompt Currant for rebate		18	8	14	z
June	9	To Cash for rebate			23	3	—
	29	To Cash payed for House-hold expence and servants wages		23	130	—
	30	To several accompts lost on them as *per* Journal		..	253	5	4
—		To Stock for the neat gain		1	103	11	—
		Summa L	506	10	6

which private stock let him keep a Book, which he may easily do apart. [page 5]

In the specimen sets of books, however, Colinson includes household expense and servants' wages, and wagers (see below). Perhaps he regarded the last as a business transaction!

The accounts in the two specimen ledgers show a number of interesting variations from 20th-century practice. The Profit and Loss Account in the first ledger is reproduced below.

The first thing to notice is the absence of any reference to sales, purchases and opening and closing stocks of goods. Instead we have, *via* two entries in the journal, two items of £386.16.0 [8] and £253.5.4 summarising the gains and losses on various accounts. £35.5.0, for example, is lost upon " Wines of France ", that account being debited for the cost of wine bought, £430.0.0, and charges, £6.15.0, and credited with various sales amounting in all to £472.0.0. A separate column is used to record volume in " Tuns " with a loss of half a tun " in lackage ". There are similar accounts for Seck of Zeres (*i.e.* sherry), Iron, Mader, Indigo Lauro, Clothe, Sarges, Salmond, Herrings, Stockines, Hides, Wheat, Mum-Beer and, in the second Ledger, Tallow. None of the goods accounts illustrated by Colinson has a closing balance, nor does he anywhere in his book discuss the valuation problems involved.[9] He contents himself with stating (page 20) that:—

" Debet side of goods Accompt is what they cost me with charges, Credit is what is sold or sent away, or otherwayes disposed of."

The gains and losses in the summarising journal entries also include:—

(*a*) References to a number of voyage accounts. £71.13.4, for example, is gained from a Voyage to Rotterdam in the Ship Bonaventure, goods being bought from David Mills in Aberdeen for £970 and sold by William Cornelisen in Rotterdam for £1,041.13.4.

(*b*) £30 " gained by wagering ".

(*c*) Commissions received, £47.13.8.

[8] The figure in the journal entry heading is actually £393.16.0, but the items in it add up to £386.16.0.

[9] For a historical survey of the valuation of stock-in-trade see R. H. PARKER: " Lower of Cost and Market in Britain and the United States: An Historical Survey "; ABACUS, vol. 1, No. 2, 1965, reprinted in R. H. PARKER and G. C. HARCOURT (eds.); " Readings in the Concept and Measurement of Income " (*Cambridge University Press*, 1969).

(*d*) £158 " lost by insuring other mens goods ".

(*e*) £30 " lost upon Sea hazard by Skippers ".

The first four items on the debit side of the Profit and Loss Account reproduced all refer to rebates allowed; the first two items on the credit side are rebates received. The remaining items are £130 " payed for House-hold expence and servants wages "; £100 for a " Prentice-fee " (the apprenticeship was presumably for a period of years but no part of the fee is carried forward); and £15.4.6 commission received from Gilbert Callant.

The fixed asset[10] accounts, *e.g.* House called Black-Hall which is debited with the original cost plus reparations and rents payable and credited with rents receivable, follow what Yamey calls the arithmetical balance basis of valuation. No attempt is made to transfer revenue expense items to the Profit and Loss Account or to revalue the asset. The balances on such accounts are obviously rather meaningless.

The last account in each ledger is the " Balance " account, to which are transferred all account balances still open after transfers to the Profit and Loss Account and transfer of the " neat gain " therefrom to Stock [*i.e.* Capital]. It is in effect an unclassified Balance Sheet contained within the books of account.

Bibliographical Note

There are copies of Colinson's book in the libraries of The Institute of Chartered Accountants of Scotland and The Institute of Chartered Accountants in England and Wales, and also in Edinburgh University Library, the National Library of Scotland and the British Museum. It is referred to in:—

(*a*) B. S. YAMEY, H. C. EDEY AND H. W. THOMSON: Accounting in England and Scotland: 1543-1800; (London: *Sweet & Maxwell*, 1963), which includes three extracts from *Idea Rationaria*.

(*b*) R. BROWN (Ed.): A History of Accounting and Accountants (Edinburgh: *Jack*, 1905; reprinted by *Frank Cass*, London, 1966).

(*c*) D. MURRAY: Chapters in the History of Bookkeeping, Accountancy and Commercial Arithmetic (Glasgow: *Jackson, Wylie*, 1930).

The above three references are all available in the Scottish Institute's Edinburgh and Glasgow Libraries.

[10] Colinson does not classify assets into groups and does not use the term " fixed asset ".

© R. H. Parker, 1974.

31

Edinburgh , Anno 1682.

PROFITE and LOSS, Credite.

Febr	16	*Per George Dane*	5	3	—
	—	*Per Alexander Norman*	5	1 10	...
June	29	*Per Cash* for Prentice-fee	23	100	—
	30	*Per Gilbert Callant* in *Aberdeen*	16	15 4	6
	—	*Per* several accompts for so much gained on them, as *per* Journal		386 16	—
		Summa L.	506 10	6

Capsules and Comments

The Historical Development of Internal Control from the Earliest Times to the End of the Seventeenth Century

T. A. LEE*

Introduction

Since about 1900 accountancy writers have paid increasing attention to internal control, particularly in relation to the activities of the auditor.[1] This may give the impression that the concept of internal control as a part of business management is a relatively new idea and that auditors have only recently become concerned with it. However, auditing and accounting are known to have been practiced widely in developed economies which existed years before the birth of Christ. Nevertheless, little has been written about the history of internal control as a subject in itself. The purpose of this paper is to summarize some extracts from previous research in order to provide some insight into the development of internal control.

A Definition of Internal Control

The definition of internal control as used in this paper is the one adopted by Paul Grady:[2]

> Internal accounting control comprises the plan of organization and the co-ordinated procedures used within the business to (1) safeguard its assets from loss by fraud or unintentional errors, (2) check the accuracy and reliability of the accounting data which management uses in making decisions, and (3) promote

---

* Lecturer, University of Edinburgh.

[1] One of the earliest writings on internal control and the auditor was Lawrence R. Dicksee, *Auditing* (New York: Ronald Press, 1905), p. 54.

[2] Paul Grady, "The Broader Concept of Internal Control," *The Journal of Accountancy* (May, 1957), p. 41.

operational efficiency and encourage adherence to adopted policies in those areas in which the accounting and financial departments have responsibility, directly or indirectly.

Thus, the term will be used to refer only to the financial and accounting functions and will cover two related activities: internal audit (the management function which is intended to verify many of the aspects of the defined internal control system) and internal check (the procedures designed to safeguard assets against defalcations, etc.).

The Earliest Times—The Babylonian and Egyptian Eras

Williard E. Stone states that the first signs of internal control and in particular, internal auditing, can be found in the records of the early Mesopotanian civilization—the Sumerian—around 3600 to 3200 B.C.[3] He quotes Kenneth S. Most as saying:[4]

33

> It was customary for summaries to be prepared by scribes other than those who had provided original lists of payments. Further, the documents of the period reveal tiny marks, dots, ticks and circles at the side of the figures, indicating that checking had been performed.

Thus, the business managers of the time appear to have had a firm idea of control through an adequate division of accounting duties, and this is more easily seen in the description by Richard Brown of the activities conducted within the Treasury of the Egyptian Pharaohs:[5]

> Nothing was given out of the treasury without a written order. Peculation on the part of the workmen was provided against by the records of one official checking those of another. When the corn was brought to the storehouses each sack was filled in the sight of an overseer and noted down, and when the sacks were carried to the roof of the storehouse and emptied through the receiving opening the scribe stationed there recorded the number received.

Brown also notes that the above system was described in pictures in the tomb of Chnemhôtep, clearly portraying the basic rules applicable to internal control systems.

Other early indications of the existence of internal control include the use of test checking procedures by Zenon (the estate manager to Appollonius, a finance minister of Hellenic Egypt[6]), the internal audit of the financial records of Persian government officials, and the audit of money collected by the Hebrews for repairs to the Temple in Jerusalem.[7]

---

[3] Williard E. Stone, "Antecedents of the Accounting Profession," *The Accounting Review* (April, 1969), pp. 284, 285.

[4] Kenneth S. Most, "Accounting by the Ancients," *The Accountant* (May, 1959), p. 563.

[5] Richard Brown, *A History of Accounting and Accountants* (Edinburgh: Jack, 1905), p. 21; also described by Stone, *op. cit.*, p. 285.

[6] Most, *op. cit.*, pp. 564, 565.

[7] Stone, *op. cit.*, p. 286.

The Roman and Greek Empires

Brown goes on to describe the use of checking clerks in the city states of Greece around 500 B.C. as part of the control of governmental receipts and payments. These checking clerks were public officials who verified in great detail the business transactions pertinent to government establishments. At the time, all governmental receipts and payments had to be legally authorized and ordered by appointed magistrates. This rather resembles that part of contemporary internal control exercised by company boards of directors and senior executives when authorizing major capital investments through their minutes and meetings.

However, Stone writes that the earliest Greek civilizations had little time for formalized accounting, with the result that internal auditing was a somewhat unsophisticated affair:[8]

> Slaves were preferred as accountants because the law prohibited the torture of a freeman. The statements of the slave under torture was felt to be more conclusive evidence than those of a freeman under oath.

This rather primitive form of audit was superseded by somewhat more civilized forms. For example, Stone mentions the time of Pericles (451–429 B.C.) in which each citizen effectively became an auditor "by the custom requiring contractors of buildings to report their receipts and expenditures on tablets chiselled in stone on the walls of the building." [9]

The Romans displayed perhaps the most perceptive awareness of the need for internal control, and this is well documented by Brown.[10] They instituted a firm system of control over their governmental activities, particularly those involving tax collections, by distinguishing "between the person who imposes taxes and authorizes expenditure and the person who is responsible for the actual receipt and payment."

The following is a summary of a typical system of internal control in the Roman Republic as described by Brown.[11]

(1) Overall control of public revenue and expenditure was the responsibility of the Senate.

(2) Administration and authorization of these receipts and payments was entrusted to the *consuls* and, subsequently, to the *censors*, these persons having to account for their activities to the Senate.

(3) The actual collection of receipts and the making of payments were the responsibility of the *quaestors* of the treasury, provincial *quaestors* being directly accountable to the town or city *quaestors* who were in charge of the public treasury itself.

(4) In addition,

> All expenditure had to be legally authorized and regularly ordered by a competent magistrate, and could only be discharged by the production of a formal

---

[8] *Ibid.*, p. 287.

[9] *Ibid.*

[10] Brown, *op. cit.*, pp. 29–40.

[11] *Ibid.*, p. 32.

order, supported by documents tending to guarantee the existence and liquidity of the debt, the title of the creditor, and the execution of the work indicated by the order. The identity of the magistrate ordering payment and of the creditor, had, if necessary, to be attested by witnesses.

During the period following that of the Republic, the control of financial matters in government was ultimately vested in the Emperor.[12] Indeed, there is an example of an early attempt to control the use of funds set aside for public expenditure by use of budgets and cash reconciliations. Authorization of the actual payments made was the responsibility of either the *consuls* or *censors,* but subject to the limits of the budget and the overall control of the Emperor. The administration of the whole system was carried out on a regional basis with local officials responsible to centrally located superiors.

The third period of the Roman civilization—the Diocletion era—saw a series of reforms intended to strengthen internal control in government. This was undertaken by dividing the whole structure into four main centers of administration and rearranging the provincial governments in each of them. The four main areas were divided into provinces, each containing twelve *dioceses* (local districts), with the Emperor determining the total taxes to be collected by each area. The *praefects* of each area then determined the amounts to be collected in each *diocese* under their control, and thus, by further reallocations, each citizen in every town was allotted his share of the tax burden. Details of the individual amounts due by citizens were then entered in an assessment roll, copies of which were sent to the official responsible for collecting the taxes at *diocese* and main area levels of the organization. The taxes actually collected were thoroughly checked against the details of the assessment roll before eventually being sent to the central public treasury.

35

The main idea of this system was to ensure that each administrator at every level knew how much tax was to be collected by those persons for whom he was responsible. The work of the tax collectors, cashiers, and accountants could be checked by reference to the monies actually received and the predetermined and prerecorded sums that were due to be collected. In addition, each central treasury had a team of inspectors to conduct an internal audit of the system and procedures.

Another form of control used by both the Greeks and the Romans was the extensive use made of *arbiters* or auditors. Brown comments on their use by the Athenians around 500 B.C. to scrutinize the public accounts of all government officials at the end of their respective terms of office. These auditors were appointed officials, entitled *euthuni,* who had assistants called *logistae* to help them operate this internal audit function.

Internal Control in the Dark Ages

During the period following the fall of the Roman civilization and up to the beginning of the twelfth century, the developed economies rapidly

---

[12] *Ibid.,* p. 34.

rejected existing monetary systems and reverted to barter systems (particularly between 300 and 600 A.D.).[13] However, around 1100 to 1200 A.D. the tally stick was introduced into the business and financial affairs of both private and public enterprise. This device served as a form of receipt and was very quickly accepted to help in the internal control of business transactions.[14] When a particular transaction was completed and had an ascertained value, the tally stick was notched in accordance with this value, with different notches representing different values. The stick was then split in half, one half being kept by the debtor and the other by the creditor. This procedure was used, for example, as evidence of monies entrusted to government officials by the Exchequer in England.[15] At the end of a set period of time these officials had to account for the money given to them (for which they had received a tally stick as receipt), with much the same effect as in present-day cash imprest systems. The sticks were used first because of their durability and legibility, and second because the people using them were illiterate. In other words, it was a relatively easy way for an uneducated man to know exactly what he owed or was owed. The use of the tally stick indicates not only a keen awareness of the need to reduce the possibilities available for fraud and error, but also the need to control government revenue and expenditure particularly when decentralization of administration was necessary.

In the beginning, tally sticks were probably used more in the public than in the private sector of economic activity. The latter was either in the form of small business units or in the form of the large landed estate where the power of the feudal system was control in itself.

Another internal control device used in England was the Pipe Roll of the Exchequer which is thought to have been first produced in the reign of Henry I (1100–1135 A.D.). The Roll was a detailed record of the revenues due to the Crown and of the expenditure incurred in its collection. The following is a summarized description by Brown of the controlling aspects of the Roll.[16]

(1) The Domesday Book contained a permanent record of all major revenues due to the Crown, from which copies of the Pipe Roll were prepared.

(2) Three copies were independently prepared annually, one by the Treasurer, one by the Chancellor's clerk, and another, in the early days of the Exchequer, by a special representative of the King.

(3) Each copy contained details of the revenues to be received by the Exchequer on behalf of the King, and of the actual receipts and payments made.

---

[13] P. Grierson, *Numismatics and History* (The Historical Association, 1957).

[14] For a full description of the use of tally sticks, see R. Robert, "A Short History of Tallies," in *Studies in the History of Accounting*, ed., A. C. Littleton and B. S. Yamey (London: Sweet and Maxwell, 1956), pp. 78–85.

[15] Brown, *op. cit.*, p. 42.

[16] *Ibid.*, pp. 41–43.

(4) Each Sheriff responsible for collecting revenue due to the Crown in nis local area had to account for what he had collected to the Exchequer at Michaelmas, having made an interim payment to account at Easter, for which he was issued a tally stick as receipt. At the annual reckoning, he produced the tally stick together with vouchers supporting his various transactions during the year. The latter were recorded and compared with what had originally been recorded as due in the Pipe Roll.

(5) The various copies of the Roll were then audited.

The above system was obviously intended to control the funds coming into the Exchequer as well as controlling the actual collections of money due. The auditors used as part of this procedure were initially justices or barons and subsequently specially appointed officials entitled *Auditores Compotorum Scaccarii.*

The End of the Dark Ages

37

One of the most frequently advocated methods of control in private enterprise in the Middle Ages was the internal audit which was more often than not conducted by the estate owners themselves or by their appointed officials. D. Oschinsky describes several treatises of the time written by teachers of accounting, in which they suggested the use of internal audits and the means by which the auditor could tell if the various financial records were fraudulently drawn up.[17]

> He [the auditor] is instructed, for instance, as to how much salt should be allowed for the salting of a specified quantity of meat, and is told to inquire after the hides and fleeces of beasts which had died during the year, and to compare the corn yield with the seed corn in the previous roll and with the acreage in the extent.

Brown offers statements which document that these warnings were recognized in practice.[18]

Around 1300, the nature of private enterprise was undergoing a rapid change, with alterations to the actual structure of the existing business unit predominating. As businesses grew, more and more partnerships were formed with a consequent need for better internal control of transactions and resources. It was found that the existing accounting procedures had to be improved in order to deal with the increased trade, and gradually, through a process of trial and error, double entry bookkeeping was evolved, probably simultaneously in several important trading centers of the time such as Genoa, Milan and Venice.[19] The Italian monk and teacher of that time, Luca Pacioli, collated the bookkeeping practices of

---

[17] D. Oschinsky, "Medieval Treatises and Estate Accounting," in *Studies in the History of Accounting*, ed. A. C. Littleton and B. S. Yamey (London: Sweet and Maxwell, 1956), pp. 91–98.

[18] Brown, *op. cit.*, p. 53.

[19] For a detailed description of this development, see R. de Roover, "The Development of Accounting Prior to Luca Pacioli According to the Accountbooks of Medieval Merchants," in *Studies in the History of Accounting, op. cit.*, pp. 114–74.

others, and in the late fifteenth century, presented his famous work *Summa de Arithmetica*. It is clear that Pacioli and subsequent writers looked upon double entry as a control device as well as a recording procedure. Pacioli emphasized this in chapter 4 of his book, stating that bookkeeping would help the merchant control his various business activities.[20] Some of his recommendations from later chapters are given below:

(1) proper crossreferencing of bookkeeping entries and dates of transactions in order to facilitate easy tracing of entries when this was necessary (chapter 6);

(2) the appointment of a mercantile officer in every town to act as a registrar of accounting books kept by each business existing in his alloted area (chapter 7). This officer would keep a register of accounting books and any changes affecting them would be notified to him in order that he could seal the relevant books. Duplicate books were not to be kept by businesses;

(3) a stores ledger account for every store of goods in order to prevent fraud in relation to stocks (chapter 23);

(4) the prohibition of erasures in the books of account (chapters 31 and 36). All alterations were made by a further entry.[21]

This marked the beginning of a long period of complacency over internal control during which too much trust was placed in the ability of double entry to completely control and check human behavior in business.[22] However, there is evidence that the internal audit function was being employed with more frequency during the fourteenth and fifteenth centuries. For example:

(1) In 1298, the accounts of the City of London were audited by the Mayor, Aldermen and Sheriffs of the City.

(2) In 1333, the accounts of the City of Dublin were similarly verified by the Burgesses or the Earl of Desmond.

(3) In 1346, the warden's accounts of the Worshipful Company of Grocers of the City of London were audited by chosen members of the Company.

(4) In 1457, a *cont* of the Burgh of Pebillis (Peebles) was made by the Provost, Council and inhabitants of the Burgh.[23]

Stone states that in the early part of the thirteenth century the accounts of the cities of Pisa and Venice are known to have been audited, and even Columbus in 1492 was accompanied to the Americas by an auditor representing Queen Isabella.[24]

---

[20] Translated by John B. Geijsbeek, *Ancient Double Entry Bookkeeping* (Denver: Geijsbeek, 1914).

[21] Luca Pacioli, *Summa de Arithmetica*, 1494, translated in Geijsbeek, *op. cit.*

[22] This point is strongly made in B. S. Yamey, H. Edey, and H. W. Thomson, *Accounting in England and Scotland 1543–1800* (London: Sweet and Maxwell, 1963), p. 12.

[23] Brown, *op. cit.*, pp. 77–82.

[24] Stone, *op. cit.*, p. 290.

The Sixteenth and Seventeenth Century Development

In Geijsbeek's book, frequent mention is made of Simon Stevin, sometime government engineer, soldier of fortune, accountant and writer. Stevin (1548–1620) acted as an accountant and auditor, and in 1604 wrote a book, *Verrechning Van Domeine*, in which he described various internal control methods. Despite this, as Geijsbeek explains, "no credit is given him for the ingenious devices he mentions and which we now call internal checks." [25] Examples of these devices, given in the context of military administration, are as follows: [26]

(1) Payrolls should be sent direct to the auditors for immediate verification by them.

(2) The cook should report independently to the auditors on the number of meals served by him to the troops; Stevin advocated the use of a budgeted cost per meal to ensure no fraud or error was occurring in the cookhouse.

(3) Arrears of rent should be reported monthly to the general treasurer for suitable action. Geijsbeek also states that Stevin was the first advocate of control accounts for debtors, creditors, etc. These accounts were verified by the monthly detailed reports sent in by the officials concerned with the day to day accounting for such transactions.

Further evidence of the importance placed in this period on internal control by means of adequate bookkeeping procedures is given by Yamey, Edey, and Thomson. For example,

(1) Jan Ympyn Christoffels in his book, *A Notable and very excellente woorke, expressyng and declaryng the maner and forme how to kepe a boke of accomptes or reconynges*, published in 1547, stated that the pages of each book of account should be properly numbered "because that the fewer frauds and wronges maie be wrought therein."

This suggestion was repeated by other authors of the time such as John Weddington in 1567 and John Mellis in 1588.

(2) Gerald Malynes in *Lex Mercatoria* in 1656 suggested that no space should be left between entries in the journal in order to prevent fraud.

Conclusion

The concept of internal control relevant to accounting and finance has developed over a considerable period of time with its progress frequently retarded. That it remains a fundamental part of business management today in many ways is due to the generations of businessmen, government officials, accountants and writers who have either applied the concept in practice or at least advocated its use. This summary of the development of the concept reminds us that it was also recognized in many past civilizations, which reinforces its usefulness in business activity today.

---

[25] Geijsbeek, *op. cit.*, p. 12.

[26] *Ibid.*, p. 115.

39

A Pitman's Notebook

THE DIARY OF EDWARD SMITH
Houghton Colliery Viewer 1749

INTRODUCTION

In the year 1750 Edward Smith the Manager (or 'viewer') of the Colliery at Houghton in the County of Durham was one of the few people in the neighbourhood who could write. He seems to have been a respected member of the community, a person who could for example, be trusted to take notes of an agreement between a farmer and his customer. He apparently was a man who was interested in his work and displayed some of the characteristics of what would be today called modern management thinking. The rudiments of such management techniques as production planning, cost estimating and profit planning can be traced. The whole picture is of a professional manager who reduced his daily problems to writing in order to see them more clearly and to provide a basis for future reporting to his superiors.

43

Mr. Smith's responsibilities extended to the management of Houghton Colliery which comprised a coal drawing pit called "Hope", an "Engine" pit from which water was drawn and a "Sinking" pit which when completed was named "Success". The latter pit began to draw coal at the end of 1750 and the records show that it promised well for the future. The Viewer's responsibilities were wide as they covered all aspects of the venture. He was mining engineer, mechanical engineer, labour officer, planner, wages clerk, cost clerk, estimator and to some extent, a farmer.* In terms of current colliery outputs the operation was of course a small one, but an average weekly output of about 270 tons whilst a major shaft sinking and development were in progress, was nevertheless a most successful achievement for the times.

*Amos Barnes' View Book (N. of E. Inst. of Mining and Mech. Engineers) shows that Edward Smith was, twenty years later, also a consultant valuer. He used what is today thought in some quarters to be a modern method—that of calculating the present value of a future income stream by reference to a rate of interest.

"*Mr. Edward Smith's Valuation in Mr. Swinhoe's Estate at Hetton November 27th 1773.*

What is the present worth of £6,000 to be got in 60 years allowing for the first 40 years Nothing to be got and for the remaining 20 years to be got £300 p year allowing the purchaser £5 p Cent for his money.

Answer It's Worth in present Cash £531-0-0

N.B. if a yearly rent of £300 for 20 years were to be sold and to be entered upon immediately it would be worth in present Cash allowing £5 p Cent as above £3738-4-0"

Little has been recorded of everyday life in a pit village in the mid-eighteenth century. The housing was probably typical of what may be seen in some of the older pit villages of Co. Durham today. Pitmen's houses were built in the form of a single street or 'row'. Reference to the County archives gives the addresses of the mining community as "Collier Row", Houghton. The scene is one of drab uniformity in living conditions coupled with long, uncomfortable and dangerous working hours. A child born into such a community, if he survived the enormous yet normal hazards of infancy, had little to look forward to other than a life of toil. A man and his male children would normally go to the pit, perhaps at midnight (for Houghton shift times see 6th - 30th March 1751 below), the father and eldest son to hewing and putting and the younger children to operating the trap doors. It is probable that in the dark winter months of the North country, children working in the mine might not see the light of day, other than on Sundays; much of their life being spent in entire darkness.

44

A pitman was closely bound to the mine, if not in actual serfdom as obtained in Scotland, something closely akin to it. A binding fee of sixpence or a shilling was a customary payment to colliers with a fine of £18 if the contract was broken. The coal owners agreed among themselves that no man would be employed unless he could produce a certificate of leave from his master. In times of labour shortage a master would not issue such a certificate and the collier was therefore bound for an indefinite period. A type of remedy did exist however in the form of a Magistrate's release and a note of the exercising of this right is shown below (see 28th February 1751 - 4 March 1751). It would require very determined men to seek out a Magistrate who would listen sympathetically to colliers' complaints against a powerful coal owner. A deserting collier could be pursued, returned to the pit and fined for absenteeism. There is thus considerable significance in the wording of a certificate which states that a man may leave 'without molestation'.

Whereas much of the notebook is naturally concerned with 'pit work' it does contain some notes of more general appeal. Residents in and around Houghton-le-Spring may in the time records of both Colliery and Colliery Farm, recognise the names of their ancestors. Richard Stonehewer, B.A., M.A., LLD. who was the

Rector of Houghton in 1750 has his name recorded in the records of Church and University, the registrations of the Christening and early deaths of some of his children appear in the Parish Registers in County Records, Durham. A less important aspect of his life - the purchase of Fothers of fire coal from the local pit, is also preserved due to the meticulous recording of the Viewer (acting in his capacity of Despatch Clerk). It is in such trivia that history is seen to be a live, warm subject concerned more with people than with material and dates, and no apology is made for their inclusion together with data of more academic interest.

Today all that remains of the Success pit is the old heapstead which is grass covered and unsuitable for anything other than pony grazing. The shaft was filled in (1957) with stone from the nearby New Herrington mine as it was considered dangerous in its original state. At that time the shaft was approximately 350 feet deep*.

45

The naming of the pit "Success" was the decision of the owner Mr. John Nesham (see 3rd September 1750). At that time some miners travelled considerable distances to their work, others being housed in "hovels" provided by the coal owner whilst new pits were opened (see North Country Life in the Eighteenth Century, Edward Hughes, p.257). Pits were sunk where coal was most easily found and these were quickly worked out, new sinkings taking their place, perhaps at some distance from the original "Colliers' Rows". Success pit however did continue to work long enough to give its name to a hamlet and in that hamlet the name is preserved to this day. Collier Row is now a sizeable village called Colliery Row.

The sites of Hope pit and the Engine pit are almost certainly the two unnamed shafts shown on the six inch map, page 37, Nicholson's Farm, in 1749/50, the site of the Sinking pit, is now (1970) part of Stotts pastures, farmed by Mr. A. E. Smith.

In the following pages Edward Smith's notebook has been transcribed and arranged in chronological order. A brief explanatory commentary has been included where this has been considered necessary to a layman's understanding of the entries. The

*The following entry in the official List of Abandoned Mines shows that Success was finally abandoned in 1909:-
"Newbottle: Jane, Margaret, Success.
Low Main, Busty. Abandoned 17th July 1909
Harvey. Abandoned 13th July 1907"

original spelling and grammar has been maintained throughout the transcript.

In the case of repetitious material (output records, stores, etc.) an example is given and a summary provided in the Appendices A and C. A "roll call" of names mentioned in the notebook arranged in alphabetical order is included at Appendix B and a short Glossary of old mining terms forms Appendix D. A summary of Deliveries of Fire Coal forms Appendix E.

BIBLIOGRAPHY

1. The Compleat Collier 1708
2. The Miners of Northumberland and Durham. *R. Fynes* 1873
3. A Glossary of Terms used in the Coal Trade. *G. C. Greenwell* 1888
4. The Coal Industry of the Eighteenth Century. *T. S. Ashton & J. Sykes* 1929
5. The Rise of the British Coal Industry. *J.U.Nef.* 1932
6. The Great Northern Coalfield 1700 – 1900. *F. Atkinson* 1966
7. North Country Life in the Eighteenth Century: The North East 1700 – 1750

Edward Hughes

46

6 November 1749

A cost and profit estimate for a Colliery owned by Mr. George Humble a gentleman who owned land on the North side of the River Wear.

Measurements (up to the 1830's) were local and approximate and only the roughest estimate of costs per ton can therefore be made. The estimate below may indicate a cost of 2/2d. per ton at the pithead and a selling price of 3/5d. A cost estimate for Houghton Colliery is recorded on 10th January 1751.

At Lemonton Colliery belonging to Mr. Humble they pay for working p. Score with a 12 peck Corfe . . . . . .

	s.	d.
To Hewing p. Score	*1*	*8*
To Putting do.	*1*	*0*
To Headways do.		*2*
To Overman shifts and Candles		*6*
To deals props Smith and wreight		*3*
To drawing 6d. sleding 3d.		*9*
To Corveing 2d. wailing –1d. ropes 1d.		*4*
	4	*8*
To Colliery Rent	*1*	*0*
To engin charge Sinking drifting	*1*	*7*
	7	*3*
A score of coals as above will answer to 10 Chalders at 9/-p.	*11*	*3*
Profitt	*4*	*0*

16 and 17 February 1750

Mine drainage. This is the first of many notes on the constant battle against water in the mine. Tubing or 'Tubbing' was of wood and it was not until 1795 that metal tubing was introduced into the Northern Coalfield for shaft lining – at the King Pit, Walker Colliery.

These days putt in a length of wett Tubing to outsett the levell of the water.

24 July 1750

This day having got the Main Coal in the Borehole or Sinking pitt in Houghton Colliery.

This evening having lett in a Bargain to Robt. Humes and Willm. Hull for drawing out the Brattish in the above pitt for One pound one shilling.

16 August - 6 September 1750

Maintenance work on the Hope pit shaft.

Days wrought at the Hope pitt in Houghton Colliery From the 16th

Augt. to and wth. the 6th of Sept. 1750 . . . .

Cutting out five planks in the low length of Tub & etc. inside cribs. Putting in a pipe & Examining the shaft.

28 days . . . . £1. 8s. 0d.

1 September 1750

The Hope pitt in Houghton Colliery under of bank levell of the 1st. pitt in Ironsides' Ground

	fathm.	ft.	Ins.
this 1st Sept. 1750	1	0	6
From Surface to the Top of the wett tub	12	5	10½
	14	0	4½
The first pitt in depness from the Surface to			
. yd. water.	14	0	6
Diff			1½

3 September 1750

An important day in the life of the Colliery. The owner named the shaft sinking the " Success Pit." The Colliery now comprised two coal drawing pits named "Hope" and "Success" (although " Success " did not produce any coal until November) and an " Engine " pit which drew water from the mine. Mr. John Nesham was the owner and his " over Viewer " or agent was Mr. Amos Barnes. At the time of the naming of the sinking pit Nesham and Barnes did a little " long range planning " - or rather speculation about the future. This the Manager recorded fully. The "planning" was confined to discussion of the probable life of the colliery and pumping capacities. Barnes estimated that a life of three years might be expected. The Manager calculated 4 years, a year consisting of 46 full weeks work.

Some of the calculations are in cubic yards, thus it is possible to estimate the weight of a Houghton land chalder at that time, the final yield expected and the annual output. The expected annual output was not in fact achieved during the period documented, Hope's output diminishing as Success' output increased until in 1751 all output was being drawn from the Success shaft. For further commentary on outputs see Appendix A.

Sept. 3rd. 1750. This day at Houghton Mr. John Nesham gave a name to the Bore Hole or Sinking pitt being the Pitt last sunk and is from this times to be Called the Success pitt.

This Day Amos Barnes was down the Hope pitt in Houghton Collry. from which Mr. Nesham Ask'd on his Oppinion in Regard to the working of her as also his oppinion how to proceed from this present time . . . . 1st in Rgd. to what has been wrot. to this present time . . . .

Mr. Nesham ask'd Mr. Barnes how many years he thought that the present two pitts would work. Allow them to work 14000 Chalders a year

his answer was $3\frac{1}{2}$ Years.

he allowd. the two pitts to work 30 Acres of coal allowing 90 Tens an Acre in the whole coal the 1st time working over.

Allowing 9 yds to a winning Viz:-

	yds	ft	ins
Thickness of the wall	5	1	6
Breadth of the bord	3	1	6
Totall allowed for a winning	9	0	0

Supposeing that the present two pitts in Houghton Collry. to work 30 Acre its Req'd how many Chalders of Coals will be wrot. the first working. Over in the whole . . . . . .

> *66 Tens allowg. to be wrought in an Acre*
>
> *30 Acres*
> ___
> *1980*
> *16 Chalder allowing in a Ten*
> ___
> *11880*
> *1980*
> ___
> *31680 Chalders of coals . . . . .*

Supposing to vend 14000 chalders in a year.   7000 Chalders to work a pitt in a Year . . . .

Char. a Ten

```
16)7000(437,5 Tens
   64
   —
   60
   48
   —
  120
  112
   —
   80
   80
  ——
```

                                    Tens
                                    437,5
                                        176 Corves in a Ten
                                        ———
                                    26250
                                    30625
                                     4375
. . *corves in a score*   ———
                        21   )770000(3666 scores a year
                             63
                             —
                            140
                            126
                            ———
                            140
                            126
                            ———
                            140
                            126
                            ———
                             14

51

Allowing to work 46 weeks in a year and to work as above 3666 Scores . . . . 79 scores a week.

```
158,4   Tens in an Acre Height of seam 5ft 4 ins
    3
 ———
4)475,2
```

  118,8   *Tens to be wrought in the whole coal and broken . . .*
   30   *Acres*
 ————
 3564,0
   16   *Chalders in a Ten*
 ————
 213840
  35640
 ————
 57024,0 *Total, chalders of coals*
  14000 *Chalders a year . . . . 4 Years*

Calculations - Pump capacities.

The quantity of water an Engin will draw with a 9 inch bore 6 foot the length of a stroke and 10 strokes in a minute . . . . .

$$
\begin{array}{ll}
63,6174 & \text{sq ins} \\
72 & \text{Ins length of stroke}
\end{array}
$$

$$
\begin{array}{ll}
4580,4528 & \text{cu ins} \\
10 & \text{strokes a minute}
\end{array}
$$

$$
\begin{array}{ll}
45804,5280 & \\
60 & \text{minutes in an hour}
\end{array}
$$

Ins

282)2748271,6800 (9745,64 gallons

63 gallons a Hodgshead . . . . .154,69 Hodgsheads an hour. Its also Reqd. what a 10 inch bore will draw in an Hour 6 ft stroke 10 strokes a minute

As 63,62 Sq of 9 ins is to 154,69 Hodgsheads what will 78,54 Sq of 10 in . . . . 190,96 Hodgsheads in an hour

An Estimate made of the Materiall in Iron work thats in an Engine that draws water 40 Fathm. with a 9 inch bore at two Setts . . . .

   3   *Fathom two Barrells*

		Tunn	Cwt	sto	lbs
37	*Do. of wood pumps in every fathom 4 hoops each to weigh one stone*		18	4	0
40					
16	*Screwbolts each 12 lbs wt.*		1	5	10
8	*Plugplates each 16 lbs wt.*		1	1	2
40	*Fathom of spear having 8 Joynts each joynt will take plates & bolts each 5 sto*	5	0	0	
	The bottom rods for each spear 6 stone		1	4	0
	Two swords for the bucketts		0	3	0
	Two Us for the top of the spears		1	6	0
	For the Jackhead pumps and other Geer		2	0	0
	Carried over	1	11	7	12

52

	Tunn	Cwt	Sto	Lbs
Brot. Over	1	11	7	12
Three great chains	1	10	0	0
Arch plates & Bolts	0	1	0	0
Two Arch pinns	0	2	0	0
Great Gudgeon & Geer	0	2	0	0
Four spring plates & bolts	0	0	5	0
Cylinder bolts	0	1	0	0
for plugframe without Iron leggs	0	0	4	0
Moving Geer	0	1	4	0
Spanner for the Regulater....	0	0	1	7
Fire door and frame	0	0	6	0
Coal rake & two pokers	0	0	6	0
Piston Shank	0	1	2	0
Three screw keys	0	0	2	0
	3	13	6	5

Errors Excepted

I R p n

17 September 1750

The Height of Houghton Colliery Main Coal Seam

	....	ft.	ins.
From thill in coal		2	3
a stone band			1
In coal		1	3½
a stone band			1
In coal		1	5½
a stone band			
In coal			
Workable		5	2
in coal at top to bind the roof		1	1½
Totall height		6	3½

N.B. The above Dimensions is taken of the coal upon the Hitch
in the Hope pitt workings . . . . .
Gentlemen Coal Owners in the River Wear 1750
So. Side.
Hen Lambton Esqr.
John Tempest Esqr.
Nich. Lambton Esqr.
Sir Richd. Hylton Barrt. & Mr. Nesham

53

No. Side.
Sir Ralph Milbanks & Sir Rich Hylton.
Misstress Allans & daughters
Wm. Peareth Esqr.,
Mr. Thos. Donnison
Mr. Geo. Humble

19 September 1750

The manager today had a visit from Lawyer Fawcett who made enquiries as to the extent of the workings. The note is not comprehensive and one cannot therefore determine whether the lawyer was concerned with a claim for royalties, surface damage, or for some other purpose. Royalties claims would be fairly normal but surface damage claims were not unknown. At Elswick in 1609 tenants of a manor claimed against a partnership for subsidence damage (there were no roof supports in the headways workings).

This day Lawyer Fawcett was at Houghton Colliery Engin. he enquired of me where that the dike was I told him in Hutton Moor he ask'd me how it runn I told him and show'd him the ground He ask'd me whether we had wrought into the Butchers pasture I told him not . . . he told me that he was informed that the coal was wrought into it . . . he ask'd me if that the Colliery Rise to the South I told him that the depth to the So. to the New pitt. . . .

Days cross girding the Levells to the 20th Sept.

To Wm Hull	....	....	*9 days*
To Robt. Humes	....	....	*10 Do.*
To Ralph Taylor	....	....	*10 Do.*
			29 days

Levell taken out of the sump at Thos Bells pump . . . .

To Wm Hull	....	....	*1 day*
To Robt. Humes	....	....	*1 Do.*
To Ra Taylor	....	....	*1 Do.*

To 4 days Sluding the drift . . . .

Robinson's Brewery, Houghton-le-Spring.

25 September 1750

A note of some hard bargaining between a farmer (?) and customer.

This evening at Houghton at Thos Robinson I was in company with him and Martin Wind when that a bargain was made between the above two persons for bigg or barley. Martin Wind is to let Thos. Robinson* have all his barley which he computes to be near 80 Bushl. for 1s 11d per bushl. nothing agreed on to be returned. Mr. Robinson would fain had of have had a bushl. of wheat but could not prevail . . .

17 October 1750

No comment!

This day John Blenkinsop and his son Mathw. Turnbull went to work at Staith to repair the Trunk.

27 October 1750

The bargain note for driving the headways to win coal from the Success pit. The South headways were commenced later (see 12 January 1751).

This day let in a bargain to Robt. Harrison the Headways that is to go out of the New Pitt called the Success pitt he is to have 1s 2d per yard the Wall between the Headways is not to exceed 8 yds between Holeing and holeing he is to drive her 40 or 50 yds. in length as I choose it I am to pay no Consideration for wett working but obliges myself to continue the levell along one the headways . . . .

Edw. Smith.

The above Harrison is to supply The Headways with men double handed & to work 12 or 24 hours every day as is reqd.

1 November 1750

Mr. Barnes was over at Houghton Colliery.

There is little to report this month. Output from Hope Pit declined and as the Success Pit headway advanced a small quantity of coal was gained from the new area being opened for exploitation.

(See appendix 'A')

27 November 1750

(See also 1 – 10 January 1751)

This evening lett in a Bargain to Jno. Selby, White, Banks & Ra.

---

*See the photograph page 33 shewing the old Houghton Brewery built about the middle of the eighteenth century by the Robinsons – a well known local family (from information supplied by Mr. C. A. Smith, Sunderland)

Burrell the Levelling of the Success pitt Heapstead. Its mean length is 52 yds & breadth 26 yds. Which contains 28 Sq. Rood & to have ten pence p. Rood.

Totall   £1. 3   4d. . . . .

8 December 1750

This day let in a Bargain to Thos Nicholson Thos Scorer and four other partners to drive the East drifts in the Hope pitt Each 6/4 Quarters wide and to be continued Night and day to have for Each drift ten pence p. Yd. the putting to be at the Masters Expence.

26 December 1750

This day Measured over the Oates in the Grainery & finds 280 bushl. Having putt into the chist 9 Bouls to serve till New Years day . . . .

1 - 10 January 1751

Work wrought levelling the Success Pitt Heap Room in Houghton Colliery From the 1st to & with the 10th of January 1750/1

		s	d
To Ra Burrell	7½ days	5	-
To Jno Banks	6 Do.	4	-
	13½	9	-

3 January 1751

A note of a visit to Long Benton Colliery in which the following depths are given for the pits there.

	Fathm.	Yds.	ft.	Ins.
The 3rd Pitt a Coal Pitt in depness	60	0	0	0
The 2nd Do. a Coal Pitt Do.	50	1	0	0
The 1st Do. a fire engin Do.	56	0	0	0
The 2nd Do. a fire engin Do.	60	0	0	0
The lane pitt a Coal pitt Do.	58	1	0	0
The Dyke pitt only sunk (no coal)	35	0	0	0
The Meadow pitt Coal Pitt	58	1	0	0
Gosforth Engin pitt in depness	40	0	0	0

At Long Benton Colliery they allow ten Yards to a Winning, (viz) 4 Yards the breadth of the bord & 6 Yards for the thickness of the Wall or Pillar . . . . By a survey of Long Benton Colly. There is supposed to be 661 Acres of Coal . . . . The Leading Ten of Coals is Accottd. . . . . 22 Waggons. Each Waggon to hold and carry 19 Bouls that is 418 Bouls to a Ten. . . . .

The bargain made 8 December 1750 was amended. It seems that the drifts were driven at least partially in coal and this would account for the continued drawing of coal from Hope shaft in the first three months of the year.

This day having agreed with the above men for to Hew and putting the coals at 1s. 3d p. yard.

Houghton Colliery Cost Estimate.

On the assumption that 1 Chalder = 53 cwts. and that the estimate was in respect of 20 peck corves the pithead cost would be 1/10 per ton and the selling price 3/5 per ton.

58

	s	d
To Hewing p. Score	2	1
To Putting p. Score	1	0
To Headway p. Score		3
To door keeping p. Score		1
To Barrowmen's candles, ridding, making up Stopings nails & etc. p. Score		3
To Overman's wages p. Score		2
To driving gutters putting down sumps & pumping water p. Score....		3½
Wailing the coals		1
Ropes, Ginns & Repairs, Smith and Wreight p. Score		3½
Corving p. Score 2½		
Drawing p. Score 1 0		
Sledding p. Score 4		
——	1	6½
To Deals and props p. Score		4
To Engin Charge p. Score		8
To Sinking drifting & etc.	1	6
To Colliery Rent p. Score	1	8
	10	2½

D. A. R. Forrester
UNIVERSITY OF STRATHCLYDE

"WHETHER MALCOLM'S IS BEST OR OLD CHARGE & DISCHARGE"*

Abstract: In 1775 A.D. the recommendation was made that the accounts of Glasgow College be changed from the traditional charge and discharge type of records to a double entry bookkeeping system. This touched off an academic controversy that lasted for many years and generated much bitterness among the Faculty of the College.

59

Public sector accounting in the 18th Century was still in most countries clearly derived from medieval practice. But important innovations in Exchequer practice in Britain began in the 1780s. Some of these reforms were anticipated in a dispute at Glasgow College which illustrates certain themes, and the resistance innovators could encounter. In Scotland and not least in Glasgow a new liberalism flourished at the same time as the American tobacco trade brought prosperity. For the University, a period of peace and international repute ended as Adam Smith resigned his Chair in 1764. Subsequent efforts to reform the university constitution and administration aroused donnish disputes of growing intensity.

John Anderson, Professor of Natural Philosophy, advocated the University's accounts should be kept in journal, cash book and ledger, referring to Alexander Malcolm's "Treatise of Bookkeeping or Merchants' Accounting" (1743 A.D.). Principal Leachman supported the traditional stewardship accounts being maintained by the factor, Professor Morthland. A local satirist observed:

"No strife about book-keeping sharpened their range
Whether Malcolm's is best or Old Charge and Discharge:
Of which as examples of learning and wit,
Long speeches were made and huge volumes were writ.
and still as their noodles were puzzled,
They got swarms of book-keepers' clerks to unravel the knot;
When after rewarding with thanks and with plate,
They let loose on their steward a tempest of hate."'

*The author acknowledges advice generously given on earlier drafts by Professors B. S. Yamey, W. E. Stone and G. A. Lee.

The Visitation System

The University, the second in Scotland, had been founded by a papal bull of 1451 A.D. It was reformed in 1577. After the Glorious Revolution of 1688, and the establishment of Presbyterianism, the revenues of the former archbishopric were granted under lease to the University, with its single college. Income was also received from a sub-deanery. General revenues were brought together in a third, ordinary account. In addition, specific bequests or mortifications had to be separately accounted for.

In 1727, there had been accusations of malpractice against the Principal, leading to a special Royal Visitation. The powers of dean and professors or masters were at this time clarified, leaving the principal responsible for practical matters and for chairing faculty meetings. Professors resided during term-time in houses on the campus. The close, collegiate life prompted disputes, the settlement of which, along with other functions, was entrusted to the College Visitors.

The visitation system originated in the supervision of medieval religious houses. In 1772, when applying to the Courts in Edinburgh for some constitutional reforms, John Anderson referred to William Blackstone's "Commentaries on the Laws of England", which noted:

> ". . . the tendency for individuals and corporations to deviate from the end of their institution. The law had therefore provided proper persons to visit, enquire into and correct all irregularities in such corporation." (1765, I, cap. p. 46)

(Blackstone in 1753 had written a treatise for his fellow Bursar of All Soul's College, Oxford, where the accounting system was "of as high Antiquity as the Mallard or College Mascot.")

In Dr. Robertson's History of Scotland published in 1759, Anderson also found support for asserting that societies are never reformed from within but always as forced by some "foreign hand".

An alternative course was suggested by Adam Smith in 1776, when he implied that the invisible hand of competition could guide, motivate and correct the efforts not only of the butcher and baker, but also of masters, provided they were remunerated from fees and not from funds.[2]

The Visitors of Glasgow College could scarcely, however, be described as "a foreign hand": One was himself a master, in his office of dean of faculty. The second was the Presbyterian Minister of Glasgow, a post combined somewhat later with that of college principal. Only the third, the rector, was elected by masters and students each year. Normally, he was a national figure. In 1775, the rector was the 9th Lord Cathcart, to whom John Mair dedicated his "Book-keeping Modernized". In 1776, it was Baron Montgomerie of the Scots Exchequer. In 1783, Henry Dundas was elected: he was twice Treasurer of the Navy and in 1806 was unsuccessfully impeached for privately holding state funds. In 1784, the rector was Edmund Burke, who four years before had proposed "Economic Reform" of the Exchequer. In 1786 and '87, Adam Smith was elected. The long-drawn out controversy over college accounting came to the attention of important people, and may be set in national perspective.

Auditor independence could thus scarcely be guaranteed, especially when the rector's inauguration was accompanied by much conviviality, the expenses of which in 1755 are fully detailed and vouched. (The food and drink were not as rich, however, as that provided for feasts of the audit at Trinity College, Cambridge early this century, commemorated by turtle shells on the old kitchen walls!) In addition to the Visitors, Glasgow magistrates normally signed the college accounts, until 1778, when they refused, and the Principal appended a note of his disagreement with the Visitors' docquet approving an experimental and minor change of form, thus constituting himself "Visitor to the Visitors", Anderson claimed.

61

New Professionalism

While Lords and Magistrates were accustomed to audit functions, a new professionalism of administration was emerging in this century. The Royal Visitation had prescribed that the college books should be kept by a single factor, who was to be a near relative neither of the principal nor masters. Yet the interests of incumbents were preserved! Professor Morthland continued to act as factor at that time; and in 1745, the college factor's duties were taken over by his son Matthew, a writer with some legal training.

It was Matthew Morthland's accounting which Anderson found so hard to change. One of those brought in to help was James Hall, who succeeded Morthland in 1784. Hill's son later joined him in a partnership, which with changing membership continues as legal factor to the University till the present day.

Gradually, therefore, professionals took over administrative and accounting functions from the faculty, whom Anderson sought to involve in technical matters:

"The art of book-keeping never was and never will be disparaged by those who know it. It is the duty of every mem-

ber of this College to know as much of it as will enable
him to judge whether the Factor's accompts and his Cash
book, Journal and Ledger be properly kept."[3]

The Principal confessed he had neither talents nor taste for such
accounts as required deep skill in book-keeping but, after thirty
years of application and drudgery, felt that he knew how tot keep
accounts in the best order. Of his colleagues he wrote:

"The Faculty satisfied with the accuracy of the account . .
did not think it of much importance to enquire minutely
into the particular modes of book-keeping which few of
them understood and fewer had leisure to study from constant application to the business of their profession."

Charge & Discharge Accounts

The controversy in 1775 focused on the form and timing of
Morthland's accompts, which were inscribed in three large volumes
and submitted annually to the faculty. For each of the three classes
of revenue, to sums outstanding from the previous year were added
current revenues, and from this total charge were deducted payments made by the factor and his salary, leaving a balance due for
settlement, or carry forward. The system had originated in the
Exchequer of the Norman kings in the 12th Century. It was traditional, widely spread and emphasized personal accountability. The
Principal was "the accountant" for the Archbishopric revenues, and
had to appear at the Scots Exchequer every three or four years to
have accounts derived from Morthland's passed by the officials and
auditors, paying fees of £33 before receiving his quietus *(See Illustration I)*.

In 1775 Professor Anderson appealed to the Edinburgh Law
Courts for changes to be made in the accounts, but the matter was
remitted for decision to the College Visitors. They met first in
Glasgow and then at Lord Cathcart's Schaw-Park house. Their de-
gree prescribed a scarcely amended form of account *(Illustration II)*.
A footnote suggested that:

"the order of articles is a matter of indifference:
only to facilitate the comparing the accompt that
is examined with the preceding year's accompt, one
and the same order should be preserved."

Anderson held that clarity depended upon the distinctness of order
in which articles were stated. Later the faculty resolved that the

ILLUSTRATION I

"In the book of foreign Accompts, In the nineteenth year of the reign of his Majesty King George the Third—

Doctor William Leechman Principal of the University of Glasgow and the other Masters and Professors in the said University Accounting for the Tack Duty of the rents and duties payable to the late Archbishop of Glasgow as per Tack from his present Majesty under the Privy Seal, dated the 12th day of May 1779 to the said Principal and Masters and to their Successors in office for the use and behoof of the said University for the space of nineteen years, commencing from the term of Midsunday 1773 and ending at the term of Whitsunday 1792 being for the crops and years of God 1773, 1774, 1775, 1776 which is the first four years of the present Lease, and of their issuing, paying and disbursing the same rendereth an account of ₤MM.CC. vi: s d xix: vi 8/12 the yearly sum of ₤551. 14.10 8/12 sterling as the tack duty payable by them."

(From the total Charge above was deducted bursaries, salaries and grant for instruments for making experiments in Natural Philosophy).

63

Excerpts from

The Principal's "Quietus" from the Scots Exchequer" (Scottish Record Office, E215/3 p. 57).

same order and form must be used in the primary books and in the final accounts.

Double-entry Books

In appearing before the Visitors and subsequently, Anderson pressed for double-entry books.

The Royal Visitation of 1727 had prescribed that the factor should keep an accurate cash-book, journal and ledger. Thomas Harvie, a merchant, had at that time put the College books in order. But a half century later there was a problem of interpretation. Morthland insisted to Anderson that his cash-book was rightly kept, meaning his rental or collection book. When earlier asked for his ledger, he claimed to have a book of that kind which would give every satisfaction.

Anderson with a small committee was put in charge of the implementation of the Schaw-Park decree. For this purpose they may well have bought a handsome folio book still preserved in the university archives and inscribed "The Factor's Ledger": inside there are no entries whatsoever! The problem, of course, was to adapt Italian, traders' book-keeping, as described by Mair or Malcolm, to the needs of estates and stewards. Principal Leachman and others

ILLUSTRATION II

The Factor's Annual Accounts

Approved for Glasgow University, according to the
Schaw-Park Decree of October, 1775.

Charge or Dr.   *Discharge or Cr.*

1. Balance of last Account when due by the Factor and not paid

1. Balance of last account when due by the College and not paid

2. Deductions or rests, judged not be absolutely desperate stated in one article as they stood in the discharge of the last account.

2. Disbursements stated and casual, including the Factor's Salary.

3. Rental divided into its different articles as normal.

3. Deductions or rests judged to be absolutely desperate and irrevocable and therefore unnecessary to be carried to the next accompt

4. Annual Rents or sums belonging to the account which the Factor is empowered to levy within the year accounted for.

4. Deductions or rests, judged not to be absolutely desperate, refering to a particular list, signed and dated by the Factor and examined by the Faculty, which the Factor is to charge himself within the second article of the next account.

5. Casual articles that come into the Factor's hands: such as donations or legacies to the College, gross sums, etc.

5. Balance of Account when due by the Factor.

6. The Balance of this account when due by the College.

Source—"The Management of the College Revenues" p. 184.

64

doubted whether the visitors of 1727 had meant to tie the factor to the artificial modes in use among merchants who had extensive and complicated dealings: neither journal nor ledger could be applied in a normal sense, they submitted, nor were the rules of the art really necessary except as always applied. The Principal felt that the *origo mali* or real source of conflict would appear to a disinterested spectator as lying in a perhaps bigoted attachment to long established practice on one side, and in an enthusiastic admiration of speculative rules of art on the other.

Fears were expressed that the new system to be introduced might be found cumbersome, tending to the utmost confusion.

Anderson admitted that the new system could be abbreviated, if accompanied by an accurate ledger and a bill of arrears. Against the outdated practice, Anderson claimed, there were three laws: the law of reason, the laws of book-keeping, and the Statute of Visitation.

Professor Anderson was sanguine that improvement could soon be obtained since in 1776, he said, there were in Glasgow five hundred persons who had studied and understood the regular method of book-keeping, as taught by many: a few guineas would be enough to arrange the accounts better than Morthland had managed. Some time later he challenged the Principal to pay the fifty or hundred guineas due, or to get people willing to put the accounts in order and take nothing for their trouble.

The first practitioner brought in 1776 to open the new books was Carrick, a banker: after a month or two he declared himself averse. Then Marshall, Hill & MacNae were each set to work. By 1778 the work was at a standstill and Anderson tried to blame Morthland for the delays. Then, in 1780, McNae & Hill

65

> "declared that in their opinion the complex, laborious and expensive mode of keeping accounts which may be necessary in complicated mercantile business is not necessary nor proper nor useful in accounts as plain and simple as the college ones indisputably are."

Principal Leachman called that if all the masters of book-keeping in Europe were assembled they could devise no shorter, simpler and safer form that charge and discharge. The law courts had ordered accounts presented in the artificial form of book-keeping "to be thus simplified for the examination of persons not adapt in the art."

Finally the Principal offered to submit all Morthland's accounts as being in conformity with the Decree to the opinion of any three merchants, such as Glassford, Speirs & Henderson: and engaged under penalty of £500 to exhibit a form of College accounts acceptable to those merchants or any three noblemen's factors. The old forms of accounts, he was ready to show, were clearer and better by induction of particulars.

Accountability

Further significant differences emerged over whether Morthland was accountable for cash received or for a "full charge". Anderson believed that a cash accounting system was best. Although Morthland's duties included the raising of revenues and the enforcement of dues, Anderson held that he should be accountable only for his "intromissions", or the actual levies received by himself and subordinates. A distinction was made between a tax-farmer responsible for the precise amount bid and a factor or agent; and Morthland should not be seen as "some mongrel kind of being". The Principal explained that Balliol College accounted to them on the basis of full charge, while they accounted to the Treasury for a bequest by King William III in terms of *proventus et expensae* formally, but in practice for full rentals collectible. Caught within the traditional and state system, Leachman asked if it would be for the general benefit of all civilized nations to account for actual receivings and actual disbursements, without the check and control of a rental or charge. Morthland defended the accuracy of his rental and demanded:

66

> "What is the authority the college goes upon in making any alterations in their original charge given to me and my predecessors past memory, whereby you account with the Lords of the Treasury and with the Court of the Exchequer who have the rental of the Archbishopric recorded exactly the same as in your charge."

Many of the misunderstandings focussed in the balances carried forward and in the requirement of the Schaw-Park decree that the debts on the three branches of revenue be brought together "hereby a full and single accompt may arise yearly, and the whole estate and condition of the University may appear at one view". The inventory on which Italian Book-keeping builds is not readily derived from the charge-discharge system.

The Glasgow faculty in 1776 voted monies for a new chapel and college frontage only to have the Visitors refuse approval till they knew the debt and surplus monies and unappropriated funds available. Anderson protested later that:

> "in the year 1778, in Britain and in a great commercial town, there is an incorporated body, Glasgow College, which keeps its accounts in such a manner that their debt and wealth cannot be ascertained, nor had they a proper bill of arrears nor even an accurate rental."

Some of these needs were met by a simple listing of the securities in the College chest, after noting "in their bosom or on their backs" the fund or funds to which they were appropriated. Anderson was particularly sensitive about misapplications of college funds, for instance to commercial ventures such as canal building. He opposed a contribution of £1,000 to raise a battalion to fight the American rebels. Morthland was expected to clarify the funding and the flows and the wealth in his accounts.

Failure to distinguish personal and cash accounting had significant consequences. The link could be found in the "bills of rest" and the bad debts allowances made every dozen years. Anderson complained that Morthland had only once been able to submit a list of rests or dues unpaid. The balance carried forward in the charge-discharge accounts was thus made up in unknown proportions of debts irrecoverable or recoverable by Morthland, and of excesses of receipts over payments due by him. Undoubtedly he had difficulty in enforcing annual payments of small sums from thousands of debtors. Rentals and tithes were fixed largely in quantities of specific grains, salmon, capons and poultry. These were converted to money at prices struck at "Friars Courts" held each Candlemas, due for payment at Whitsun "with a mark furder for each boll of meal in case of non-payment at or before that term". The 1775 rental still shows cash due in Scots pound, although English sterling had been the legal currency since 1707. Scots money values were shown in the books till 1762. At 1/12 of sterling value, Scots pence and half-pence thereafter appeared as very vulgar fractions in Morthland's very precise accounts. In 1762 there had been a special drive to collect dues outstanding in some cases for 39 years. Morthland at that time was allowed "interest" of £500 Scots for his special expenses.

67

From 1775 there was pressure for quicker collection, even of very small dues, symptomatic perhaps of a move from networks of debts which remained open at least till death towards a cash and bank transaction society. There was also pressure on stewards and others to operate with smaller or nil balances and to account for interest earned on longer term funds. On one mortification or special fund alone, Morthland suddenly found himself charged with interest over 20 years amounting to £800. The rests or balances outstanding in his other accounts were reduced for ground annuals no longer enforceable at law, and for rents owed by "broken tenants": for the remainder he was forced to grant a bond on which he would have to pay interest. Thus at the same time as there was a new effort to collect punctually and to distinguish each year's income and expenditure, there was an innovation going on in depriving stewards and tax collectors of their banking functions, and concentrating these last in ever fewer specialized firms.

Conclusions

Efforts to prove incompetence or dishonesty against Morthland were far from successful. Anderson's committee found errors of £3, £5, and £2, the largest being a balance of £383 in 1776 which he showed as due from rather than to himself! Formally his rights were secured by his heirs to uplift and appropriate outstanding dues for which he was said to have made 'thankful payment' to the College *(Illustration III)*. Such wording, however, Anderson rightly described as a farce which could be dangerous and unjust to the factor. Many another factor of the time was broken on retirement, or relieved of debts for sums which he may never have been able to collect.

In 1782, Morthland retired, Leachman ensuring for him the praise of the faculty and the award of an inscribed plate. (The account for this long remained unpaid). But large sums due in "rests" were then demanded from Morthland, he claiming discharge on grounds of "long service, vast buildings and immense additions to collect revenue". Retrospectively over 37 years, he then claimed expenses with interest accruing, in total exceeding his debt. When this was disallowed he was declared bankrupt shortly before his death. Intricate legal process was initiated against his cautioners or guarantors and their heirs. The degree of specific funding and obligation was investigated by William Keith, a sub-auditor to the court and a fore-runner of the Scots accountancy profession.

68

ILLUSTRATION III

Morthland's Discharge

7th May, 1761 A.D.—The whichday the Masters of the university having seen and examined the above Accounts in Charge and Discharge given by Mathew Morthland their factor of his intromissions . . . and compared the Charge extending to (£9,587.17/10½ Scots.) with the Discharge extending to (£8,124.4/8 Scots). They find there is resting by the said M.M. to the Masters, the sum of £1,463.13/2½ with which sum he is to charge himself in his next year's Accounts, and which accounts the said Masters do allow . . . and hereby . . . discharge the said M.M., his heirs and executors for the said Cropt and year (excepting the above Ballance.) But also by these presents impower him and his foresaids to uplift and receive what is resting and owing unpaid by those liable in payment . . . and to appropriate the same for his own use in respect he hath made thankful payment to us thereof (excepting the above balance as said is . . .)

                                   Sgd. Will Leechman VR
                                   Adam Smith D.F.
                                   . . . . John Anderson P.N.P.

Source—University Archives 2667.

Anderson after increasing alienation from his fellow professors died in 1796, founding in his Will an 'anti-university', which grew steadily until it was granted a charter as the University of Strathclyde in 1964. An incompatibility was thus imperfectly resolved at this time between accounting systems appropriate to landlords and to the "Tobacco Lords", and other tradesmen of Glasgow with whom Anderson was on friendly terms. Neither the books nor the form of final accounts altered significantly from the tenure of Morthland through that of his immediate successors. Gradually through small sequential changes, income and expediture accounts and balance sheets for the university emerged.

But charge-discharge forms and terms remained long in use in Scotland especially for trust or benevolent funds, (such as that for the Edinburgh Chartered Accountants, where the accounts were thus headed up till 1948. Through the controversy, one can sense the robust simplicity of stewardship accounts, presented for audit for successive periods in columnar form.

69

FOOTNOTES

[1]Murray, p. 106.

[2]Smith Book I, p. 120 & Book II p. 247.

[3]Precise References to Faculty Minutes, etc. are given in Forrester,, passim.

[4]The accounts and vouchers of the period have been safely stored in the university archives. One voucher of 1756 records the supply to Dr. Black of a Papin's digester which in 1761 proved invaluable in the development of the steam engine with separate condenser. (See Law, pp. 10 & 16). The supplier was James Watt, who had a shop on the campus, and in co-operation with Black patented this improved engine. The transaction of 1756 is recorded in Watt's Day-Books which are preserved in Birmingham (C. F. Swinbank P.)

BIBLIOGRAPHY

Anderson, J. and Others, "The Management of the College Revenues", being the papers in the case printed by Anderson at his own expense.

Binney, J. E. D. *British Public Finance and Administration, 1774-1795* (O.U.P. 1958).

Coutts, J. *History of the University of Glasgow* (Maclehose, 1909).

Devine, T. M. *The Tobacco Lords* (Donald, 1975).

Forrester, D. A. R. *There are Three Laws,* (The Philosophical Journal, Glasgow, January, 1975).

Law, R. J. *James Watt & The Separate Condenser* (H.M.S.O. 1969).

Murray, David *Chapters in the History of Book-keeping, Accountancy and Commercial Arithmetic* (Glasgow, 1930).

Smith, Adam *The Wealth of Nations* (Everyman edition).

Swinbank, P. *"James Watt's Glasgow Shop"* and *"James Watt's Partnership"*— Papers available from the Department of the History of Science at Glasgow University.

Early Canal Company Accounts: Financial and Accounting Aspects of the Forth and Clyde Navigation, 1768—1816

D. A. R. Forrester

Economic and accounting historians have tended to study railway developments, and companies incorporated under the British 1856 and 1862 Acts, rather than the earlier experience of Parliamentary or statutory companies out of which general, consolidating legislation and limited liability for companies evolved.

The Forth and Clyde Canal or Navigation is of interest insofar as private finance was subscribed in Scotland and London in 1768, adequate according to first estimates, and postponing the need for Exchequer support. As work progressed, retrospective and prospective statements of sources and applications of funds were required, anticipating more general charge-discharge annual statements sent from Glasgow to London from 1791 to 1856. Transactions on credit were curtailed; receipts were lodged in and payments made from the Bank. New corporate and cash accounting systems thus emerged at precisely the time of Exchequer reforms of the Imprest system. Periodic income was quickly ascertained, tabulated, classified, and graphed as early as 1815. A final significant innovation in printing and circulating reports and accounts to proprietors took place after Glasgow interests outvoted the London and landed shareholders.

Account books as such have not survived, but minute books and a series of reports and accounts sent from Glasgow to London from 1787 are available in the Scottish Record Office. These records have been used by Lindsay to describe the Canal's general history, but do not permit replication of J. R. Ward's socio-economic analyses of the finance of English canals;[1] but

they offer contemporary vignettes which can be supplemented in local archives. The stature of individual entrepreneurs becomes clear as the freedoms advocated in Adam Smith's *Wealth of Nations* were increasingly realised. Administrative and accounting skills learnt in the mercantile field were applied effectively to this Canal, which was not completed to the Firth of Clyde until 1790, and paid no dividend till 1800, thereafter liberally rewarding the patient investors.

We therefore find here examples of inter-sectoral migration of skills, of relationships between Exchequer, legislature and a private company, and also of a coordination of private interests and common weal. The infrastructural development described was of importance not merely in facilitating and cheapening the transport of passengers and freight (almost 3 million tons were to be carried in 1866) but also by its direct tendency to make different districts and different places feel that each had need of the other, as Buckle wrote in his *History of Civilisation in England*.[2]

Introductory

A canal through the narrow central belt of Scotland had seemed attractive since the 1660s: both naval and commercial traffic would be facilitated. A century later, Edinburgh's interests with the Continent and Glasgow's booming trade with the Americas promoted rival plans, until that for a Great Canal for sea-going ships received effective support.

Glasgow's promotion of a shallower canal could be replaced by a 7-feet deep navigable cut[3]

71

---

[1] Works referred to are listed by author in the Bibliography. FCN1/- indicates Scottish Record Office files.

[2] J. T. Buckle, 1867 edition, vol. III, p. 181.
[3] Progressive deepenings to 10 feet took place up to 1814.

only if support was obtained from public funds, it was thought. But negotiations proved fruitless. Tired of delays, aristocrats and merchants and bankers, chiefly in Edinburgh and London, opened a subscription list to raise the £150,000 required according to John Smeaton's, the great civil engineer's, plans and estimate. Meetings were held in both cities, and a Private Bill was presented to Parliament for incorporation. This received royal assent as 8 Geo III cap. 63 in 1768.

Twelve more times up to 1820, the company had to obtain Private Acts amending its constitution, altering its fund-raising powers, or for acquiring land on modified routes. There was thus advantage in having members and influence in the Houses of Commons and Lords. Parliamentary companies may well have seemed 'little republics',[4] growing up in the shadow of Westminster till they reached the independence which Robert Lowe aspired for them in 1856. The experience then gained by the legislature enabled incorporation by simple registration.

But with poor communications and parochialism, tension and problems inevitably arose, especially as the cut proceeded westward from Grangemouth on the Forth and reached the vicinity of Glasgow in 1776. Thither the management was moved and Edinburgh found itself increasingly ignored in negotiations between London and Glasgow. London's control was tightened after funds had run out in 1773 with the sea-to-sea canal scarcely half complete. The position was made specially difficult by the collapse of Douglas Heron & Co.'s Ayr Bank.

Economies were insisted on, and more formalised sub-contracting. Faith in the contract method was later voiced by Superintendent Colquhoun who found it the least expensive mode of conducting the business, and proposed that his estimates of maintenance and operating costs under twelve heads be the basis for putting these operations out to contract: 'in spite of every kind of vigilance on the part of those entrusted with management, like all public undertakings there is a propensity to waste ... which if not checked by the most vigilant eye of an auditor, will accumulate and increase year after year'.[5]

Accounting

In addition to the Chief Engineer, Smeaton, a site engineer, MacKell, and a surveyor or estimator, a

---

[4]The phrase is Robert Lowe's, used in the debate on the 1856 Companies Act. (*Hansard*, 3rd Series, CXL, col. 134.)
[5]FCN1/37, p. 186.

key appointment at the start was that of Oversman or Clerk to the Cheque for the whole works. Nine candidates applied for the post in June, 1768, including a factor, a former Carron Iron company clerk, and an army lieutenant. Several had powerful patrons. The successful applicant, a former merchant in Edinburgh called Alexander Stephen, was awarded a salary of £70. His duties at first were to pay wages and to keep accounts, with a journal of work done, reporting to the Law Agent in Edinburgh weekly. Some months later he was instructed to make a full and distinct account of monies received and disbursed. Invoices for more than £20 were required to be checked against current and agreed prices, and to be signed by the Engineer before submission to the Committee for approval. Stephen was also instructed to draft a State of Accounts owing, and to prepare an Account of Utensils and Materials. This was later described as a Ledger of Ware, distinctly accounting for the diverse applications of wood, etc. In 1771, Speirs sent over from Glasgow an assistant to keep this record at a salary of £30. The task was not facilitated by MacKell who attested receipts and uses of wood without informing Stephen. From 1769, a General Account of materials on hand was to be laid before Quarterly Meetings. No such stocks appear in the 1792 or 1815 Balance Sheets, even though in January 1797 it was prescribed that an annual inventory of materials and utensils should be taken, and the value fixed 'by some disinterested person'.

The Edinburgh Agent had early opened a Minute Book, a Letter Book, a Book to register precepts or cheques drawn on the Bank, a share or Stock journal and Ledger for transactions. (The Book for bank precepts has been reduced today to cheque counter-foils; but in the 18th century Treasury at Westminster, such a system had replaced cumbersome instructions to the lower Exchequer by means of tallied foils and counterfoils.) The agent had been ordered to prepare a plan of share transfer books in the manner of the great companies in England, but instead adopted the 'plan' of the Royal Bank of Scotland. All these books, together with Stephen's Accounts, were ready for examination in November, 1768, when a full Committee was adjourned so as not to interrupt the Lord Provost and Mr. Speirs in the examination sub-committed to them.

But the auditing of ever increasing expenses proved onerous for Committee members. Relations with the Royal Bank were so close that, in 1770, its Secretary was made part-time Comptroller and auditor of Accounts to the company. After he had taken the oath of faithful administration, and provided sureties or guarantees of £1,000, Archibald Hope's salary was to be £60 per annum. He was to audit the accounts of the London and Edinburgh Agents, and of Stephen, while his account would be audited by a committee member. Full committee approval of expense might be necessary in special circumstances. The title of Hope's function was borrowed directly from the Exchequer. But the days of combining many offices which could be delegated to assistants were numbered, after the 'one man, one job' reforms in the Treasury from 1776–82 spread out.[6]

London of course required an over-view of sources and applications as work proceeded. Those in Parliament required from Hope an abstract of bank Accounts, and a clear statement of proposed works and expenses before they left town in March, 1771. Later that year, the Committee approved the books audited by Hope as 'giving full satisfaction to all concerned, especially the distant proprietors, who have no opportunity of seeing the works and inspecting the respective Accounts'. Next spring, London requested estimates of sources and applications for the coming season, and to the completion of works, along with Accounts of work to date including information on average costs per yard dug and of masonry built, which had to be obtained from those on site. (The best estimates or forecasts, we will see, were prepared by Colquhoun for the last stages of canal construction.)

As work moved west and finance became increasingly hard to find, responsibilities were transferred to Glasgow in 1775. London resolved that Stephen should be Agent in Scotland and cover all meetings, while Hart in Edinburgh should be demoted to company solicitor, after he had transferred the books to Hope. An Edinburgh General Meeting however continued Hart as chief clerk, agent, accountant and book-keeper at a salary of £200, to include all his assistants and office expenses.

In May 1775, the Committee in Glasgow invited a member, Jackson by name, to examine the Books and vouchers of the company from the very start. He replied that it would be too time consuming and distracting from his own business; he was doubtful of the propriety of interfering with Accounts contracted under the former Committee, and refused to take custody of the books.

By March, 1776, it was resolved in London that there was no occasion for an agent, clerk, auditor or comptroller in Edinburgh. Hope was downgraded to company cashier at a salary of £30; and even this appointment was terminated subsequently.

Many responsibilities thus rested with Stephen: he was ordered to receive toll receipts each week, and to lodge Accounts and vouchers monthly with the member of Committee responsible for 'contingent affairs' between meetings. By 1779 London was complaining of his slowness in transmitting committee minutes. From the start of 1781, Accounts of Revenue and Expenditure were demanded quarterly.

Edinburgh felt even less well served. A General Meeting there in 1782 appointed a committee to investigate problems in the Falkirk area, and were told from London that this was contrary to regulations. Edinburgh complained of this reaction to 'a very innocent recommendation': but the value of meeting subsequently was not clear to members, only two of whom attended that September. Early in 1883 Stephen was ordered to transmit Committee of Management minutes to Edinburgh. Yet in 1784, Glasgow and London had got a Bill through first and second Readings in the Commons before news of it reached Edinburgh. The Bill was designed to put the whole Canal under control of a new Glasgow Customs House, and to reduce proxy powers at London meetings. Edinburgh was goaded to self-defence, and to demand that the agent in Glasgow forward a full report monthly, and copies of accounts which a committee of five were to audit. Unless the system of management was entirely changed, wrote John Knox in Edinburgh,[7] there was risk of a total loss of capital. The Glasgow Committee also asked for a clarification of the roles of general meetings and committees.

By 1786 many influential Glasgow merchants had added to their interests in West Indian trade or in cotton importing and processing some shares in the Forth and Clyde Navigation. Such names occur in the list of proprietors at that date as Henry Glassford and his collaborator Patrick Colquhoun, who as Provost of Glasgow had chaired Committee meetings for two years prior to 1784. Other members were the Speirs, who had intermarried with the family of Sir Thomas, later Lord, Dundas of Kerse on whose lands stood Grangemouth. Dundas was established as a rich government contractor in London. Together then,

73

---

[6] cf. Roseveare, pp. 85, 181/2.

[7] His pamphlet is quoted by Pratt.

the London and Glasgow interests secured the outnumbering of the Edinburgh vote, and the passing of an Act confining General Meetings to London. The Secretary of the company there was required to keep a true and perfect account of all Acts, Proceedings and Transactions of the new Governor, Council and General Meetings. Sir Thomas was elected Governor, and re-elected in each of the next 26 years.

Meanwhile, perhaps before demitting office as Provost in 1784, Patrick Colquhoun had instigated proposals for a new ledger, which were approved by London. In August, 1785, Richard Smellie, Accountant and book-keeper, was appointed because of:

> the absolute necessity of employing an able accountant to post up the books of account in a methodised and accurate manner and upon the principles of double-entry, showing the stock of the company and specifying such heads of expenditure as shall be thought necessary to give the proprietors a clear and distinct view of the application of the money.

Three terms in this suggest the varied derivation of the accounting to be applied. *Methodised* was familiar from the title of John Mair's *Book-keeping* in its first eight editions. *Heads* was a typical Exchequer accounting term. *Application* suggests fund or trust accounting, where misapplication had to be guarded against. The supremacy of the traders' forms is indicated by the instruction to Smellie to buy a waste-book, journal and ledger. Stephen was to supply evidence, and the accounts of the proprietors were to come from Edinburgh.

The new books were to cover transactions since 1775. Tersely, Smellie was told to record receipts only from clear and distinct vouchers. Soon it became clear that there were more than trivial errors in Stephen's accounting. In April, 1786, he acknowledged blunders and inaccuracies, the largest of which was a failure to record £825 received from the Carron company. His Account showed total debits of £25,287 and credits of £23,683. After some eighteen adjustments his debt to the company (cumulated over the years) was agreed at £1,223.14s.8½d. This sum the Committee had to recover by the sale of his house, and from his sister and James Dennistoun, who were his guarantors. Stephen had been ill and was put on half-pay, before he was brusquely replaced by Patrick Colquhoun.

Stephen suffered like many another of the period not so much through dishonesty as from imperfections in accounting. He had had to cope with the first commitment of proprietors' funds to unprecedentedly large engineering works, with changes in administrative centre and responsibilities, and with financing problems now to be examined. These imperfections could not be remedied by book-keepers or officials trained to this type of operation, for there were none. The problems arose within the tradition of stewardship or factor's accounts, where interim audit and even discharge of accountability for one period were less important than the final reckoning. In Exchequer and similar accounting, only on death or retiral was the final settlement demanded.[8] Security was obtained not from fool-proof, ongoing accounting and audit systems, but from a continuing personal responsibility of office-holders, guaranteed by the sureties which they had to provide on appointment. But novel in many respects as the systems introduced to the Forth and Clyde after Stephen's retiral might be, the traditional ideas and form of Charge and Discharge account continued to co-exist alongside them till 1856.

Financing

The financial history of the Forth and Clyde Navigation may conveniently be studied with reference to calls on subscribed capital, bank lending, bonds and annuities, and government aid. (Later we will describe a dispute on whether improvements should be financed from retained profits or from borrowing.)

Accountants in Britain have been neither knowledgeable nor sensitive on how their techniques have evolved and may evolve to meet changing circumstances and to exploit changing technical media. Accordingly the system of progressive calls on subscribed capital, which was developed by statutory companies in the 18th and 19th centuries to finance extended infrastructure developments was still covered in book-keeping texts until very recent years, even though such companies and such developments had long been absorbed into the public sector of the economy. The history of the system has to be sought in such books as O. C. Williams' *Historical Development of the Private Bill Procedure and Standing Orders in the House of Commons.* F. Clifford's earlier *History of Private Bill Legislation* is there referred to, showing how Parliament's accumulated experience of local initiatives proved invaluable, and

---

[8] cf. Forrester, *passim.*

was eventually applied in the general enabling legislation for companies in 1844, 1856 and 1862, complemented in the case of infrastructure companies by increasing bureaucratic interventions prior to nationalisation.

Canal legislation has not received the same attention as that for railways. But the first problem of competition from alternative navigations had been faced in 1761/2 for the Duke of Bridgewater's Canal Bill. With the Forth and Clyde Bill, Glasgow's alternative Bill and the proposal of Bo'ness that a cut be made east to serve that town were each withdrawn on the offer being made to repay their legal expenses.

The problem faced by the legislature was to ensure the seriousness of each proposal, and that finance was adequate. Estimates by respected engineers were therefore sought, together with sufficient subscriptions by persons of worth to carry through the works which often yielded little income till complete. With experience the problem of subscribers being unable to honour all calls was encountered and partially overcome by the transferability of part-paid shares. In the case of the Forth and Clyde, the financing problem was accentuated not only by Smeaton's initial underestimating of construction costs (which may appear typical of most projects), but also by the 8 years before toll income became considerable, the 22 years before sea-to-sea navigation was completed, and the 32 years before dividends were paid and the shares ceased to be a speculation. More particularly, in the year after the Canal was incorporated, Douglas, Heron and Co, formed the so-called Ayr Bank, with the Duke of Queensberry in its chair also, and with the Duke of Buccleuch involved. The management operated with a mixture of 'aggressiveness, euphoria and self-deception' which was extended also to the proprietors, a nation-wide speculative frenzy giving way to the Bank's collapse along with thirteen Edinburgh private banks in 1772.[9] Such events lay ahead as the Forth and Clyde began.

Of the £128,700 nominal value of shares subscribed for, 10% was due before incorporation. The first call of £5 was payable to the Royal Bank of Scotland by 1st December 1767, and the second 2 months later, till which date new subscribers were admitted. These calls of course would be absorbed in initial legal expenses and compensation monies. The incorporating Act permitted calls to be made each of not more than £10 per share, nor less than 3 months apart. Sub-

sequent calls, payable to the Royal Bank or at Drummond's Bank in London, may be traced from the Minute Books in part but were not always approved by General Meetings.[10]

By 1773 the tenth to twelfth calls were advertised for funds to cover the work which had proceeded briskly but expensively towards the west. Many contributed promptly, but for others it appears to have been a semi-voluntary matter. The company's powers to forfeit shares or charge interest on unpaid calls were extended by private Act in 1771, and appear to have been more readily enforceable in Scotland. Counsel's opinion was there obtained that October; and in May, 1773, a Court of Session summons was to be executed. In November 1780, the Carron Iron company had to be forced to pay interest due by Court of Session decree. Complicated relations could, however, arise with individual proprietors. In 1787, new powers were obtained from Parliament for partial forfeiture after crediting actual payments to a proportion of shares now treated as fully paid; and this was done for George Chalmers, a lawyer who had been active in initial flotation and was then allowed his expenses, but denied a similar claim in 1788 for charges possibly incurred in representing Edinburgh's interests against London and Glasgow.

In England the enforcement of calls was always a matter of imperfectly documented difficulty.[11] A Forth and Clyde meeting in 1769 felt that 'arrears from noble-men and gentlemen require only a reminder'. In February 1774, slow payers were to be reminded prior to Drummond, the bankers, calling on each, bearing a receipt. In November 1779, the Lord Chancellor advised that a Bill in Equity was not to be recommended, but that declarations should be filed in the Court of the King's Bench. If a subscriber died, his executors might be forced to pay £1,000 overdue, plus the cost of King's Bench process, as for Luke Scrafton's shares in 1781. In February of that year, £14,300 was still recorded as outstanding; two members in total arrears were struck off; and a polite reminder was sent to Lord Elphinstone! In May 1783 law charges in one case alone totalled £100; 10 months later it was decided to debit such charges to the subscriber. In March 1785 as subscribers' capital in relation to the Exchequer participation had to be confirmed, interest on arrears was demanded because thereafter 'interest on interest' (i.e. compounded) would

75

---

[9]Checkland, pp. 124–134.

[10]cf. Issues in Accountability, III/12.
[11]Ward, p. 118.

be payable. Yet legal process against Henry Isaac's executors in March, 1787 was dismissed with costs.

In 1789, Colquhoun calculated the situation as follows: The statutory capital was 1,500 shares; 213 shares not initially subscribed had been entrusted to Sir Lawrence Dundas, and 136 had subsequently been sold. Thus 77 shares had not been issued; 85 had been forfeited under the 1771 Act, and 41 more under 27 Geo III cap.55 leaving 1,297 shares in the hands of 136 proprietors. Under this latter Act, capital which had received no reward for up to 17 years had interest allowed at 5% per annum from the date of each individual contribution. Each share issued at £100 was thus revalued at £167.3s.6d, with total paid-up capital showing as £216,125.19s.6d.[12] This of course represented an 'opportunity cost' to the proprietors rather than actual capital paid in. Extra cash was then, as earlier, needed.

On several occasions, additional finance was offered. Glasgow pressed to finance from its own resources a connecting canal in 1771. In March, 1773 additions to subscriptions of £16,700 were proposed, Glasgow expressing a willingness to subscribe if other proprietors were also willing.[13] In March, 1781 a new subscription of £30,000 was also discussed. In 1789 the Glasgow Committee urged that the 203 remaining shares should be issued above par, increasing the private capital to 5/6 of the whole, with the Exchequer's share reduced to 1/6. But London vetoed the idea of a prospectus for circulation to shareholders.

More effectively and frequently the Royal Bank of Scotland helped with finance. It had agreed to charge only 4% interest on its loans to such a 'national concern' in 1768, on condition that all payments should be made in its bank notes.[14] But the Bank was unwilling to lend to a company without personal security. In 1770, the Praeces or Chairman in Edinburgh was to accept bills of exchange presented by the company's agent, and discount them at the Royal, thus raising immediate funds which were to be repaid out of the receipts from the sixth call on the shareholders. In this and other ways, £11,500 was owed to the Bank in June, 1770: and the debt increased to £19,600 by 1772.[15] On subsequent occasions we learn of the company seeking to relieve the Dundases and others of their liability on its behalf to the Bank. In 1794 Bonds of Relief are mentioned

12FCN1/35.
13Marwick, VII, p. 399.
14Three Banks Review, December, 1964.
15Checkland, p. 233.

as issued by the company under its seal to the Governor and proprietors who had signed personal bonds to the Bank.

A new source of finance was clearly required by March, 1773. A London Minute recorded Smeaton's estimate 5 months earlier that the cost of works from the Logie Water to the 'West Sea' would amount to £70,000, and in addition a further 243 acres of land would have to be purchased at £30 per acre. Salaries were estimated to add £4,500 before completion, and £19,610 was due to the Royal on bonds given by Sir Lawrence and Thomas Dundas. Funds still required were estimated at over £102,000, but arrears on calls, and the 15% of subscribed capital still to be called were estimated to bring in £39,000. Allowing for £6,500 contingencies, some means of raising £70,000 was sought.

This was to take the form of an issue of bonds resembling in many ways those by which Queensberry and Buccleuch were seeking to pay off the debts of the Ayr Bank. They had raised £450,000 by placing 'annuity bonds' on the London capital market, despite the opposition of the East India Company.[16] Precedent for the new means of raising finance also came from the toll-roads. By Act of 13 Geo. III, cap. 104, the company was permitted to print bonds for £70,000, granting or assigning the navigation and its future tolls as security. Books recording these assignments 'by way of life annuities or otherwise' were to be open at all times to proprietors and creditors. In March 1774, the London Meeting minuted its confidence in this form of finance; further bonds should be issued to complete the canal.

But whether owing to the interruption to trade resulting from the American War of Independence or for other reasons, no further work was undertaken for several years after the canal had reached Hamiltonhill one mile from Glasgow. Bond interest must have remained a heavy, prior charge on the revenues of the incomplete canal. In 1787 Colquhoun noted that bonds bore interest at 5% as compared with bank interest of 4%. In preparation for the final stage, in 1787 he calculated the sums held or owing to the company or likely to be received in each of the three following years. A surplus over requirements of £30,000 was disclosed until 1790; and this surplus he suggested might be used to repurchase the bonds for £26,000 held by Messrs Forbes and Cumming. In March 1788, bonds for £20,000 were redeemed and delivered to the proprietors who had signed

16Checkland, p. 132–3.

them. In the 1792 Balance Sheet two bonds total-ling £25,000 are shown as due to the Royal Bank. Typically for the period, Colquhoun proposed that a surplus of £5,000 could form a sinking fund, but with the purpose of repaying cash-credits and overdrafts. Recourse to bonds, of £100 up to £1,000 each nominal, was adopted again in 1799, for the purpose of repaying the Exchequer participation.

The flexibility and other advantages of Scot-land's unique Bank 'cash-credit' system[17] gain further evidence after the transfer of management to the West, where the Royal had no branch at first. In 1783 Stephen was ordered to lodge receipts punctually with the Glasgow Arms Bank. In that year, David Dale and Scott Moncrieff started operations on behalf of the Royal, and by 1786 were entitled to receive a copy of Committee of Management Minutes.

A new importance for cash accounting and for Bank records can be discerned, displacing aperio-dic, personal and imprest accounts. From 1st January 1781, a quarterly Account of Receipts and Expenditure was required for London. In that month, a copy of the Account from 1786 was provided by the Royal, £5 being charged for this 'work of much labour'. By 1786 the Royal Bank Account was being copied monthly and trans-mitted to London, where it took up about 100 pages of the Reports which were bound together each year. With the monthly and annual classified summaries, this Account obviously played a cen-tral role as a Day-book for a company which sought to avoid imprests or debtor accounts.

A very similar transfer to cash accounting, year by year, was being instigated in the Treasury by the Commissioners for Examining appointed by Parliament to reform outmoded procedures.[18] One of these Commissioners was George Drum-mond, possibly related to John and Adam Drum-mond who were proprietors of the Forth and Clyde Navigation. It is not necessary to attribute to individuals a natural extension of state accounting developments which would be known to every parliamentarian.

In the north the Balance Sheet of 1792 shows that £2,761 was still imprest with the company servants or contractors, and was due to become part of the cost of the canal when accounts were settled. In January 1794, it was specified that all accounts and outlays formerly paid by the sur-veyors and others from advances made to them,

should be paid monthly and quarterly at the com-pany's offices by drafts on the Bank. All revenue and expenditure were to pass through the com-pany's account at the Bank, and be directly debited or credited to respective nominal accounts for receipts and disbursements. The account was to be examined, compared with vouchers and initialled monthly by a member for the Committee.

In 1791, the offer of a leading proprietor, Hop-kirk, to lend £12,000 for 5–7 years at 4¾% was rejected because of the flexibility of the Bank's overdraft system. In 1795, it was decided to pay off all small sums which bore interest so that the company would pay interest to the Bank only.

From July 1775 toll-collectors had been urged to avoid giving credit, and to pay in takings weekly to the agent, and by him to the Bank. Even Henry Glassford was pressed to settle accounts for lime moved from his quarries each month; this was modified however, since, pro-vided these dues were brought to account within the year, it was felt of little consequence in which month.[19] In general, means were sought to facili-tate punctual analysis of monthly revenues and speedy year-end accounts.

Government participation

Government systems were not always copied or welcomed. The story of Exchequer aid must now be told, marking as it does an early rejection by nobles and merchants of the mercantilist ideas which had informed the applications for state support for the Canal in the 1760s and again in 1776. In 1780, the Board of Trustees for Fisheries and Manufactures was approached once more without success. Further efforts were made, how-ever, and in 1783, the Dukes of Argyll, Buccleuch, and Queensberry, and the Lord Advocate, with Sir Thomas Dundas waited on the Earl of Shel-burne at the Treasury. Only in February 1784, after a similar deputation to Pitt and the Treasury Lords, was agreement reached for an intricate manoeuvre. This related to the estates of former Jacobites, which after the '1715' had been sold but which after the 'Forty-five' had been retained in a major effort to civilise the Highlands.[20] Forty years later those disinherited had shown their loyalty to the Hanoverian kings so clearly that resale of lands to them could be considered. The Forth and Clyde Navigation appeared first

77

[17]Checkland, p. 267.
[18]cf. Binney, passim.

[19]FCN1/14–9/vi/1801.
[20]cf. A. M. Smith, passim.

among the petitioners for the funds to be realised from the sale, and indeed bore £200 of the cost of the Disannexing Act. The company was to receive £50,000: and this sum was to rank equally for dividends with subscribed capital as increased by interest up to Martinmas 1784. The Act 24 Geo. III, cap. 57 prescribed that dividends were to be declared from the free annual produce of the canal, once the company's debt had been paid off, and a sufficient fund retained for contingent expenses and repairs. The Exchequer's dividends were earmarked for road and bridge building.

The Act required the company to deliver to the Court of the Exchequer annually an abstract from their books, showing the state of their funds and debts as well as the gross revenues and deductions therefrom. (Significantly the basis of state accounting in specific funds was altered through their consolidation in 1787—since which time the plural form 'funds' has lived on in state and company accounting from which specific, earmarked revenues and funds have progressively disappeared.)

Between London and Glasgow, detailed debate took place as to what precise accountability was required. Colquhoun in Glasgow advocated a 31st December year-end, rather than accounts to Martinmas (11th November). He also supported a General Account Current, clarifying charges and discharges rather than a Cash Account. By 20th May 1789, the Scots Exchequer demanded accounts for the previous 5 years.[21]

London transmitted Accounts which were to be sent on from Glasgow. James Loch for the Exchequer then wrote that the Accounts submitted did not sufficiently convey the information intended by Parliament. He proposed that the King's Remembrancer should travel to Glasgow and obtain a more particular state, to give the Court a complete view of the situation in 1784 and of alterations since, 'adjusting with the managers a plan of the Accounts for the future.'[22]

Glasgow was at this time instructed to co-operate, while later negotiations were reserved to London. But resistance to the Exchequer was hardening: in December 1788, it was ordered that an account showing the Exchequer as proprietor of 2,999 shares should be replaced by one showing the £50,000 as 'Money granted by Parliament ... from the Act it could not be inferred that the government were either partners or pro-

prietors, with any voice or control in direction or management'.

In March 1797, Glasgow defended itself against further Exchequer criticisms. In 1798, the company felt able to offer repayment of the initial sum with interest. Two accounts of the Cost of the Navigation, with and without interest, went to the Chancellor. But when the time came, confusion arose as to whether repayment should be to London or Edinburgh.[23]

Tolls

The toll-charging of the canal also reveals influences from the mercantilist period, and in particular from Customs and Excise. On incorporation, rates were fixed at 2 pence per ton-mile, except for ballast or ironstone which was to be charged at one penny. This was by agreement with the Carron Iron company, which in March 1773 suggested that if the produce of lands in the neighbourhood of the canal was to be exempt, all their materials, which were listed *extenso* might be similarly treated. Such requests were typical of the pressures from particular interests, in resisting which Smeaton was asked for the experience of the River Calder Navigation in Yorkshire. Its Schedule and Book of Rates was obtained from a Mr. Simpson of Halifax.

Adam Smith in *The Wealth of Nations* ignored the effects of speed and wash in suggesting that charges based on weight were the most equitable for such works.[24] But the problem of calculating the weight of mixed cargoes was speedily reported by the Stockingfield collector, and was resolved by equating a barrel to 5 cubic feet or 1/8 ton, as in the Customs service. By 24 Geo. III, cap. 57 the company was authorised to calculate tonnage on this basis, and was relieved of the obligation to apply equal rates throughout, provided due notice was given and maximum charges were not exceeded. Endless committee hours were spent in discussing rates for specific commodities, with few underlying principles of pricing or rate-moderation emerging. Yet in 1787, a further Act reduced rates for cargoes of lime, ironstone and manure only at times of ample water supply over the locks. It was thus sought to secure marginal traffic and income without need for further reservoirs.

In the 1790s frequent requests for lower tolls

[21]S.R.O.–E.310/2, p. 326.
[22]FCN1/38–8/viii/89.

[23]In Edinburgh, public records preserved are confined to a request from the south that payment be accepted. SRO–E307/10 p. 329.
[24]II, p. 216.

78

were received to favour specific cargoes or persons, but were forwarded to the Governor. From 1794 to stimulate export of coals dug beside the Monkland Canal, such coals were charged at ½d per ton-mile provided that water was ample. Two years later, resistance to a proposal by Pitt to tax canal traffic was successfully organised with the English canals. But in 1806, war-time inflation prompted a Bill authorising full freedom in setting tolls up to 4d per ton-mile.

As in the Customs service, receipts were analysed by commodity carried, and neatly tabulated for months and years. Indeed they formed the subject of a lithographic chart which presented these statistics up to 1814, in mode pioneered for economic data by William Playfair. Playfair's brother John was Professor of Natural Philosophy at Edinburgh, and suggested that whatever can be expressed in numbers may also be represented by lines. William's drawing skills learnt for engineering with Meikle, Boulton and Watt were applied to statistical presentation in his *Commercial and Political Atlas* (1786) and *A Statistical Breviary*. The method soon found imitation in France.[25] Evidence of earlier application than this to company statistics in Britain has still to be found.

But Customs procedures and dues had a detrimental effect on the growth of canal traffic, especially via the Firth of Forth to Leith; dues payable equalled the complete cost of land carriage from Edinburgh to Glasgow. Sea-to-sea passage was secured just before the French wars made the English Channel dangerous and greatly increased traffic. But Customs problems were typical of those prompting campaigns for laisser-passer and free trade which were finally successful only years after the Napoleonic wars were over.

New control systems

We may now return to our study of the company's administration. The engineer MacKell had died in November, 1779. His successor with the title of Surveyor was Nicol Baird, who had been a toll collector. In 1785, Robert Whitworth who had worked with Brindley became engineer with the task of completing the works from Stockingfield to Bowling on the Clyde estuary.

With Stephen's dismissal a new strong administrator was also required. The Glasgow Committee proposed that Patrick Colquhoun be appointed Inspector and Superintendent from April 1786.

Ten years before, at the age of 31, he had returned prosperous from Virginia and became closely involved with the Glassford interests. In 1778 he helped raise money for a regiment to fight against the American rebels. As Provost of Glasgow he founded the first Chamber of Commerce in Britain (preceded by one in New York), and from 1782–3 chaired Canal committee meetings. The *Dictionary of National Biography* records his later effective advocacy of poor relief, and of a London Metropolitan Police force, as well as his authorship of *The Wealth, Powers and Resources of the British Empire*, which C. R. Fay described as 'the statistical bible of the early English socialists'. These activities are said to have been based in London from 1789 till his death in 1820. Other less known activities include the arrangement of trading outlets on the Continent during the Napoleonic Wars. In 1806, he became London agent for the Senate of Hamburg, and established thereafter a Chamber of Commerce on Heligoland where Scots exporters had their agents.[26]

All this, however, lay in the future for Colquhoun, whose energies and abilities are documented in volume after volume of the Forth and Clyde Navigation's records. On his appointment no salary was mentioned, but in 1787 a sum of £300 was approved supplemented later by a gratuity of £100 plus £50 for his clerks. His chief task was to support Whitworth in the completion of the Canal. We have already seen how he estimated and scheduled future expenditure balanced against funds as they became available. Probably when he took over the chief account for the company was a 'General Account Current' to which all expenditure was debited, but where also operating expenses and income were reflected leaving a balance at any time called 'Cost of Navigation to date'. The Duke of Bridgewater's canal was similarly accounted for, deficit balances being inflated each year with interest at 5%.[27] For the Exchequer's purposes Colquhoun preferred an alternative calculation which showed the proprietors' contributions together with interest thereon, as accepted in the Disannexing Act, plus the grant from Parliament, all increased by simple interest since 1784 at 5%. The total of £371,000 was then increased by outstanding debts of £39,000, less sundry disposable properties and debtors to give 'a total and exact cost of the Canal in its finished state' of £394,545. This he preferred to the £294,473.18s.3d shown in the

79

²⁵See Funkhouser and Walker.

²⁶Crouzet, p. 190.
²⁷Ward, p. 27.

ledger 'General Account Current' which included no interest since 1784, and had been reduced by £104,000 of toll dues.[28]

Colquhoun's final account on demitting office may now be examined. It was accompanied by a meticulous report on the whole venture to date. The Balance Sheet is described as a 'General Aggregate of the Affairs of the Company'. Property is itemised on the left side starting with debts receivable. The seven realisable forms of 'property' are aggregated with forfeited and unappropriated shares to give a total at the bottom of 'Property which can be turned into cash'. Items 8–13 appear to be capable of producing rents or other income in several cases. The canal itself is shown in terms of net costs of old and new lines, with sums still outstanding on the latter, 'impressed' and not yet accounted for. We may note that the forfeited shares were valued including interest, while the unissued capital was shown at par. These two items appear identically in the Capital Section on the other side of the Balance Sheet, emphasising the sense of a fixed stock, authorised and modifiable only by statute. Of the debts due by the company, the largest is the bonds of £25,000.

This Balance Sheet shows a final account of the period, but interim reporting systems had been developed and formalised immediately on Colquhoun's taking over. From 1787 it was necessary to account to London only. On sheets all of the same size were transmitted Committee Minutes monthly, a General Report and Abstract of Tolls quarterly, a copy of the Ledger and Journal annually, copies of all stock transfers, and 'an authenticated General Abstract of the State of the company's Affairs as they stood at balancing'. Annual Reports were to reach London 10 days before the Annual General Meeting on the first Wednesday of February.[29] The year's reports were then all bound together. That this system was arranged jointly between London and Glasgow is suggested by the fact that a copy of the Standing Orders of the House of Commons relating to Canal and Navigation Bills was sent north in 1786 to assist deliberation on a new constitution for the company, which would require parliamentary approval. The reporting procedures just described were adopted as company 'standing orders' by a General Meeting in August, 1791. Thus terms in use in 'the Mother of Parliaments'

were adopted naturally by the companies to which she gave birth.

Difficulty was encountered in meeting the tight deadlines for reporting. The 1788 Accounts were delayed; and in March 1791, London enjoined obedience to Standing Orders. In 1794 a timeous submission was urged so that 'every proprietor in England may, when he requires it, have all the necessary information relative to the company's affairs'.

But Colquhoun's effectiveness is evident in every line of his reports. On resigning in March 1792 he proposed a mode of arranging and estimating the annual expenditure under heads of repairs to locks and bridges, banks, tow-paths, reservoirs and houses; for wages and salaries of artificers, lock and bridge-keepers, and officers. After Repairs, the sixth head was for Adventitious Damages and Accidents; and a tenth head was for Contingent Expenses. While many expenditures could be forecast, and indeed, as we saw above, made matter of subcontracting, reserves would presumably be built up to cover these sixth and tenth classes. In his estimate of annual expense at £1,961.4s.0d., however, Colquhoun modified his classification, and based his calculation on numbers of locks, bridges, miles and persons employed.

An additional report was prepared to explain to the Governer how the debts of the company had increased during 1791. The Books, Colquhoun wrote, were

> kept upon the Principles of Double Entry, and every transaction is detailed according to the most accurate and approved Rules of Accomptanship... but as this mode admits of being shaped into any Form that may be most familiar to the mind, and as the idea of a Factor or Steward's Account has been suggested as a kind of model I shall adopt this system...

He proceeded to consider himself responsible to the company of proprietors for all the debts, property and effects at year-start, charging himself with revenue received and new debts contracted, and to show what became of this property, or 'in other words the exact Application, not departing at all from the statements in the Books'. His illustration showed a *Charge* for debts, from arrears, etc., plus properties, adding increases in debt during the year and the revenues. His *Discharge* showed closing debts to the company and properties, an increase in sums imprest out for new works, expenses, interest and salaries, balancing

[28] FCN1/37 Appx. 2.
[29] FCN1/27–25/iv/1789.

to a ½d. He added a two-sided illustration showing only increments or changes during the year.
Such a report from one trained in trader's
double-entry to a Governor accustomed to
stewardship accounts, must represent an antece-
dent of our present day Sources and Applications Statements.[30] Accounts of 'Charge and
Discharge—both on Account and in Cash' continued till 1856 to be transmitted from Glasgow
and tabled at meetings of the Forth and Clyde
Navigation.

The London Minutes of 1792 evidence doubts
about Scots accounting: Mr. Black, a local accountant was to be employed to inspect the Journal and Ledger 'for any mode more eligible for
keeping the same and to have proper allowance
for his trouble'. His account for £46.15s.0d was
submitted in 1794, but consideration of his report
was postponed, apparently indefinitely.

Audits, as we have seen, were usually a matter
for Committee members. In 1796 the Glasgow
Provost compared Journal and balanced Ledger
with every statement in the State Book, before
copies were sent south. In 1821 when Mr. Wallace
of the Committee was unable to examine the
Books and Accounts on his own, Robert Grahame and Professor Millar were appointed a
Committee of proprietors to assist. But at all
times, and especially at General Meetings, the
Books or copies of them were available for inspection by proprietors.

Share transfers

A few facts may be added to what is known of
stock markets at this period.[31] One of the essen-
tials of a joint-stock and continuing company was
an ability for membership to change: indeed this
was secured by the Forth and Clyde's incorporating Act, which laid down a form of share-transfer
certificate. We have already noted that the company preferred to copy the Transfer Books of the
Royal Bank to 'the Plan of the great companies in
England'. Transfer responsibilities were moved to
Glasgow, at least by 1787. In June 1792, it was
instructed that transfers were to be booked only
on original instructions, an extract of sale, by
heredity or probate of will. A memorial on the
subject was prepared by an advocate, Archibald
Campbell, in 1800. One year later, transfer fees
paid to the Superintendent were fixed at 1 guinea

for five shares, and 2 guineas for more than ten,
payable by buyer or seller and excluding stamp
duty and postage. Two guineas including stamp
duty was reported as the fee in all general companies in England. By 1779, 192 transfers were
recorded; and by 1848, a total of 1715.[32]

The prices at which transfers took place are not
evident in the early years. In 1794, the Secretary
in London enquired of Glasgow as to what the
Superintendent considered a justified price. From
this time, the latter charged himself with the price
received from the buyer, and in his discharge
showed his payment to the seller. Thus the market appeared to be made by and through the
company. Once dividends were declared, prices
were more readily calculable. Sometime before
1831 transfers were normally completed through
brokers. From that year dates the first list of
stock prices printed by James Watson, a Glasgow
accountant and stock-broker, who quoted the
price of the company's shares of £400.16s.0d
nominal with dividend of £28 at £560–562.

Dividends

The opening of the canal from sea-to-sea was
followed by war with France, which made the
English Channel dangerous and the use of the
canal more attractive. Toll revenues increased,
and exceeded £20,000 from 1796. At first the
income was absorbed by new works and improvements as by the repayment of debt. But in 1800,
the long-patient stockholders received a first dividend of £10 per share. Such payments continued
till 1814, with the company paying the new
Income Tax equal to 11s.4d per share. In 1814 the
dividend was raised to £15, and next year to
£17.10s.0d. In 1817, it was raised again; and
officers, surveyors and master carpenters, who
had been refused an increase in wages, were
assured they would benefit with shareholders
later. Five years later, proportionate changes in
dividends and wages and salaries were considered
'in order to identify as much as possible the two
interests'.

Glasgow take-over

Glasgow's trade and manufactures had on the
whole flourished during the Napoleonic Wars.
This is documented in the ledger of James Finlay
and Co. for 1800 (stored at Glasgow University).
Therein are accounts for agents in St. Petersburg,
Berlin and other German cities, Alsace and Italy.

---

[30]As suggested by B. Yamey, p. 43. Origins of this Statement
may thus be traced 65 years before those suggested by Park or
by Rosen and DeCoster.
[31]R. C. Michie, passim.

[32]Copy transfers are found in Vols. FCN1/48–90.

81

(Friedrich Engels' father was their agent in the Rhineland.) In all, Kirkman Finlay claimed, they had 700 correspondents on the Continent prior to 1803.

In the history of James Finlay and Co. published in 1951, only very brief reference is made to Kirkman's chairmanship of the Forth and Clyde Navigation from 1816 till his death in 1842. He most ably represented brash, new Glasgow energies which had over the years come into increasing conflict with Lord Dundas whose estates lay at Grangemouth, who had family ties with the Speirs and contacts in the House of Lords. The conflict was fought out over long-standing personal resentments, partially in legal forms, and climaxed in an important accounting innovation.

Dundas adopted a proprietorial attitude, and had forgotten about his long-standing debt of £3,000 to the company. The expense of the first ever steam-boat experiment was also held against him. Also recalled was confusion about the purchase of gravel beds at Bantaskine to provide ballast for ships without cargo. In 1803, he informed the Royal Bank that the land had been acquired by the company.[33] But in that year of 'uncommon pecuniary distress', neither the company nor Dundas nor Speirs had available the necessary funds. A Glasgow Committee member had then stepped in and bought the land in his own name—to the profit, he claimed, not only of himself but also of the company since ships had access to ballast at cheap prices. Personal enterprise thus complemented corporate efforts, but did not receive credit for so doing!

More serious were the doubts raised from London about the competence of Scots law-courts to intervene in the affairs of a company whose meetings could only be held in Westminster, since 1787. This the Scots held was a matter of internal regulation, since the property, profits and cash of the company were in Scotland: there share-transfers were registered; and there creditors of individual shareholders could 'arrest' their shares. In 1786, 1,213 shares of the company were held by natives of Scotland, and only 130 by English people.[34] Now, in 1815, out of 127 shareholders only 40 owning 365 shares had fixed residences in the south. The lawyers had to consider whether the real estate of the company could be considered real estate 'in the person of a partner'. If shares were personal property, then personal

rights had no *situs* or fixed location. Such matters had not been resolved in the decision *Syme v. Balfour* of 1804, and formed part of the controversy in 1815.[35]

The immediate cause of the open rift was financial. Glasgow shareholders led by James Hill and Robert Grahame of Whitehill objected to the application of surplus revenues not to dividends but to the extension of the docks and other works at Grangemouth, which they suggested would chiefly benefit Dundas as landowner. The Governor replied in print that projections of revenue under four new 'heads' might total £8,849.10s.0d per annum and thus equal a return of 6% on the project's cost, the investment appraisal being undertaken by Rennie the engineer. But no such justification had been given to the 'packed' meeting which Dundas had got to approve the application to Parliament for the private Bill necessary: the objectors replied that a less warrantable estimate had never been palmed off upon any company! The Londoners had meanwhile attempted to transfer the surplus of £23,000 from a Scots to an English bank, only to have an interdict successfully raised in Scotland. No mention was made in the controversy of the drop in canal revenues nor to the need for more employment which would result from the end of the Napoleonic Wars.

Thus at the same time as the House of Commons was rebelling against an extension of wartime income tax, the shareholders in the Forth and Clyde were revolting against restrictions on their dividends in order to finance new works—which if necessary at all they felt should be financed from new borrowings. The war of pamphlets brought alternatives into focus. Did the Scots believe, asked the Governor, that the extraordinary (or capital) expenditures of £76,000 in the previous 22 years should not have been taken from revenues? Where full profits were distributed without abiding by a fixed annual dividend and without reserving against eventualities, 'the stock would bear no fixed or determined value in the market': speculators might examine minutely the company's books and see the precise state of its affairs; but no person unacquainted with business would think of buying its shares: 'The immediate injury to the stock and to the credit of the company by any diminution of dividend is much greater than any advantage arising from any temporary increase'. Referring to an Irish Canal scan-

---

[33] *Three Banks Review*, December 1964.
[34] Lindsay, pp. 29/30.

[35] The pamphlets printed during the controversy are stored in the Strathclyde Regional archives.

dal, the Governor suggested that only stock jobbers would want a temporary increase in dividends and share prices, before selling out and leaving the company to shift for itself. He observed:

> As English capitalists could not derive any consequential benefit from the canal except by making it productive as a navigation, they might be supposed to be altogether unbiassed as to their views of management.

He quoted the opinion of legal Counsel in Edinburgh:

> Every corporation has a discretionary power to fix upon a sum as neat profits, leaving surpluses ... as undivided profits which may be applied by the company to any expense whatever that occurs in the management of its affairs, subject to the claims of creditors till distributed.

Finlay and his supporters first submitted calculations that an increased dividend was reasonable: dividends should be related not to the nominal value of capital, nor to the value of £325 per share enacted in 1799, nor to the value of £420 calculated by the Governor by adding the short-fall of dividends not equal to legal interest rates. Instead they applied compound interest to capital contributed since 1768, and deducted dividends when paid, and thus calculated a value per share of £643, using what would now be called 'opportunity costs'. The Governor, they said, would adopt simple rather than compound interest when it suited his purpose. Current dividends were still not equal to 4% of share values as calculated in Glasgow.

At one stage Hill and Grahame suggested that each proprietor should lend the company for its new works his share of the surplus revenue, and receive therefor a transferable document. But the chief Glasgow case was that all shareholders should be kept informed and allowed to decide. In 1804, an abstract of accounts had been printed; but the motion at the meeting held in April, 1814 that a printed abstract should be furnished to each proprietor at the same time as his dividend was paid, had been negatived. 'To make such information public and general', one of the pamphlets suggested, 'would tend more than any other thing to prevent jobbing in shares of stock, either in buying or selling.'

The Governor wrote in justification:

> It is a thing which is never done in any copartnery. It never was heard of that a chartered bank or any company ... printed and published to the world annual states. ... It is sufficient for every proprietor that he has access at London and Glasgow to examine the books at all times—as they have twice a year to call for their dividends, they can easily make this examination.

The cost of posting statements to proprietors was avoidable. Any proprietor who was in Parliament could and did take advantage of free mail services for all purposes. It was suggested that James Finlay and Co. saved about £1,000 each year in postage while Kirkman was an MP.[36]

The outcome may be briefly recorded. At a General Meeting held in the British Coffee House in the Liberty of Westminster on 20th March, 1816, there was a large turnout of nobility, six redoubtable Glasgow spinsters, and Glasgow merchants including Robert Owen as executor of David Dale.

Tabled at the meeting was a weight of books and documents: the Journal and Ledger; an Abstract of Accounts with the Royal and the Bank of Scotland; accounts of tolls and commodities for the year and previous decade; accounts of Charge and Discharge for the company as a whole, for toll collectors and two others. There were also abstract or summary Receipt and Expenditure accounts for passage-boats, a General Account Current and a Balance Account. Such were the forms of corporate reporting to this company in session—supplemented by copies of the Interdict case, and Counsel's opinion on the attempted transfer of funds south of the Border.

The battle was quickly over. Dundas and his relatives and supporters were voted out of office and Finlay was elected Governor. The capital expenditure at Grangemouth was rescinded as was the transfer of funds from Scotland to England. Indispensable works were to be financed from borrowing.

A dividend of £25 per share thus became possible and was approved. (Share prices rose promptly to £500).[37] It was also ordered unanimously that the Governor and Council prepare and print States of the Company's affairs, as at present, and furnish each proprietor with a copy,

83

---

[36]cf. Binney, p. 46-7 and the *History of Jas Finlay*, p. 28.
[37]Michie, p. 161.

and in the future prepare states of affairs and of their Revenues and Expenditure by 10th March yearly. Longer notice was to be given of any bills proposed for Parliament.[38]

Thus more participation at meetings was sought by proprietors—as also by providing a Memorandum Book for their suggestions at the Glasgow office from 1824. And from 1831, they also were to receive a printed Chairman's statement. Whether attendance and participation, or the opposite, were thereby promoted is open to discussion. But the Forth and Clyde initiative is clear, and was not promptly imitated.

The next stage in publishing company accounts may have come in 1837 when the London Joint Stock Bank found its results good enough to be used as an advertisement. Other joint stock banks followed suit, chiefly in the London area; although Sir Robert Peel in 1844 replied to suggestions:

> I do not wish to pry into the affairs of each bank.... It has frequently been proposed to require from each bank a periodic publication of its liabilities, its assets and the state of its transactions generally. But I have seen no form of account which would be satisfactory.[39]

In 1847, Peninsular and Orient Company shareholders were informed that:

> it was not considered for their interest that such a course should be pursued... Proprietors at a distance forming their opinion of the future position of the company from published accounts of past transactions could scarcely avoid arriving at erroneous conclusions.[40]

The 1855/56 Companies Acts in an optional schedule made it easy for a company to adopt Articles of Association requiring printing and circulation of accounts, a week before the meeting. Thus far in advance was the Forth and Clyde in 1816.

Conclusion

History is composed of both fact-finding and generalisation or theory-building. Here we have been chiefly engaged in the former, providing footnotes for a survey of Company Accounting which cannot start in 1856, since so much had by

then been decided, and which need not spend too long on the earlier incorporations and monopolies of a pre-industrial age. Our footnotes relate to a company not of adventurers, but of proprietors of a thin strip of land through the narrow waist of Scotland on which was dug a waterway with a capacity for ships large for that time. In that company were landowners, bankers and merchants, led by the provosts of Glasgow and Edinburgh and by noblemen in London. It was necessary that they contributed more than capital, since rights had to be obtained or modified by legislation, engineers had to be appointed, and supervision exercised over the progress of work and the details of expenditures unprecedented in the north.[41] Audit was an early and continuing responsibility.

Since shareholders included some proprietors of the ground through which the canal was to pass, a system of shareholders' accounts had to be created to which sundry debits and credits could be posted. The initial impression is of shareholder democracy working through regular meetings and agreement rather than through voting and a delegation of responsibilities to directors. Throughout, books of accounts and other records were open to inspection as a result of the repeated copyings necessary where there were three centres. Only gradually formal reporting procedures from Glasgow to London were established derived from a new set of accounts.

In these accounts, as is appropriate to a transport undertaking, 'cash' transactions were the prime entries, with regular payments into the bank of revenues, month by month and year by year, while expenses were also paid from the bank account instead of by officers from imprests. The bank which had helped in the early years and provided a Comptroller and Auditor for the Company was unable to provide the large sums necessary to complete the cut to Glasgow and later towards the sea. In the mid-1770s bonds had to be issued, yet we find the Bank holding these. In the 1780s state participation was accepted in return for investment of monies realised by Highland land sales. The Scots Exchequer required a very precise accountability. Once the canal was complete and profitable the private shareholders hastened to repay the state investment before declaring a dividend.

In such negotiations some may see precedent for a cooperation of public and private interests

---

[38]The Accounts are reproduced in full in *Issues in Accountability*, No. 3.
[39]W. F. C. Crick & Wadsworth, pp. 20, 30, 284.
[40]Quoted Naylor, p. 12.

[41]Military road-works in Scotland cost only £300,000 from 1730–1800. See Haldane, p. 11.

two centuries later, although others will sense the death-throes of mercantilism. But in the controversy which climaxed in 1816, more is to be found than Scots resistance to manipulations from London. (This Glasgow had earlier condoned when it was Edinburgh interests which were threatened.) A system of proxies had been built up at the start to enable those sufficiently interested to be represented in both centres. Proxies could not act effectively however, unless their principals were informed. Glasgow accordingly pressed for fair notice of proposed Parliamentary bills, and for precirculation of abstracts of accounts. The focus of attention of accounting historians has thus moved from the Great Book or Ledger where Roger North sought 'a perpetual and limpid state of all accounts',[42] to the Balances and printed abstracts derived from it since 1816. A one-way stream of information is now accepted, very different perhaps from the improvements intended by the innovators of 1816.

References

Binney, J. D., *British Public Finance, 1774-92* (Cambridge University Press, 1968).

Buckle, J. T., *The History of Civilisation in England* (Longmans 1867 edition).

Checkland, S. G., *Scottish Banking* (Collins, 1975).

---

[42]Yamey, Edey & Thomson, p. 36.

Crouzet, F., *L'Economie Britannique et le Blocus Continental, 1806-1813* (Presses Universitaires, Paris, 1958).

Finlay, James & Co., *A History of the Firm, 1750-1950* (Glasgow, 1951).

Forrester, D. A. R., Whether Malcolm's is Best or Old Charge & Discharge. *Accounting Historians Journal*, V, 2, Fall 1978.

Funkhauser, H. S. and Walker, H. M., 'Playfair and his Charts', *Economic History*, February 1935.

Haldane, A. R. B., *New Ways Through the Glens* (Nelson, 1962).

Issues in Accountability III, *The Great Canal which linked Edinburgh, Glasgow & London* (Strathclyde Convergencies, 1978).

Lindsay, Jean, *The Canals of Scotland* (David & Charles, 1968).

Marwick, J., *The Records of the Burgh of Glasgow* (Scottish Burgh Records Society, 1876-1917).

Michie, R. C., 'The Transfer of Shares in Scotland 1700-1820', *Business History*, July 1978.

Naylor, G., *Company Law for Shareholders* (Institute of Economic Affairs, 1960).

Park, C., 'Funds Flow Statements', in *Modern Accounting Theory*, ed. M. Backer, 1966.

Pratt, E. A., *Scottish Canals and Waterways* (Selwyn & Blount, 1922).

Rosen, L. S. and De Coster, D. T., 'The Funds Statement, a Historical Perspective', *Accounting Review*, January 1969.

Roseveare, H., *The Treasury, 1660-1870* (Allen & Unwin 1973).

Smith, A. M., 'The Forfeited Estates, 1752-84' in *The Scottish Tradition*, ed. Barrow, (Scottish Academic Press, 1974).

Three Banks Review, 'The End of an Enterprise—The Forth & Clyde Canal', December 1969.

Ward, J. R., *The Finance of Canal Building in 18th Century England* (Cambridge University Press, 1974).

Williams, O. C., *The Historical Development of Private Bill Procedures and Standing Orders in the House of Commons*, HMSO, 1948.

Yamey, B., 'Accounting in England, 1500-1900' in *Studies in Accounting Theory*, ed. Baxter & Davidson (Sweet & Maxwell, 1962).

Yamey, B., Edey H. C. and Thomson, H. W., *Accounting in England and Scotland, 1543-1900* (Sweet & Maxwell, 1963).

A Scottish farmer and his accounts: 1822-23

Tom Robertson, FCA

In the early 19th century Scottish farmers in the Lothians were highly thought of; indeed they were considered to be on a par with farmers in the wealthy English counties. Alexander Trotter of Dreghorn was one such farmer and this article examines the sophisticated farm accounting system he introduced on his farm at Colinton, concluding that many of his ideas remain relevant today. This article is published posthumously: Tom Robertson, who was senior lecturer in accountancy at the University of Edinburgh, died in 1981.

Farming in the Lothians in the 19th century

In 1842 the high standard of farming in parts of Scotland was illustrated in an article in *The Manchester Guardian* by a Hereford farmer, R H Greg, entitled "Scotch Farming in the Lothians" (the still fertile region surrounding the City of Edinburgh). Greg's enthusiasm for the competence of the Lothians farmers and labourers allows us to forgive him his frequent referal to them as "Scotch":

With a system equal to that of the Lothians

established throughout England, landlords might receive double rents, farmers be rich and prosperous, and the country be rendered, for two generations, independent of foreign supplies, notwithstanding an abolition of all protective duties. I am confident the agricultural produce of England, Wales and the West of Scotland, might be doubled; and that of Lancashire and Cheshire be tripled, and this without any material addition to the agricultural population.

A typical Lothians farm would comprise 200 to 500 acres; the farm buildings would be small and compact and situated near to the centre of the farm. Mr Greg observed that they "always have a steam engine of 6 to 8 horse power for thrashing and other purposes". The corn was stacked in the stackyard, which was situated as close as possible to the threshing machine, and the stacks were of a size to provide one day's work for the machine. The grieve's (or bailiff's) cottage was situated at the entrance to the farmyard, and this position enabled him to act as a "security check". The grieve was a supervisor and received one shilling per week more than the ploughmen. So much for the premium placed on managerial ability! Greg attributed this small recompense for responsibility to the fact that the general standard of education of the peasantry in that part of Scotland was so high that outstanding ability was a natural requirement of grieves, bailiffs and overseers. He found the grieves whom he met to be:

universally clever, acute and sensible and their minds open to what was passing in the world, beyond the limits of their own farm, or immediate neighbourhood.

The farmers themselves were men of a superior education and of civilised manners. Their style of living was equal to their counterparts in the wealthy counties in England, "even Lincolnshire and Norfolk", where the farms were comparable in size. *Few are without a handsome phaeton, for the use of the female members of their family; they are hospitable; except at seed time and harvest, they have company at home or dine out three times a week.*

A great uniformity of crops was noticed by Greg throughout the Lothians, farming having been "reduced to a science" and leaving nothing to chance but the seasons. (Fields in the counties of England, on the other hand, were usually between 20 to 50 acres each.) Hedges were seen to be "clipt low and thin", and the ditches were covered in to occupy as little growing space as possible. There were no trees in the hedgerows and—

few furrows, the land being laid down flat–thus the entire area of the farm is made productive and the expense of fences and gates minimised.

Permanent grass was virtually unknown at the time in the Lothians, hay being produced from grass seed specifically sown for the purpose—this was known as "artificial grass". Accordingly the grass crop was found by Greg to be heavy compared with other less scientifically run concerns, 16 acres supporting 234 sheep (which Mr Greg counted personally!). The same acreage would support 20 cows, feeding them on white clover, which was abundant and of high quality.

The Lothian tenant farmer held his farm on a 19 years lease (at that time considered a long period for a lease), which had far-reaching effects on the attitudes of the farmer towards the enterprise he was operating. A short lease would not encourage a man to invest his capital, but would encourage a short-term view of his occupancy. He would be motivated to think of the best way of increasing his return with the minimum of investment, knowing that he would shortly relinquish it to his landlord.

On the other hand, a long lease encouraged the tenant farmers to invest their capital, to have an independent outlook, and (in Greg's view) "to hold themselves higher" than the most wealthy of English farmers. It encouraged men of superior rank and education to enter into the business of farming, where they saw the possibility of utilising their undoubted talents in a pleasurable and profitable pursuit.

The rents paid to landlords in the Lothians were, compared with English rents, high (£3 10s 0d to £5 per acre) and were linked (either wholly or partly) to the price of corn, that is, "corn rents". The actual monetary rental value, when related to the then current price of corn, resulted in any fluctuations in the value of the farm (because of, say, a change in the Corn Laws) being borne by the landlord and not the tenant.

The division of proceeds from farming operations throughout the Lothians was approximately, according to Greg, rent 33%, expenses 47%, profit and interest 20%. Greg believed education to be at the root of the success and efficiency of the farmers in this region.

The more generally diffused and more practical education of the Scotch is at the bottom of the improved state of things.

Education has quickened the intellect and given knowledge which has enabled them to apply their capital with success.

Mr Trotter of Dreghorn 1822-3

Let us now look at one of these Lothian farmers—not a tenant, but a man who owned his land. He not only confirms the observations of Mr Greg in his management of his farm at Colinton, near Edinburgh, but he has also left a record of the

87

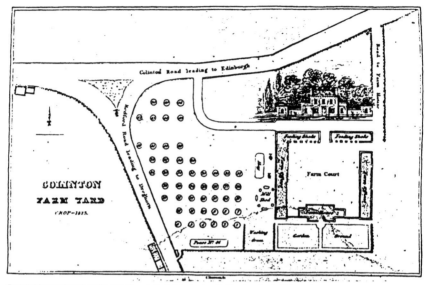

Farm Yard Crops 1823: an illustration, from Alexander Trotter's book on farm bookkeeping, showing his farm at Dreghorn. In the stackyard the stacks are numbered for the accounts. The road plan is basically the same today, with Redford Road still dividing as shown.

accounting system which he devised.[1] This therefore adds the dimension of profit and loss, cash flow and inventories to the life of the farm in the year 1823.

When Mr Trotter decided to take over the management of his farm at Colinton for the agricultural year 1823 he recalled (in a letter to Professor Coventry of the Chair of Agriculture at the University of Edinburgh) that in recent years he had had to spend a great deal of effort on his farm at Dreghorn, which had been "wrought to the bone" or "scourged" by an outgoing tenant. This experience he had used to some advantage by evolving a system of accounting to control and record all expenditure which he had incurred in bringing Dreghorn up to what he considered to be an acceptable standard of husbandry.

Mr Trotter thought it essential, in the case of the Dreghorn farm, to determine with substantial accuracy the amount spent upon each separate field "in bringing it again into proper condition". He went into considerable detail in accounting for a normal operation such as that at Colinton—for example, keeping records of how every man and horse was employed each day. This sort of detail he considered unnecessary once a farm was restored to sound working order.

My ignorance of husbandry would have deterred me from this measure [of working Colinton farm himself instead of letting it], had I not been fortunate enough to have had, at that time, an overseer [Robert Guthrie] in whom I have the

fullest confidence, regarding his knowledge of management ...

He was well aware of the failures of other gentlemen who had found that, in their efforts to work their own farms, they had not been able to generate sufficient income to cover the normal rent expectation (generally assessed at one-third of normal receipts). Mr Trotter, viewing the causes of failure from his position as a landowner, came to the conclusion that there were four basic reasons for such failure:

(1) Improper selection of an overseer.
(2) Failure to allow the overseer to get on with the job of management without interference.
(3) Luxury spending on ornamentation.
(4) Keeping incomplete or incorrect records.

It is tempting to draw parallels with management pitfalls of today such as poor personnel selection (particularly for managerial positions), failure to delegate properly, indulging in low productivity capital expenditure, and the keeping of incomplete, inaccurate and irrelevant records—all well-known problems to accountants, bankers, and others concerned particularly with small business.

Accounting problems

As with any business, the problems of accounting are directly related to the nature and complications of the technical operation of that business. In 19th-century Scotland the farmer entered upon his lease

at Martinmas, ie, 11 November. He took over stock from the previous tenant and then found that he immediately had to begin spending money on the following two years' crops. Mr Trotter took over his Colinton farm at Martinmas 1822 and spent £1,000 in the acquisition of stock from the outgoing tenant.

In order to determine the profit for the year 1823 he found it necessary to separate the costs and incomes of "manufacturing, selling and carrying" any crop he had bought from the previous tenant from any expenses and incomes related to 1823 and to outlays in respect of 1824. Moreover, during 1824 his men and horses would be engaged not only in work for the current year but also for 1823 and 1825. For example, the men and horses would carry the crop of 1823 to market and return with dung for the green (growing) crop of 1824 and, later in the year, with dung for the fallows of the 1825 crop. As Mr Trotter observed:

It follows that neither of the three crops should be charged with the whole of the labour of such men and horses for the days they were so employed.

This principle was also applied to related operating costs such as turnpike charges, which had to be apportioned to the crops receiving the benefit of the transport. This complicated apportionment of a cost among three outputs had to be accomplished with a minimum of administrative effort, for, educated or not, the farm labourer of 1823 was probably no more enthusiastic about filling in forms than his equivalent (wherever situated) would be now. All other expenses, including wages, maintenance, wear and tear on horses and implements, were also apportioned among the three crops under management.

The selling crop (in this example 1823) was closed off under this system at Martinmas in the year following that in which it had been reaped—that is, at 11 November 1824. Any stock which remained at that date was "made over" to the ensuing year's crop "at the prices of the day". For example, in the case of the work horses, which had been acquired for £187 0s 0d at Martinmas 1822: these were valued at Martinmas 1824 at £192 10s 0d, and this amount was in effect credited to the 1823 crop. The "holding gain" of £5 10s 0d was not apportioned between the two crops of 1823 and 1824. Similarly, implements bought in 1824 increased the value of stock of these items by £19 13s 6d—an amount credited to implements stock 1823 and debited to 1824. These are but small examples, however, of how the profit of 1823 is slightly overstated and that of 1824 equally understated because of a minor departure from the principle of attaching costs and revenues to the appropriate crop.

Mr Trotter's system
Mr Trotter's basic system was as follows:
(1) A farm Expenses Account was opened for each of the three years and debited throughout each year with the expenses relevant to that year. Appropriate credit entries were made to stock accounts, cash, and intermediate expense accounts such as fences and ditches. The expense of day work, turnpikes, and an appropriate charge for the portion of year work related to the year were also debited. The balance on this account was ultimately transferred to the Crop Account for the year.

(2) A farm Crop Account for the year was credited with a list of the fields, their acreage, and an estimate, at a time when a realistic estimate became possible, of the value of the crop from each field. The estimate was in money terms, expressed as a rate per acre, and then extended and totalled. Sundry credits for rents from houses and cottages were also included and these amounts were eventually debited to the employees as part of their wages. The principal accounts debited from the Crop Account were the Stack-Yard Account, the Deposit Account and the Pasturage Account.

(3) The Stack-Yard Account recorded the amount of grain and pease received from the fields and put into stacks to await threshing. Each stack was numbered and located on the plan of the yard. The account was credited with the estimate (a "more accurate estimate") of the value of the threshed grain.

In the year 1823 an estimated loss appeared on this account which was de-

bited to the farm Crop Account. The grain, having been threshed, was then measured in the conventional measure of the time—the "boll" (21 lbs in Scotland). The grain and pease which were eventually to be sold were transferred to the Deposit Account and seed crops were carried forward to the Stock Account for the following year's crop.

(4) The Deposit Account for the year was debited with the amounts transferred from the stack yard, cut grass estimates, hay estimates, potato estimates and turnips "still in the ground", all taken from the crop account. The account was credited with the proceeds of sales (recorded by weights as well as in money terms) and transferred to the Work Horses and Farm Labourers' Accounts for produce consumed on the farm. An apparent profit arose upon this account due to the difference between the estimated prices debited and the realised prices credited (realised = prices of the day) which were applied both to the external sales and internal use. The profit or loss (in 1823 a profit) was transferred to the Crop Account.

(5) The Pasturage Account was debited with the estimate of value of pasture, as shown in the fields in the Crop Account, and was credited with the profits on the Cattle and Sheep Accounts. It was also credited with an amount for pasturage of the work horses, the account for the latter being debited with this as an operating expense. The profit shown on the Pasturage Account was transferred to the Crop Account for the year.

Transport costs
The control of transport costs and their allotment among crops was effected by means of a daily record of cart journeys into market and of the specific costs attaching to each journey. A simple code was used:

E = Empty, signifying a journey into Edinburgh with an empty cart and returning with manure for a specified crop of the three years under management (viz 1823, 1824, 1825).

ML = Mixed labour, being a journey for which a ploughman and his horse(s) were employed on two crops. This occurred, for example, when a cart went to market carrying the crop for sale (1823) and returned either with manure for the green crop (1824) or manure for the fallows for crop (1825).

The specific expenses attaching to these journeys were turnpikes, customs, maugs (allowances for extra work) and weighing.

Small sums were advanced as required to the head ploughman (£2 or £3) to cover the expenses incurred on each journey (Dr Turnpikes, etc, Account was closed at the year-end by transfer to the Farm Expenses Account (1823). Similarly, at the year-end a transfer was made from the Farm Expenses Account (1823) to the debit of the other years' Farm Expenses Accounts (1824 and

1825) when the carts had been engaged in transport for those years. In the "mixed" years' expenses a notional charge of two shillings and sixpence per journey was credited to the selling crop (1823) and debited to the benefiting year (1824 or 1825). This charge was "a fair proportion" of the charge for men and horses, and was part of the turnpikes, etc, expenditure. It was an estimate only, based on the journey from Colinton to Edinburgh, and would be suitably adjusted for other journeys.

The system of transfers of costs at the year-end was devised largely to avoid a great deal of recording by the grieve or head ploughman, who had to:
(1) Control the small amount of cash advanced to him and record expenditure against the appropriate heading (turnpikes, customs, etc), showing it in the selling crop column and, where coded ML, also against the benefiting crop year.

(2) Record each day, in respect of each ploughman (himself and three others) and their horses, which crop had been worked on. The guidelines given to him were:
(a) Where the man and horses were employed on one crop—to record that fact in that year's column. This would hold good for an empty cart to Edinburgh returning with manure for a specific crop (the time of the year would be a good guide as to which crop was to benefit—in addition, the driver would also be given the task of spreading the cargo or storing it on unloading).
(b) Where they were employed on two crops—to record the journeys against the selling crop (1823). The transfer of a notional charge of two shillings and sixpence per journey has already been mentioned. This was intended to relieve the selling crop year for expenses incurred on behalf of other years.

The time records were then used to calculate a cost per day rate for each ploughman and an overall cost per day rate for horses. This was a simple matter, as there was an account for each yearly employee, to which his wages, rent, meal allowances, gratuities, etc, were debited, as well as the Work Horses Account, in which all expenses of feeding the horses were recorded and the value of manure produced was credited. The capital cost of the horses was debited to the account when it was set up, and a valuation was credited at the end of the period. In the year 1823 a small gain on revaluation was recorded.

Other expenditure
All other expenditure (for example, on fences, ditches, thatching cottages, etc) was accounted for by a series of accounts which were built up concurrently for each of the years under management; they were each closed off to the Farm Expenses Account appropriate to the year in which it became the "Selling Crop Year". The Expenses Account was then transferred to the Crop Account, which had received the credits from external sales of produce and also the internal profits and losses. The

89

balance on this account was transferred to the Proprietor's Account.

Objectives

This is what Mr Trotter had to say about the system and its benefits:

I do not mean to assert that the accuracy of my farm-books will benefit my crops; but I feel well assured, that the system I have adopted will, at all times, enable me to judge whether, in prudence, I should continue to keep my farm under my own management, by having it in my power to compare my profits with the rent for which I could let it on lease; and I cannot be deceived in respect of my profits, as I have shewn that not a shilling can escape from my pocket, without my being aware of its application.

I am sensible that, by an improper management, I may be involved in much improvident expence, which the correctness of my books may not altogether have the effect to guard me against, or to remedy. More men or more horses, for example, may be employed on the farm than are absolutely necessary to cultivate it, or I may not have adopted a proper rotation of crops; but, as I have already observed, I have very little anxiety on this score, under the opinion I entertain of my present overseer, who, instead of being jealous of me taking the opinion of some very intelligent farmers in my neighbourhood upon the merits of his management, rather courts investigation; and I have the satisfaction of obtaining the approbation of those who, from a local knowledge of my farm, or other circumstances, have had the best opportunity of judging of his operations.

Mr Trotter therefore made no extravagant claims for his farm accounting system, but he did make three important points which would be valid today:
(1) He could, through the system output, decide whether to continue farm management or revert to letting out his land for rent.

(2) He had a tight control over expenditure and also, by means of his estimates of expected outputs from his fields, a guide to the yields therefrom. These physical controls also extended to the time spent by men and horses. Idle time was recorded to cause, such as the lameness of a horse.

(3) He had, with his overseer's approval (or at least without his open opposition), instituted a form of peer review, in which the opinions of other local farmers were sought and obtained about the working and management of Colinton Farm. It may be noticed with interest that this same principle of review was well known in the operation of coal pits in the 18th century, when colliery viewers regularly visited each other at their mines, noting methods employed and exchanging advice.

That Mr Trotter's farm was profitable in the first year of his own management is apparent, although he is slightly cautious in not quoting the precise prices he obtained for his grain sales, incorporating instead the "Midlothian Fiar" prices[2]. In this respect, the profits as shown in the accounts summarised above differ to some degree from the actual profits he realised, but did not reveal.

90

Summary of Colinton Farm Crop Account 1823

To Stack-Yard Account	£	s	d		By Estimated value	£	s	d
loss	111	7	8		of growing crop	2,146	4	6
Farm expenses total	1,016	5	1½		Deposit a/c	354	1	6
Alex Trotter Esq, balance on this account, or, in other words, profit upon crop 1823	1,422	17	2½		Pasturage	46	17	0
					Meal	3	7	0
	£2,550	10	0			£2,550	10	0

Summary of Inventories and Capital at Martinmas

	1822				1823		
	£	s	d		£	s	d
Horses	187	0	0		192	10	0
Cattle	105	0	0		131	0	0
Sheep	18	0	0		29	16	0
Implements	308	13	0		328	6	6
Sundry Stocks	62	12	4		99	10	0
Dung	93	7	10				
Payments in advance	37	7	8				
Cash	187	19	2		366	19	8½
	£1,000	0	0		£1,148	2	2½
Capital increase on account of the 1823 crop					£148	2	2½
Cash withdrawn during the year					1,850	0	0
					£1,998	2	2½
Cash introduced during the year					400	0	0
Total net funds for the year					£1,598	2	2½
Being profit on crop 1823					£1,422	17	2½
interest at 4% on £1,200					48	0	0
reimbursement of Dreghorn Estate*					127	5	0
					£1,598	2	2½

Proportion of overseer's wages, overseer's horse, incidental expenses and general policy of insurance.

Farm management now, and the future?

Certainly there have been developments in the spread of knowledge of agricultural economics, but we suspect that only in the larger units will there be found anything approaching the sophistication of accounting system pioneered by such men as Alexander Trotter of Dreghorn. The agricultural colleges and the universities teach their students about the merits of marginal costing, and there are published examples of yields (poor, average and good), together with specimen cost/income/margin and net profit results for a range of crops and animal products.[3] A scrutiny of the yields quoted as examples shows how modern farming methods have outstripped the results obtained by Mr Trotter's men:

Crop		1823	1978
Wheat	per acre	105 lbs	36 cwts
Oats	per acre	2 cwts	34 cwts
Pease	per acre	31 lbs	22 cwts
Barley	per acre	1½ cwts	32 cwts
Potatoes	per acre	1 ton 13 cwts	11 tons

Intensive farming, artificial fertilisation, and genetic engineering all contribute to satisfying the needs of a hungry world, a constantly changing fast-moving world, remote from the leisurely pace of Mr Trotter's ploughmen and his horses plying between Colinton and Edinburgh. But the ideas of Trotter are as relevant today as when they were first developed. □

[1] *Alexander Trotter, A method of farm bookkeeping exemplified by the forms and accounts actually practised by the author (Edinburgh, 1825). There is a copy in the Antiquarian Collection of The Institute of Chartered Accountants of Scotland, at the National Library of Scotland. A short article on the book appeared in TAM, December 1978, p 517: Anna B G Dunlop: "Mr Trotter's Method of Farm Bookkeeping".*

[2] *... Average prices of grain determined annually in March in each county of Scotland by a jury of farmers and landholders from actual sales made of the preceding crop from 11 November of the previous year up to the time when the Fiars are struck.*

[3] *See, for example, Nix J Farm Management Pocketbook (School of Rural Economics and Related Studies, 1979).*

24

"A Careful and Most Ingenious Fabrication of Imaginary Accounts": Scottish Railway Company Accounts before 1868

WRAY VAMPLEW, B.SC.(SOC.SCI.), PH.D.

91

This article examines a major fraud practised on Scottish railway shareholders which was made possible by the accounting techniques of the day. The author is a member of the Scottish Committee on Accounting History.

Introduction

" We have frequently had to characterise the reports issued by the directors of this company [the North British Railway] as having in them much of the quality and force of state papers . . . we look in vain, indeed, to the half yearly or special missives of any other company for explanations so full, so convincing and so efficient in aim . . . the board have deemed it their duty invariably to put the shareholders in possession of the grounds and objects of every important step taken on behalf of the company . . . nothing has been withheld or disguised." (RAILWAY TIMES, March 17, 1866.)

" The latest report and accounts of the North British assuredly surpass all that have gone before." (RAILWAY TIMES, August 25, 1866.)

Question: Have the annual accounts as laid before the shareholders been systematically cooked so as to mislead them as to the true position of the revenue and expenditure of the company, and simply to exhibit an ability to pay the dividend desired by Mr Hodgson (the chairman), regardless of the free revenue of the company being adequate for the purpose?

Answer (from the company accountant): Yes, that has been the plan. (Report of the Committee of Investigation into the Affairs of the North British Railway Company, October 1866.)

This revelation of the financial irregularities of the North British Railway, at that time with a capitalisation of nearly £13 million probably the largest company in Scotland, railway or otherwise, shocked its shareholders, the financial press and the investing public at large. But should they have been so surprised?

What follows is first an examination of how this financial façade developed and then some general comments on one of the major contributory factors, the state of railway accounting in Scotland before 1868, the year which saw the passing of the Regulation of Railways Act, which aimed to promote the standardisation of such accounting.

Deception revealed

In the decade following the great railway mania of the mid-1840s the North British had become a prime target for the snipers of the financial press. Its dividends were negligible, its management deplorable and its equipment decrepit. In contrast, over the next decade the company apparently prospered under the chairmanship of Richard Hodgson. Dividends and shareholders became more than passing acquaintances, and the same journals that had earlier strictured the company now proclaimed that " the growth and increased stability of the North British . . . has been altogether marvellous ".[1] So marvellous, in fact, that it was too good to be true, as was discovered by a new company secretary, John Walker, who had begun to investigate the company's books after coming across an irregularity in the surplus property account. His scrutiny revealed that, far from being prosperous, the company's finances were in dire straits with revenue inadequate to cover the dividends which were actually being paid out of capital. When Hodgson insisted, against his advice, that a 3% dividend was to be declared in September 1866, Walker informed the directors of his suspicions as to the company's true financial position. The board decided to investigate his allegations, with a private internal enquiry by a committee of directors. Hodgson, as chairman of the company, was to be a participant.

Unfortunately for Hodgson a leading shareholder, James White of Overtoun, worried about rumours of internal dissension, had determined to request a shareholders' enquiry. White, a strict Sabbatarian, was not disposed to look with favour on Hodgson who willingly operated the North British on Sundays. On hearing of White's manoeuvrings Hodgsontri ed to tempt him with a promise of the next available directorship, but White was not to be bought and pressed ahead with his demand for a full investigation into the company's affairs; a demand which was readily agreed to by the

[1] RAILWAY TIMES, March 17, 1866.

shareholders at the statutory half-yearly meeting, perhaps because the proposed 3% dividend had been reduced to 1% because of an inability to raise funds.

The report of the investigation committee did little to relieve the anxieties of the shareholders, for it revealed that " a careful and most ingenious fabrication of imaginary accounts " had been perpetrated in order to disguise the illiquid position of the company. Far

An extract from the evidence of the company accountant, Mr J. P. Lythgoe, to the 1866 enquiry.

MR. J. P. LYTHGOE.

The Chairman.—We want some information from you as to the Company's accounts, and as to the mode of keeping these accounts, and the details of the department over which you have the oversight. How long have you been connected with the Company ?—I have been the Traffic Accountant since November 1852 up to August 1862.

All the principal financial books are kept by you ?—I had only the Traffic Accounts to July 1862, and I have had the general accounts in addition from that to the present time.

So that since 1862 you have had complete command of the books and accounts of the Company ?—Yes.

Mr. Simpson is under you ?—Yes.

Do Mr. Simpson's instructions emanate from you ?—Yes.

All the entries in the books are made by Mr. Simpson under your instructions and at your light ?—Yes.

You are cognisant of them all ?—Yes.

Do you hold yourself responsible for the correct statement of the accounts in the books of the Company ?—No, I do not.

Then, who is ?—Well, my superior officer, I believe,—Mr. Rowbotham.

You mean that you make entries in them according as he desires you ?—Either him or Mr. Hodgson,—one or other. Of course, nothing is done without Mr. Rowbotham's concurrence.

In speaking of that, I suppose you refer more to cross entries in the books, keeping one account larger and another smaller ?—No ; I refer to the accounts generally. If the Board had held me responsible for the integrity of the accounts, the accounts would have been very differently made up from what they are, in my present position. I have no access to the Board whatever, nor to any of the Directors, or Committee of Directors. That is one complaint that I have.

In short, you were not an independent officer ?—No, I was not.

When did there first begin to be any irregularity in the mode of keeping the accounts, or in the entries made ? Or, perhaps, you had better first exhaust the present half-year, and explain the irregularities as to it. Taking the Revenue Account for the half-year ending July 1866, will you explain in what respects the statement of it is inaccurate ? Can you assure us that the receipts entered in the Revenue Account, p. 13, are correctly stated, and that these items honestly embrace the traffic and revenue of the Company for that half-year ?—Subject to certain deductions which have been made.

As they appear here ?—No, subject to certain deductions which I shall hereafter explain, I believe this is a fair statement of the revenue, made up according to the custom of the Company.

Is this a correct statement of the revenue of the Company ?—Certainly this is not an account which I should make up if I had myself to look to for producing a proper statement of accounts, because it is a short charge of two weeks. It is a principle I don't admit, and never did.

But that is the expenditure. We are dealing now with the traffic earned.—The amount of the receipts from passengers, parcels, and mails is correct. In the Merchandise Account there is a sum of £6921, 10s. 3d., which was brought from the Suspense Account. That is to say, we had that sum in reserve, and it is brought into this account.

Was it at the credit of the Suspense Account ?—Yes.

How did it get there from the previous half-year ? Had you ever revenue that you could afford to part with to that extent ?—It is a part of the £84,400, charged as surplus property at 31st July 1865. On the other hand, there is a sum of about £5700 or £5900 of cartages brought into this half-year, which properly belongs to the previous half-year.

Is there £5700 included in the £26,000, more than there should have been ?—Yes.

from being able to pay the dividends that had been declared on ordinary stock, the North British could not genuinely meet some of its guaranteed and preference share obligations. By charging over £300,000 to the capital account which should have been met out of revenue, the annual accounts for at least three and a half years had been systematically faked to allow the payment of whatever dividend Hodgson desired.

The importance of dividends

The importance attached by Hodgson to the maintenance of dividends stemmed from the nature of railway capital expenditure, which tended to occur at discreet intervals rather than being spread evenly over time. This hampered the utilisation of ploughed back profits, the prevalent industrial method of financing growth, as it would have involved the creation of reserves to be used for investment at a future date, and railway shareholders took a hostile attitude towards such a policy, believing that it was unfair to retain current profits in the hope of obtaining future returns.[2]

A more modern view is that undisturbed profits, in increasing the assets of the company concerned, benefit the existing shareholder by increasing the market value of his stock, thus giving him the option of obtaining immediate returns in the form of a capital gain. However, this view has evolved through experience and in the mid-nineteenth century experience in shareholding was decidedly limited. The railways, though not the pioneers of joint stock enterprises with limited liability and transferable shares, certainly popularised such investment and were instrumental in the creation of many provincial stock exchanges, including those in Edinburgh and Glasgow. Yet this had not occurred until the 1840s and thus there was little experience on which to base attitudes; and what there was tended to encourage demands for dividends rather than a tolerance of ploughing back, for when the profits anticipated in the railway mania failed to materialise, the market price of shares fell so far below par that any possibility of capital gains must have appeared tenuous. Once bitten the railway shareholders became twice shy, at least as regards financial policy; potential capital gains appeared much less attractive than immediate dividends. Moreover, the railway companies were expanding too rapidly for profits to have financed their growth even if they had been available. It was therefore essential to attract fresh capital into the enterprises, and the obvious way to encourage this was to maintain reasonable dividends. In addition, if dividends could be relied upon, then possibly there would be confidence in that company's shares which would be reflected in their market value, and if share prices remained high this would facilitate the flotation of new issues without a discount and prevent excessive capitalisation.

The North British was therefore not unusual in its desire to maintain dividends; where it differed from other companies was in going to the extreme of paying them out of capital. However, had Hodgson not stooped to false representation in order to avoid any default in payments to shareholders, it is feasible that confidence

[2] W. Chambers, ABOUT RAILWAYS, 19 (Edinburgh, 1865).

in North British stock would have slumped so low that operations would have ceased through an inability to raise funds.

Reasons for the predicament

There were two main reasons why the revenue of the North British failed to match up to the company's financial obligations, excessive capital expenditure and receipts that were too low to provide for a dividend on even the most frugally constructed line.

One factor making for an inflated capital account was the number of companies taken over by the North British. This frequently involved the creation of nominal stock used as an inducement to the shareholders of the other companies to exchange their stock for that of the North British. Much of this paper capital bore preferential or guaranteed dividends, producing a position where the North British had a greater proportion of its capital bearing such dividends than any other Scottish railway. In addition the spate of amalgamations undertaken in the 1860s left the North British with large numbers of inferior rolling stock which had to be rebuilt or replaced. As for genuine North British construction it can be suggested that capital was seriously misallocated. Estimated to cost £218,000, land for the original main line and branches eventually soared to over £571,000. This was mainly attributable to the sellers demanding more than the land's agricultural value because they knew the railway could not do without it. High land costs were not peculiar to the North British but such unproductive outlays must have contributed to the difficulties of Hodgson. Even if costs had been minimal, some North British branches could never have yielded a reasonable rate of return. To claim that " more than half of the North British is made up of branches to mouldering old towns and cross lines over hills sacred to sheep and wandering botanists "[3] was an exaggeration, but an ex-official of the company could justifiably state that several branches were built " which it was thought would be valuable feeders to the main line. They have proved to be the very opposite, and have sucked it financially dry."[4]

Both amalgamation and over-construction can be attributed to the same basic cause: inter-company rivalry, and, more especially, rivalry with the Caledonian Railway. The prevailing attitude was that attack was the best form of defence: a company should get in first and occupy a territory, either by building or by take-over, and then battle in parliament to prevent the introduction of hostile lines. This was one reason why the North British had spent over one million pounds on parliamentary expenses. Unfortunately, although every company seemed to accept the idea of having an exclusive right to occupy certain territories, they could not agree in whom the divine right had been vested. Both the North British and the Caledonian seemed prepared to pursue the other virtually everywhere it went. In turn this led to rate wars punctuated by periods of uneasy peace.

[3] THE RIALTO, March 30, 1889.
[4] E. D. Chattaway, RAILWAYS—THEIR CAPITAL AND DIVIDENDS, 26 (Edinburgh, 1855).

94

Railway accounts

How was Hodgson able to wield practically independent control over such a large concern? Limited liability enabled railways to be the property of many, but day to day management rested with a few individuals, though at least twice a year shareholders could challenge the directors' policies. Generally shareholders remained sleeping partners, but, once aware that something was wrong, they could be roused; in the depression period following the railway mania almost every company in Scotland was subjected to a committee of inquiry. The important point is that the attention of the shareholders had to be drawn to any trouble; perhaps the most obvious sign was low dividends, so if reasonable dividends were paid regularly, as was Hodgson's policy, there was less likelihood of an uprising. Moreover, the shareholders could judge only from what they were allowed to see, and the Committee of Investigation revealed how imperfect was the flow of information from the management to the shareholders. Such was the standard of accountancy at the time that Hodgson was able to hide what he was doing not only from the shareholders but also from fellow members of the board.

Well into the nineteenth century railway accounting was scarcely a formal science, either in doctrine or technique. The keeping of accounts was obligatory but personal judgment so often decided their format that there was little uniformity between companies or even, over time, within the same company. Items in one set of accounts could find no parallel elsewhere. In the case of the North British the accounts were so distorted as to be intelligible only to those who set them out. This company was not alone in its deception. The accounts of the other major Scottish railway company, the Caledonian were once described by THE TIMES as being in " just such a tangle as one might dream of after supping on lobster salad and champagne ".[5] By careful camouflage the directors had £95,000 paid to lawyer relations and published accounts showing a profit of nearly £32,000, whereas the true profit was less than £400.[6] Further north the Great North of Scotland line's apparent prosperity in 1865 turned out to be because interest on the cost of the branch lines was being debited to the wrong account.[7]

That, until 1868, each company was " at liberty to adopt the form [of accounts] it considers most convenient, and to vary that form from time to time "[8] obviously made it difficult for the auditors to perform their task effectively, especially when their duties were rather ill-defined. The auditors of the Scottish Central Railway were not alone in their complaint that it would " have been a great satisfaction to them had the nature and extent of their duties been more specifically defined than they are by the existing Acts of Parliament ".[9]

In July 1841, early in the Railway Age, the RAILWAY TIMES, a leading financial journal for investors, criticised railway company accounts and complained that " for want of system, and of correlative facts, their utility is

sadly limited ". A series of articles followed which examined the principles on which a uniform system of keeping railway accounts ought to be constructed. But nobody heeded their advice. Parliamentary legislation set minimal requirements in that each railway had to produce a half-yearly balance sheet, but a substantial degree of latitude was given in the calculation of profit and loss.[10] Each company went its own way. How could voluntary standardisation of accounts be expected when there was no consensus on what constituted depreciation or even capital expenditure?

Capital versus revenue

Writing on the distinction between the capital and revenue accounts, William Chambers, the publisher chairman of the Peebles Railway, declared that they must be kept entirely separate, even though this " introduces a great complexity into the financial affairs of railways ".[11] Too great it would seem for most Scottish railway companies, nearly all of which, deliberately or accidentally, exhibited a decided confusion between capital and revenue in their accounts. Even in their pre-Hodgson days the North British were not immune from switching items at will from one account to another: in 1849 a shareholders' inquiry found that " the distribution of charges between capital and revenue has been correctly made ", but only three years later another investigation revealed that almost £34,000 " had been charged to capital instead of revenue under the heads of interest discounts, salaries and general charges ".

Betterment

How was expenditure on improvements and better replacements dealt with? Some companies were aware that betterment should be distinguished in the accounts. George Graham, the resident engineer on the Caledonian, tried to convince his directors that improvement of the permanent way could be justified as capital expenditure.[12] At one point the North British did classify the " improved value on rebuilt waggons " separately in the capital account, and the Great North of Scotland so allocated the cost of the additional weight of rails after relaying portions of their track.[13] Generally, however, companies took the line of least resistance and charged all replacement costs to capital. It was much easier to do than to deduct anything from revenue. William Chambers summed up the position: " Were the shareholders to look to ultimate advantages, they would sanction the payment

[5] TIMES, September 30, 1850.
[6] HERAPATH'S RAILWAY JOURNAL, January 24, 1852.
[7] ibid., April 1, 1865.
[8] ROYAL COMMISSION ON RAILWAYS: PARLIAMENTARY PAPERS, 1867, XXXVIII, xxiii.
[9] RAC(S), 1/34, July 1849. Scottish Record Office (SRO), Edinburgh.

[10] A brief survey of the legislation can be found in H. Pollins " Aspects of Railway Accounting before 1868 " in A. C. Littleton & B. S. Yamey STUDIES IN THE HISTORY OF ACCOUNTING (London, 1956).
[11] Chambers, op. cit., 19.
[12] NATIONAL LIBRARY OF SCOTLAND, EDINBURGH, Ms. 6356, 16, September 18, 1855.
[13] RAC(S) 1/1, July 1856 SRO; HERAPATH'S RAILWAY JOURNAL, October 10, 1865.

BALANCE SHEET

OF

THE NORTH BRITISH RAILWAY COMPANY.

31st Jan. 1845.

CHARGE,—Deposit on 32,000 Shares,	...	...	£.80,000	0	0
Sums received from Forfeited Shares		...	178	10	0
Interest on Accounts with Bankers	...		1,331	8	0
Subscriptions in advance	...	...	58,533	0	0
Copies of Act sold	...	...	14	10	0
Call 4th Sept. 1844, at £2 : 10s, on 32,000 Shares			80,000	0	0
Interest received on that call	...	...	83	10	1
Call 11th Dec. 1844	...	...	80,000	0	0
Interest received on that call	...	...	25	9	11
Fees of Recording Transfers	...	...	45	11	4
Loans	...	...	8,500	0	0

Total Charge   ...   ...   £.308,711 19 4

DISCHARGE,—Arrears of Deposit	...	...	100	0	0
Ditto of Call 4th Sept. 1844	...	...	2,000	0	0
Ditto of Call 11th Dec. 1844	...	...	5,107	10	0

7,207 10 0

Preliminary & Parliamentary Expenses,£.17,825	7	0			
Office Furniture	...	...	351	6	6
General Charges	...	...	556	1	9
Land and Compensation	...	...	153,134	11	7
Expenses of Conveyancing ...	...	403	3	1
Wages to Constables	...	...	257	5	0
Salaries ...	...	...	543	11	0
Engineering Charges	...	...	793	5	0
Direction ...	...	...	500	0	0
Advertising, &c,	...	...	104	12	5
Sleepers ...	...	...	3,504	9	7
Rails	...	...	11,316	19	5
Chairs ...	...	...	2,065	4	5
Carriages	...	...	3,000	0	0
Works	...	55,882	15	11
Deposit on Subscription to the Northern Railway	...	...	1,250	0	0
Paid on Account of the Hawick Line			1,775	10	0

N. B. This last payment, although inserted here at present, may be transferred to a separate Account hereafter.

————253,294 2 8

Balance on hand   ...   48,210 6 8

£308,711 19 4

Edinburgh, 1st Feb. 1845.—Examined and certified by

(Signed)   JOHN MAXTON.
GEO. HAM. BELL.
JAS. FORREST.

JOHN LEARMONTH.

Note. In addition to the sum paid for Works,
as appearing in the foregoing State, £.55,882 15 11
There has been paid since it was made up 16,950 0 0

Making the total sum paid for Works £.72,832 15 11

The first balance sheet of the North British Railway Company.

for permanent improvements out of the current revenue; but . . . shareholders for the most part care nothing for the remote and contingent prosperity of the undertaking, and will not, or cannot, make a corresponding sacrifice."[14]

Closing the capital account

This attitude of the shareholders was directly responsible for over-capitalisation of all Scottish railway companies. Closing the capital account was a major pre-occupation of most boards. In September 1852 the North British directors announced that they were "deeply impressed with the great importance of having the capital account closed, as they are quite aware how much, in the case of this company as of others, this would add to the confidence of the shareholders and the public . . . and the directors will make it a leading object of attention to do so on the earliest possible day". The Caledonian directors too felt that "the only way to give confidence in railway accounts is to prevent the possibility of further capital expenditure" and the Peebles board elected to pay for new rolling stock out of revenue so as to prevent "original cost remaining a perpetual charge against the company".[15] And by 1858 the Edinburgh and Glasgow reported that it was nearly at the "desirable position" of closing its capital account.[16] All these plans proved fruitless in face of the shareholders' views. As one authority pointed out, "in remarkably few cases [before 1865] have railway companies been able, or been disposed to close their capital account".[17]

Depreciation

Depreciation was another major topic for discussion. Was it fair, it was asked, to "the shareholders of a railway [who] are not associated together like a common partnership, always the same parties, but [who] are a fluctuating body—in one half and out the next. To tax, therefore, one half year for the wants of another is unjust, and the injustice is heightened when the tax is not for a certain want, but an undefined one."[18] Most companies, however, made some provision but generally these were of an experimental nature. The North British, for example, decided that no depreciation fund was required for rolling stock since the locomotives, carriages and wagons could be kept in an efficient state by "ordinary" replacements and repairs. They did, however, establish a fund for the permanent way and buildings. In any case depreciation was *the* variable item in the accounts. What Pollins pointed out for south of the Border was no less true for Scotland; depreciation

would frequently be forgotten when the maintenance of the dividend required such a sacrifice.[19]

Conclusion

The techniques of railway accounting in Scotland were responsible for allowing Hodgson to deceive the North British shareholders. However, following the 1867 report of the Royal Commission on Railways an Act was passed in 1868 which, for the first time, told the railway companies in some detail what they were expected to show in their accounts. Perhaps the most important requirement was that the published balance sheet should distinguish fixed and circulating capital. Henceforth, though not eliminated, deception of railway shareholders was less easy, and fraud on the scale practised by Hodgson was not witnessed again.

[19] Pollins, *op. cit.*, 343-9.

© Wray Vamplew, 1973.

---

[14] Chambers, *op. cit.*, 19-20.
[15] HERAPATH's RAILWAY JOURNAL, September 29, 1855, October 20, 1855.
[16] Chambers, *op. cit.*, 20.
[17] HERAPATH's RAILWAY JOURNAL, March 20, 1858.
[18] *Ibid*, September 2, 1848.

Professionalism

The Emergent Professionals

JAS. C. STEWART, C.A.

Is history bunk or can we learn something from the first Chartered Accountants? We can at least learn something about them, and maybe that knowlege will help us to plan for the future.

Characteristics of a profession

In their petitions (mid-19th century) for the grant of Royal Charters of Incorporation both The Society of Accountants in Edinburgh and The Institute of Accountants and Actuaries in Glasgow refer to the profession of accountant in Scotland as having long existed as a distinct profession of great respectability. It is true that the description of " accountant " had long been used, in early directories and elsewhere, by persons who were no doubt of great respectability, to describe their calling. Whether it was then entirely justified to describe that calling as a profession is, at least, doubtful.

Submission to some form of corporate discipline is an essential element in our conception of a profession, and without the formation of associations of persons possessed of common skills this corporate discipline could not exist. The appellation " profession " itself has religious origins and still retains something of an ethical connotation.

Seven criteria which, in his opinion, distinguish professions from other pursuits are set out by John L. Carey at the beginning of his history of accountancy in America.[1] His criteria, with which it would be hard to disagree, are—

(i) a body of specialised knowledge;
(ii) a formal educational process;
(iii) standards governing admission;
(iv) a code of ethics;
(v) a recognised status indicated by a licence or special designation;
(vi) a public interest in the work that practitioners perform; and
(vii) recognition by them of a social obligation.

He then goes on to describe the purposes for which, as he sees it, the first societies of accountants were formed, in these words:—

" To secure public confidence, the public accountants had to develop professional organisations, to formulate technical and ethical standards, to establish a system of training their successors, and to acquire symbolic evidence of competence and responsibility. For these purposes the Scottish and English institutes of chartered accountants were founded."

In considering the history of the first formal organisation of this long-existing occupation two questions arise. How justly, after this formal organisation, could it be claimed that accountancy was a profession; and why should it have seemed particularly appropriate in the 1850s to set up the organisations which were to effect its transformation from occupation to profession?

Aims of the founders of the Scottish Institute

The two petitions for charter were in closely similar terms, and the rules of each body provided similar frameworks for the operations of their members. Some of the early divergences between East and West will be taken up in a later article; meantime it will be convenient to consider only the early days of the Glasgow Institute and to see how far the aims of its founders, so percipiently described by the American chronicler more than a century later, were achieved.

[1] *The Rise of the Accounting Profession 1896-1969*, in 2 volumes. American Institute of Certified Public Accountants, 1969-1970.

These aims, as was expressed in the initial letter of requisition addressed to accountants in practice in Glasgow from before 1841 by a number of those who had commenced business after that date, included the short-term objective of securing that—

" the practical experience of those parties who have hitherto been entrusted with the management of Bankrupt Estates in the West of Scotland may be properly represented and have their due weight in determining what changes require to be made upon the existing Bankruptcy Law."

In the early years of the Institute the Council, and indeed the members as a body, devoted a great deal of attention to the pursuit of this objective, and their representations had a significant effect on the form of the legislation as finally embodied in the Bankruptcy Act 1856. In contrast to this almost obsessional interest in bankruptcy, it does not seem that the Institute took any great interest in the introduction and passing of the Companies Act 1862.

The wider aims of the Institute were set out in the petition for a charter. After reciting the nature of the work on which the members were engaged, with a heavy emphasis again placed on duties in connection with bankruptcies, the petition proceeds:—

"... that it is obvious that to the due performance of a profession such as this a liberal education is essential. . . .

. . . that the object in view in the formation of the Institute of Accountants in Glasgow . . . was to maintain the efficiency as well as the respectability of the professional body . . . that this object will be further greatly assisted by the formation . . . into a body corporate . . . with power to make regulations and bye-laws respecting the qualification and admission of Members. . . ."

It will be seen, therefore, that on incorporation the Institute could fairly claim that, explicitly or implicitly, it met the criteria which might be considered to distinguish a profession from other pursuits.

The world into which the profession was born

To understand why the first steps towards professionalism should have been taken at the time and in the way that they were, it is necessary to consider the contemporary legal and economic situation.

The early part of the 19th century saw the beginning of the technological innovations which have continued with ever-increasing speed and growing complexity to our own day. These years saw also the introduction of limited liability, and of other legislation, including new bankruptcy laws, designed to meet the new developments in commerce and industry.

In particular the 1840s saw the height of the railway mania, with the frequent financial disasters which it caused. Financing of the new developments called for changes in the banking system, and in the early part of the century numerous new banking houses came into existence, some of which had meteoric and catastrophic careers. Limited liability had not been introduced, and the problems presented by the failure of a joint-stock company, financial, commercial, or industrial, the ownership of which involved hundreds of " partners ", must have produced problems the unravelling of which called not only for skill and patience but also for a high degree of imagination. We have seen in recent years how the application of advanced technology has created new problems and imposed strains on traditional financial and accounting methods. It is no matter for wonder, then, that a new professionalism was called for to deal with the problems posed by the sudden emergence of steam power and of large-scale industrial capitalism. The social and financial framework was subjected to unusual strains, and where it gave way there was the need for an expert in bankruptcy to patch up the damage, if that were possible, or to clear up the debris, if repair were impossible. The development of a more adaptable and stronger framework had to come later.

Something of the atmosphere of the second quarter of the century may be sensed from the comments of an acute and well-informed contemporary observer, Henry (later Lord) Cockburn.[1] In 1826 he writes:—

" In spite of great mercantile depression this was the period of the most violent Joint-Stock mania that ever seized this kingdom. I could not have conceived that madness could be so universal. There was no peculiar temptation, from high profits, for men not regular merchants to adventure in trade; nor were purses too heavy with unemployed guineas; nor any new field suddenly discovered. It was a mere Joint-Stock epidemic. . . . The schemes were so numerous, that after exhausting every subject to which they could be applied, there was actually a joint-stock company instituted for the purpose of projecting and organising joint-stock companies."

Lord Cockburn, from the painting by Sir Henry Raeburn, the property of The Faculty of Advocates, and hung in Parliament House, Edinburgh.

Again in April 1835 he writes:—

" Edinburgh is at present almost a mass of insolvency. Trade, except in one or two branches, has left Leith, our port; the docks are bankrupt; our college has not a shilling; the Writers to the Signet are getting so destitute that it is not easy to see how they can maintain their library and general establishment; the Faculty of Advocates is in a similar condition, but further gone. . . ."

Another ten years pass and Cockburn comments in November 1845:—

" Britain is at present an island of lunatics, all railway mad."

Against that background it is not surprising that the priority interest of the new accountancy profession should have been bankruptcy.

No merchants, manufacturers or lawyers need apply

The rules of the Glasgow Institute, as originally framed, before the charter, covered in their statement of objects and their provisions governing the admission of members most of the matters which might be thought appropriate to a genuinely professional body. They also reserved the right to expel any member, if it was reported to a quarterly general meeting by two-thirds of the whole council that in their

[1] Memorials of his Time, Edinburgh: Adam and Charles Black, 1856.
[Readers may be interested to learn that Lord Cockburn was a frequent visitor at part of Chartered Accountants' Hall, Edinburgh, since at one time the owner of No. 26 Queen Street was his son-in-law.—Ed.]

opinion he ought no longer to be a member and this was accepted and confirmed by resolution of that meeting.

The worth of a set of rules is not to be judged, however, by the words in which they are set out but by the spirit in which they are administered, and it is of interest to see how the door to the profession was guarded in these early days. An earlier article dealt with the development of the Edinburgh Society's scheme of examinations,[2] and it is not proposed to deal now with the more or less parallel development in Glasgow, but rather to look at the credentials of those who were admitted as members without undergoing any, or at most a merely formal, examination and how these credentials were checked.

The initial rules for admission were necessarily transitional. A body of members had to be recruited before a rule on apprenticeship or examination could be enforced. The earliest admissions were, therefore, decided by the Council alone, but it was provided that, after January 1, 1857, only those who had served a four-year apprenticeship, although not with a member, should be admitted. On April 30, 1855, that is, before the formal granting of the Charter, it was agreed that future applicants should undergo examination. The proposed examination was to cover elementary principles of Bankrupt Law; Bookkeeping and Accounts; the practical working of Bankruptcies, Trust Estates, Voluntary and Judicial Factories; and the rudimentary principles of Arithmetic and Algebra. When the Charter was tabled on June 5, 1855, it was decided that the whole Council should be the examinators under this new rule.

The number of members admitted up to December 31, 1854, was 52. These were all admitted without examination, but the records in the Admission Book show that two at least of the five members admitted in 1855 had been examined. It is not till 1870, however, when a hundred admissions had been recorded, that this book regularly contains copies of the applicants' certificates of examination. For some years thereafter some members continued to be admitted without examination, under what was known as Rule 8, which provided that it was competent to admit applicants who were recommended by at least two-thirds of the whole Council and whose applications were approved at two successive quarterly general meetings of the members.

The rules also provided that, in his letter of application, each prospective member should set out particulars of the experience or other qualification on the basis of which he claimed to be fitted for membership and required him to state specifically that he was not engaged in the business of a Manufacturer, Merchant or Law Agent. Under Article XI of the constitution a person ipso facto ceased to be a member on engaging in any of these pursuits.

As many of the earliest " accountants " are shown in the contemporary street directories as " accountants and merchants " these rules show clearly the intention to establish a distinct and separate profession of Accountant. Only this limited range of occupations was banned, and many of the early members had other occupations, such as stockbroking, banking, insurance or estate factoring. The exclusion of merchants or manufacturers seems to have been complete until industry and commerce, at a much later date, awoke to the advantages of employing fully trained accountants and began to recruit members as employees in ever-increasing numbers.

While it was not at first compulsory, the advantages of attendance at university classes in law were early apparent, and many of the letters of application include references to current or prior attendance at these classes as contributing to establishing the applicant's fitness for membership.

[2] JAS. C. STEWART: " Qualification for Membership a Hundred Years Ago ", THE ACCOUNTANT'S MAGAZINE, July 1974, at page 263.

(continued on page 115)

(continued from page 114)

The Council stands guard

That even before the advent of compulsory examination the admission rules were not a mere formality can be shown by a number of examples. In December 1853 the application of Mr Robert Scobie was continued, as he was personally unknown to any member of Council present when it was first considered. He was admitted in January 1854. At the same meeting the Council decided that Mr Wm. J. Carswell's " previous occupation " was not sufficient to qualify him for membership. He eventually became a member in 1857. In October 1854, when Mr Robert Forrester applied for membership, his application was deferred on the ground that it contained insufficient evidence of his experience. Later that month the application was again considered, and explanations were heard from his sponsors, but it was again deferred. On the last day of the month it was agreed to recommend an amended application to the members.

It was at this meeting on October 31, 1854, that it was decided to consider the alteration of the rules to provide for examinations.

The only expulsions from membership in these early days seem to have been on the ground of failure to pay the two years' subscriptions in succession. The first such case occurred surprisingly soon after the formation of the Institute, and in 1868 when the membership was around 60 no fewer than 8 members were removed from the list for this reason, though it appears that some of these may have intended to resign their membership.

The first exercise in public relations took place in 1854. It was reported to a general meeting in that year that upwards of 120 copies of the Institute's constitution had been circulated to, among others, the Lord Advocate, the Solicitor General, the Judges, the Clerks of Court, the Dean and Officers of the Faculty of Advocates, certain Sheriffs, Glasgow bankers, the Directors of the Merchants House Glasgow, and of the Chamber of Commerce there, and the Dean and Council of the Faculty of Procurators in Glasgow. It will be seen that in the light of the high priority given by members to bankruptcy work the list includes all who might be thought best able to influence nominations for such work. In 1858, further to differentiate themselves from lesser breeds of accountants, the members, following the example of the Edinburgh Society, agreed that there should be a general use by them of the distinguishing initials " C.A.".

The initial membership numbered about 50; the petition for the charter was actually signed by 49 members, and it might have been expected that the numbers would have grown quickly since the main qualification at first was experience. In fact the total admissions to the end of 1879, more than twenty-five years after the foundation of the Institute, numbered only 144, of whom less than half had been subjected to examination.

Some early applications

The early members covered a wide range in age and experience and it is interesting to note how this is reflected in their letters of application. In general the letters are quite short, comprising the mandatory statement that the applicant is not engaged in any of the forbidden businesses, followed by a narration of his experience, which rarely exceeds two or three lines. As might be expected many stress their experience in connection with bankruptcies.

Some specific examples may be quoted. Mr Alex Ritchie (No. 34) writes that he has been a clerk with Mr Gourlay, Accountant, from 1847 to 1852 and " had charge of the chief bankrupt estates on which during that time he was a Trustee ". Mr W. J. Carswell (No. 62), the delay in connection with whose application was noted above, states that he has been an apprentice and clerk with the late Richard Hall, Writer in Glasgow, who was the law agent of the Clydesdale Banking

Company. In that office he has been principally engaged on Sequestrations and Trust Estates. On the other hand Mr James Grahame (No. 74), after giving particulars of his experience—he had been in the Inspector's office of the National Bank in Edinburgh and then for eleven years, for seven of which he was a partner, in an accountant's office in Glasgow—, writes almost apologetically:—" Although wanting in experience as an accountant in bankruptcy I have studied the law of Scotland in relation to it . . .".

Quite a number of applicants had served in the offices of banks, and a surprisingly large number, including some of these bankers, in Edinburgh offices of lawyers or accountants. One, Robert Lumsden (No. 73), was an apprentice in the Bank of Scotland, later their Inspector of Branches, and " for the last four years employed as one of the liquidators of the Western Bank of Scotland ".

It is a curious fact that, about the middle of the nineteenth century, in addition to the railway mania already mentioned, bank shares were a common vehicle of financial speculation—perhaps to be compared with the recent market interest in our so-called fringe banks of today.

Several early applicants recite mercantile experience, including one who says that it was in connection with the failure of the business of cotton spinners in which he had been engaged that he met Mr McClelland,[4] in whose office he later trained as an accountant and of whom he was latterly a partner. Another, after eight years in the counting house of a firm of commission agents, set up in partnership in another such firm, but " as our progress was not very encouraging " the firm split up, and he started in business as an accountant " for which I had long had a predilection ".

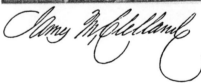

Perhaps the most varied career is described in the application of a man whose father was an original member and whose partner at the time of his application was President of the Institute. After taking a degree at Glasgow University he served some time in his father's office, and was then engaged in a mercantile counting house for three years. Thereafter he became a civil engineer, serving a regular apprenticeship of five and a half years. He later had experience of the valuation of mineral and other properties and of iron works, which

[4] James McClelland, C.A., President (the first), 1853-1864, The Institute of Accountants and Actuaries in Glasgow.

frequently necessitated the investigation of business books. Circumstances then rendered it desirable for him to adopt the profession of an accountant, and he became a partner of the Institute's President. " At present I am attending the Scotch Law Class in the university," he added.

A great many applicants describe themselves as partners of members—in a number of cases partners of relatively long standing. Whether these firms designated themselves as Chartered Accountants is not clear, but the minute of adherence of one new member is written on the letterhead of a still existing and highly respected firm, of which he had been a partner for two and a half years, and under the firm name, which includes the name of the new member, appear the magic letters " CA ". It may, of course, have been a new letterhead introduced to mark his admission as a member of the Institute!

Towards the end of the period under consideration applications from young men who had served regular apprenticeships and were submitting themselves for examination in what would now be regarded as the normal course of entry become more common, while those from men who, from the details given of their experience, must be adjudged middle-aged, become rarer.

The Institute was settling down as a respectable and respected professional body.

© Jas. C. Stewart, 1975.

102

Accountants in old Aberdeen

MOYRA J M KEDSLIE, BA

The writer of this article is currently engaged in research which is aimed at assessing the socio-economic background of the early members of the chartered accountancy profession in Scotland. When complete, it will show the educational and social class foundations of the profession; whether or not son followed father into accountancy; and if there were significant differences in the memberships of the Edinburgh, Glasgow and Aberdeen Societies. The research project is being partially sponsored by the Scottish Committee on Accounting History of the Scottish Institute. This article summarises to date the writer's impressions, in compiling a collective biography of Scottish Chartered Accountants 1854-1904, of the membership of The Society of Accountants in Aberdeen 1867-1904.

104

The Background

Prior to 1951 CAs in Scotland were grouped into three separate bodies—The Society of Accountants in Edinburgh, chartered in 1854 which, with the other two, became The Institute of Chartered Accountants of Scotland; The Institute of Accountants and Actuaries in Glasgow, chartered in 1855; and The Society of Accountants in Aberdeen, chartered in 1867.

There were accountants in Aberdeen for many years prior to the formation of the Society. As early as 1831 the Aberdeen Trades Directory lists John Smith, who became the first president of the Aberdeen Society, as an accountant. Prior to this, Smith had appeared in the Directory as an advocate. It would be impossible to pinpoint all of the factors that caused twelve of these accountants to form the Society in 1867 but several are likely. First, they had the examples of their fellow accountants in Glasgow and Edinburgh who had obtained their charters some twelve to thirteen years previously. Second, the opening of the railway to the south, in 1851, had given impetus to a healthy expansion in manufacturing activity and to the rise of an urban industry based on agriculture. Third, Aberdeen, in the 1860s, in common with the rest of the country, suffered from the greatest of all nineteenth century financial crises—the banking disaster. This was considered largely to be due to the Companies Act 1862, which limited the liability of investors and speculators and which the banks evaded by not becoming companies. In the three years from 1862 to 1865 over 2,500 joint stock companies were registered with a nominal capital of £567 million. Bank Rate rose between October 1865 and January 1866 from four to eight per cent. Several banks suffered badly. The crisis resulted in the collapse of The Aberdeen Town and County Bank[1] and of one of Aberdeen's greatest industries at that time—the linen industry. The North of Scotland Bank[1] was also badly affected by the crisis but managed to avert total disaster. It was possibly this crisis which ultimately proved the catalyst and convinced the Aberdonian accountants of the benefits to be gained by forming themselves into a Society.

The Original Twelve

Of the original twelve members, only five were natives of

Aberdeen, although they had all been in practice in the city for some years. One was a native of Edinburgh, another was born in Naples, although he was a member of an old Aberdeenshire family. The remainder came from Peterhead, Fochabers, Kintore, Stonehaven and Forfar. Their average age was fifty years, the youngest being thirty and the oldest sixty-nine.

The only apparent common factor in their social backgrounds would seem to have been that of "Victorian respectability". Those who were born in Aberdeen came from the families of merchants and shipowners. Of those who came to the city to seek their fortune, two had fathers in the professions—a minister and an army officer. The fathers of the remainder held positions which, in their own times, carried a great deal of responsibility and status in the community. James Meston was the son of a road-toll keeper at Kintore; George Marquis' father was the postmaster at Fochabers; William Steele's father progressed from being a toll-bar keeper to "riding shotgun" on the Stonehaven to Aberdeen mail coach.

The original members were, without exception, first generation accountants, the majority of them having received their early training in legal offices in the city. Only one of them had a university education—John Smith, who was a graduate of Marischal College. Unlike later members, only one of the founder members was a member of Aberdeen Stock Exchange and one eventually became Sheriff Clerk Depute of Aberdeen and Kincardine.

If type of residence is a true indication of prosperity, these accountants appear to have been men of some substance. Their homes were in the fashionable areas of that time, such as Albert Street, and Albyn Terrace. In size the houses ranged from nine to eighteen rooms and each household included a minimum of two living-in servants, a cook and a housemaid.

Eleven of the original twelve members were married, although not all of them had children who survived them. As far as can be ascertained, of the twelve founding members only John Crombie "begat" a chartered accountant.

The Development of the Society

The Society of Accountants in Aberdeen grew very slowly. In the first ten years only nine new members were admitted. The average continued to be one new member per year until

---

[1] S G CHECKLAND: Scottish Banking: A History 1695-1973, *Collins*, 1975.

the 1890s, when the average number admitted per year was three. Between 1867 and 1904, the total number of admissions was seventy. Their average age on entry—omitting the twelve founding fathers—was twenty-six, the youngest entrant being twenty-one and the eldest fifty.

More than half of these members were sons of the Granite City, the remainder being drawn chiefly from an area within a fifty mile radius of Aberdeen—the area that looked to the city as its commercial centre. Three were Englishmen, two of whom were educated in Aberdeen, the third arriving in the city when his father became manager of Her Majesty's Opera House.

Aberdeen City Libraries
Albyn Terrace, Aberdeen, in the late 19th century

Educational Background

One third of the members were educated at Aberdeen Grammar School[2] which, at that time, concentrated on the classics, its pupils going to other schools in the city in the afternoons for non-classical tuition. Somewhat surprisingly, only two members are known to have been educated at Robert Gordon's College; surprising in that, although the Deed of Mortification for the school provided, primarily, that the headmaster's principle task was "to see that the Children and Servants be brought up and instructed with Fear of God"[3], there was specific provision made for the teaching of bookkeeping. The remainder of the members were educated at Challonry House School, at Bon Accord School or at their local town or village school.

At least thirteen of the Society's members attended University. Ten were students of King's College, Aberdeen, two of Marischal College, Aberdeen and one, Stephen Forsyth, having taken his first degree at King's College, took his second degree, in divinity, at Glasgow University in preparation for forsaking his first chosen career of accountancy for that of the ministry of the Church of Scotland. Of those attending university classes, the majority *did* graduate. There were nine MA degrees from King's College, one BSc degree from Marischal College and one BL degree from Glasgow University. This would appear to be somewhat different from early findings in the Edinburgh and Glasgow Societies, where quite a large proportion attended university classes but comparatively few of them actually graduated.

Parentage

As with the original twelve, comparatively few of the first seventy members came from a professional background. Seven

[2] T WATT: Aberdeen Grammar School: Roll of Pupils 1795-1919, *The Rosemount Press*, 1923.

were the sons of ministers and three were the sons of advocates. Five came from households where there was a background of finance of some sort: the fathers of two were cashiers, one was a bank agent and the remaining two classified themselves as accountants although, in fact, one was a writer/accountant and the other a banker/stockbroker/accountant. Four, including the Rennett brothers, were the sons of teachers and, not surprisingly if one considers the area surrounding Aberdeen, six were farmers' sons. By far the largest group came from the merchants and master tradesmen of Aberdeen and its surrounding area. Among them were such diverse occupations as brewer, house-painter, tailor, flesher, meal miller, baker, polished granite manufacturer, commission agent, coal merchant, builder—all of them men of some standing in the community at that time.

As one might expect, it appears that these early CAs married into families of similar social standing. Only one, George Whyte, President of the Aberdeen Society from 1896 to 1903, married the daughter of a CA—Alice Brand, daughter of Alexander Brand, President from 1871 to 1873. The others married the daughters of merchants, ministers, farmers, advocates and shipowners.

Professional Milieu

In common with accountants of the same period in other parts of the country, a significant number of Aberdeen accountants carried on other occupations as well as that of accountant. The most popular of these was stockbroking, carried on by at least eleven accountants. Two are also known to have been actuaries and seven to have been members of the legal profession. Peter Cran was, for many years, City Chamberlain of Aberdeen and John Leslie, as has already been noted, became Sheriff Clerk Depute of Aberdeen and Kincardine.

The majority of those first seventy members spent nearly all of their professional life and retirement in Aberdeen; many, in fact, worked until their death. Some spent a year or two in London being "finished"—that is, widening their experience before returning to Aberdeen to practise. At least eight stayed in the South. One of these was Robert Fletcher, who in 1877 was admitted into partnership with William Barclay Peat, one of the founders of Peat, Marwick, Mitchell & Co. The occasional member practised in Kirkcaldy, Dundee or Glasgow and five are known to have practised and died abroad—in Calgary, Buenos Aires, Paris, Johannesburg and Perth, Western Australia. It is small wonder that Aberdeen was described in 1899 as "the intellectual Capital of Northern Scotland . . . known and respected in every corner of our world-wide Empire for its famous breed of men"[3].

The Victorians were said to wear church membership as a mark of respectability and as a sign of their standing in the community[4]. Aberdeen CAs were no exception to this and many of their obituary notices list their active church connections as elders, session clerks and treasurers of various churches in the city.

Family Ties

The first seventy members included two sets of brothers, Ernest and James Rennett and George and John McBain, whose successors still practise in Aberdeen, although now as part of Thomson McLintock. The only other related members

[3] A KEITH: A Thousand Years of Aberdeen, *Aberdeen University Press*, 1972.

[4] M MACLAREN: Religion and Social Class: The Disruption Years in Aberdeen, *Routledge*, 1974.

105

would seem to have been Walter and John Reid, who were cousins. It would seem that nine of the members had sons who followed them into the profession. George Dickie had four sons; three became CAs—only one of whom survived his father. Two of Walter Reid's four sons emulated their father's example and became CAs. James Meston, probably the best known of the original members of the Society in Aberdeen, had two sons, neither of whom reached manhood. His name, however, lived on in James Meston Dickie, CA, son of George Dickie, and in James Meston Reid, chemical engineer, son of Walter Reid.

106

James Meston, CA, one of the original members of The Society of Accountants in Aberdeen.

Conclusion

This article has described the social background of the early members of the Aberdeen Society of Accountants, but it is intended that the study will cover the three Scottish Societies up to 1904. The writer would, therefore, be delighted to hear from any member of the Scottish Institute, or casual reader of THE ACCOUNTANT'S MAGAZINE, who has any information pertaining to these early members and their successors, or who can suggest some hitherto untapped source of information.

OTHER SOURCES CONSULTED:
J C STEWART: Pioneers of a Profession: Chartered Accountants to 1879. Scottish Committee on Accounting History, The Institute of Chartered Accountants of Scotland, 1977.
Scottish Records Office: Parochial Records prior to 1855; Birth, Marriage, Death Certificates; Census Records 1841-1891.

Qualification for Membership a Hundred Years Ago

JAS. C. STEWART, C.A.

This article is a small spin-off from a study of the early Minute Books of the original Scottish chartered bodies undertaken by the author in connection with a project of the Scottish Committee on Accounting History, of which he is a member.

The methods of selection, education and examination of candidates for admission as chartered accountants, the latest report on which is that prepared for the principal accountancy bodies in the British Isles by Professor Solomons and published under the title " Prospectus for a Profession ",[1] have since the invention of the term " Chartered Accountant " been a matter of concern to all entitled to use that designation. Professor Solomons's report will stimulate much interest, will, no doubt, arouse much controversy, and lead in time to further advances. This short paper, however, does not deal with such weighty matters of immediate concern. Its humble aim is to record for the interest and, perhaps, amusement of a more sophisticated generation the results of the activities of an early predecessor of the " Lister " and " Dewar " Committees in Scotland, and some other matters relating to the admission of members which came under review a hundred years ago.

In 1874 the President and Council of The Society of Accountants in Edinburgh reported to the Annual General Meeting of the Society on the results of the first year's operation of a new system for the regulation of the enrolment and examination of apprentices.

[1] [See our June issue, at page 198, and this issue at page 248— *Ed.*]

The New System of 1874

The new system was the result of a remit by the members at the 1872 Annual Meeting to the President and Council to consider " The arrangements for the Enrolment of Apprentices and their Examination ". Having " carefully considered the whole subject . . . " the President and Council reported to the 1873 meeting. The subject was thought to be of sufficient importance for the Council to have their report printed, and this at a time when not even the Society's annual accounts were printed and circulated. Having been printed and circulated to the members the proposals made in the report were accepted at the 1873 meeting and immediately put into effect.

Although considered of such importance the printed

108

report in fact covers rather less than three quarto pages. Within these pages it contains some interesting proposals as well as some, to us, rather quaintly worded comment.

The report begins by setting out the " existing arrangements " prefaced by the statement that " No preliminary Examination is at present required before an Apprentice enters his indenture; nor is any test applied during the currency of the indenture to ascertain either the fitness of the Apprentice or his application to his professional studies." It is not proposed " to alter the general scope of these Regulations, which, in consequence of the care and trouble bestowed by the Examiners have hitherto worked satisfactorily ". It is, however, proposed to institute a preliminary examination and to introduce a rule:—

" That each Apprentice shall, during the third year of his Apprenticeship, undergo an Examination, to test the progress made by him; and in the event of any Apprentice failing to pass such Examination to the satisfaction of the Council and Examiners, at the time fixed for such Examination, it shall be competent for him to present himself for Re-examination at any time during the remainder of his Apprenticeship, and within six months of the expiry thereof. Such Examination must be passed by each Apprentice before he can present himself for Final Examination for entrance into the Society."

The Examined

For both the third year and the final examinations apprentices may " . . . profess to be examined on additional subjects, to be termed ' Voluntary ', which shall be specified by the Council and Examiners."

It is hard to imagine present-day students professing to be examined on any subjects additional to the wide range of " Imperative " subjects now covered by the syllabus, and events proved their predecessors to have no greater enthusiasm for non-compulsory examinations. Some juicy carrots, however, were offered with the view of encouraging apprentices in the prosecution of their studies. These took the form of a bursary of £20 per annum tenable for two years for the apprentice who at the third year examination should " attain the highest proficiency in all branches, ' Imperative ' and ' Voluntary ' ", and a Fellowship of £30 per annum tenable for three years for the " Candidate who shall attain the highest proficiency at the Final Examination, on the subjects prescribed in both classes, termed ' Imperative ' and ' Voluntary '. The above Bursary and Fellowship being always subject to such regulations as the President and Council may from time to time deem proper."

The Examiners

The examiners, hitherto three members of the Society, were, because the future examinations were " . . . to comprehend subjects of a varied character, such as Languages, Mathematics, English Literature, and Law . . . [to] be entitled to call in such assistance as they shall consider necessary for the proper conduct of the Examinations." They were also to have power to issue and revise a syllabus and to make regulations for the conduct of the examinations. They too, having previously been unpaid, were offered a carrot by the proposal " That, with the view of carrying out satisfactorily the above Resolutions, a sum, to be recommended by the President and Council, shall be voted annually to the Examiners, for allowances and Expenses connected with the Examinations."

The System in Operation

The proposals were accepted by the members—42 out of a total membership of 112—present at the 1873 Annual General Meeting; and thereafter detailed reports on the working of the new scheme were made to succeeding meetings. A somewhat curious feature of these reports is their references to a bursary of £10 per annum awarded to the candidate placed first in the " Imperative " subjects in the third year examination, though there is no mention of this in the original report.

The importance which the Society attached to the encouragement of a high level of general education among apprentices can be gauged by the size of the inducements offered to participate in the examinations in " Voluntary " subjects. In the first five years of these examinations the amounts paid in bursaries or fellowships amounted to rather more than 40% of the whole of the Society's expenditure, and to more than two and a half times the amount paid to the examiners for fees and expenses. But, in spite of the apparently attractive amounts of the prizes offered, and the very small number of prospective contenders—only in the preliminary examination did the number of candidates in the 'seventies ever exceed twenty—it would seem that then, as perhaps now, " stick " influenced the apprentices more than " carrot ".

After naming the winner of the award for proficiency in the " Imperative " section the report on the examinations for 1880-81 continues:—

" With respect to the Voluntary Examination also undertaken by Mr Merry [he was a classical master at the Edinburgh Academy] one gentleman only, Mr Norfor, intimated that he was prepared for it, and after considering Mr Merry's Report the President and Council and Examiners resolved not to award the Bursary for this year."

The energetic Mr Norfor, however, was not entirely deprived of reward, for it was decided that the bursary of £20 belonging to the Voluntary Examination should, as " some acknowledgement of the high proficiency attained by them . . . " be divided between the second and third candidates in the Imperative subjects, which gave him a half share.

The report then continued:—

" . . . it is evident that what is termed the Voluntary Examination is not one which has been taken advantage of to an extent sufficient to justify its continuance. As confirmation of this it may be stated that for the year 1876 no apprentice presented himself for examination; for the year 1877 while 17 apprentices underwent the Imperative examination only one underwent the Voluntary . . . "

In the light of these figures the Council's conclusion seems entirely justified. Yet they did not propose the immediate discontinuance of the Voluntary examination but merely asked that the matter be left in their hands. This part of the examination was in fact dropped in 1882.

With the small number of competitors involved it might have been expected that winners of the Bursary would frequently go on to win the Fellowship also. This did not happen, and only Mr William Hardie, who was awarded the Bursary in 1875, when he was one of two candidates, appears again as winner of the Fellowship in 1877 when there were other eight contestants.

Dealing with a small membership and a correspondingly small number of apprentices and examination candidates the Council's reports to each Annual General Meeting go into great detail as to the candidates and their performance —detail which might not be welcomed by present-day students. No doubt then all the members were known to each other, as would be a fair proportion of their respective apprentices, so that their progress would be a matter of real personal interest to all concerned.

Whatever the scope of the papers set, the general standard of the candidates' papers, and also the leniency shown by the examiners were then much as they remained, at least when this writer was an examiner. This may be judged from this quotation from the report to the Council of Mr J. A. Molleson, examiner for " General Professional Knowledge " in 1883:—

" The answers and relative states, of course, varied in degree— some of them excellent, others feeble, but as the whole of them exhibit some knowledge of the profession and the evidence of study, I have to recommend that the 13 candidates should be passed."

In the earliest days, although the time within which the third year examination was required to be passed was restricted, there seems to have been no limit on the time within which an apprentice whose period under indenture had expired was compelled to present himself for examination. The complete list of indentures outstanding at December 31, 1873, presented in accordance with custom to the 1874 Annual Meeting, shows that of a total of 130 apprentices listed the indentures of 83 had expired without the persons concerned having presented themselves to the examiners. Of these no fewer than 31 had been expired for ten years or more but were apparently thought to be to some extent still " live ". The oldest went back to 1856, only two years after the Charter was granted.

Proportionately these figures suggest a much higher drop-out rate than applies at present.

Admission in Glasgow

The Charters were originally obtained by bodies of men practising the profession of accountant in their respective cities, and the initial intention appears to have been to restrict membership to those whose activities could be so described. In Glasgow admission was formally restricted to those who had their own offices or were members of a firm, though there seems to have been a procedure for the admission of some who did not quite meet that restriction. There was also provision for a category of " associates ", being persons qualified by examination but not by the nature of their avocation. These rules, so far as Glasgow was concerned, do not seem ever to have been operated with complete rigour, although as early as 1859 a Mr John Houston offered to resign because he had become a member of the Middle Temple and deemed this to be inconsistent with continued membership. The first admission of a non-practising member noted was in 1866, but the member concerned became a partner in his office almost immediately, so no real precedent could be claimed as established.

Admission in Edinburgh

In Edinburgh the restriction took a different form. All members on admission were required to sign a declaration that " it is their exclusive object to follow the profession of Accountants as defined in the Society's Charter, that they are not now prosecuting, and that they have no intention of prosecuting any other profession or employment whatever, either alone or in partnership with others ". This, of course, would have ruled out the many Glasgow members who were themselves, or were in partnership with, stockbrokers.

The effectiveness of the declaration, and the desirability of continuing it came up for discussion at the 1873 Annual Meeting and the subject was remitted to the Council for consideration. They consulted the Society's Law Agent and he, not surprisingly, advised that the rule was really quite ineffective as it was merely a statement of immediate intention—intention which could be changed at any time. The Council then debated whether the rule should be abandoned or in some way strengthened and so made effective. Their conclusion was that it should be abandoned and at the 1874 meeting notice was given of the intention to propose a motion to that effect. This motion was passed at the Annual Meeting in 1875.

Pointer to the Future

Thus by 1875 the way was opened for the development of chartered accountancy as a wide and varied profession which in the then unforeseen future would be practised publicly by only a minority—now a relatively small minority—while the majority though remaining professional accountants would exercise their profession as officers or employees of companies, public and private, and institutions and corporations of all kinds.

This widening of the field within which members may carry on their profession has not yet led to a wider opening of the door through which the profession may be entered. That is still only by way of service with a member in public practice. The hinges of the door, however, are now beginning to creak, and the next century, if not the next decade, will see new developments.

© Jas. C. Stewart, 1974.

109

110

Accounting at Heriot-Watt College 1885-1920

F. MITCHELL, B.COM., C.A.

M. J. MEPHAM, B.SC.(ECON.), DIP.O.R.,
F.C.A., F.C.M.A.

Earlier this month Heriot-Watt University conferred the honorary degree of D.Litt. on one of its former accountancy students, the doyen of UK accounting academics, Professor William Baxter, C.A., Emeritus Professor of Accounting at the London School of Economics. At this time, therefore, it is particularly appropriate to look at the origins of accountancy teaching at Heriot-Watt College,[1] especially as the early development was supervised by three notable accounting educators. These were the Millar brothers (Robert and Thomas) and George Lisle. All three were CAs who combined distinguished professional careers with teaching and writing.

Robert Cockburn Millar, C.A., J.P. (1853-1929)

In 1885 the Watt Institution (which had been founded in 1821 as the Edinburgh School of Arts) became Heriot-Watt College, and detailed proposals were made to extend the range of courses provided. One result was that in the following year Robert Cockburn Millar was appointed lecturer in the Practice of Commerce. In evidence to a committee on commercial education in 1900, Millar recounts that he was asked by the Heriot Trust to organise a commerce class and that he did this, arranging his syllabus "very much on the

[1] Heriot-Watt College became Heriot-Watt University in 1966.

lines of the Continental Commercial Schools and mainly the Commercial Institute of Antwerp ".[2]

Millar had entered into partnership with Charles Barstow (under whom he had served his apprenticeship) in 1878 to found the firm of Barstow and Millar, of Queen Street, Edinburgh. This firm still continues with the same name. In addition to his other interests Millar was very active in the Edinburgh Chamber of Commerce, where he was an ardent advocate of the decimalisation of weights, measures and money. He was chairman of the Chamber of Commerce in 1907-08 and President of the Edinburgh Society of Accountants from 1910-1913.

In addition to articles in THE ACCOUNTANTS' MAGAZINE Millar wrote "The Accountant's Handbook ", J. Menzies and Co., 1889, which was concerned with interest calculations and related topics. He also published some of the notes prepared for his students, under the title "Notes on Money, Foreign Exchanges and Prices ", J. Menzies and Co., 1891. Other details of his syllabus are contained in " The Commercial Guide ", by Claudius Lassen, J. Menzies and Co. and Marshall, Hamilton, Kent and Co., 1891, where Lassen applauds the bookkeeping system taught at " this renowned Institution ". He says the method is ". . . superior in general utility, more easy in practice, and quite as adaptable in the business or office as other methods . . .".

Robert Millar lectured at Heriot-Watt College until 1900.

[2] This celebrated institution (founded in 1852) has been claimed as the world's first Commercial College. The College is now the Universitaire Faculteitan Sint-Ignatius Te Antwerpen.

(continued on page 261)

(continued from page 260)

Thomas John Millar, M.A., LL.B., C.A. (1866-1946)

After graduating from Edinburgh University and serving his accountancy apprenticeship under his brother, Thomas Millar was admitted to the Society of Accountants in Edinburgh in 1893. He became a partner in his brother's firm in 1894 and in 1905 was appointed to a part-time lectureship at Heriot-Watt. Millar's professional work covered a wide spread of industrial and commercial concerns, and his books —and no doubt also his teaching—reflected his wide experience.

In 1910 he brought together many of his ideas on the accounting process in his best known book, " Management Book-keeping ".[3] The book's contents reflect the originality of Millar's thinking, and a book review of the time[4] concluded:

> " It has been said that it is hard to write anything new on book-keeping, and if Mr Millar has done nothing else, he has done that."

The book contains, in Millar's own words:

> " A new method of recording business transactions with less labour and giving more, and more accessible, information than ordinary methods . . ."[5]

In comparison with many other bookkeeping texts of the period, the book is concise (114 pages) yet comprehensively lays out a " new plan " for recording and presenting accounting information. With slight modification the system could be applied to a wide range of different types of firm and, indeed, Millar had tried out his ideas in several of his clients' firms, always " with advantage " to them.

The question posed in the book's preface provides the motivation for the work and it is as relevant to the modern management accountant as it was 70 years ago:

> " Has he [the bookkeeper] ever considered what the manager needs and how it could be got for him simply and with certainty as to completeness ? "

The system outlined by Millar is geared to serving the needs of the firm's management as effectively and efficiently as possible. Briefly, he suggests:—

(1) The abandonment of Day Books, which he considered provided little useful information and the maintenance of which he saw as the bookkeeper's most time-consuming function. In their place alphabetical invoice files would be kept.

(2) " Day Sheets " recording credit purchases and sales, listed under suppliers' and customers' names, would provide useful information on trading performances. They would also facilitate the preparation of monthly abstracts of purchases and sales classified by type.

[3] Management Book-keeping, Charles and Edwin Layton, London, 1910.
[4] THE ACCOUNTANTS' MAGAZINE, August 1910.
[5] Management Book-keeping, op cit.

Robert Cockburn Millar   Thomas John Millar

(3) The adoption of the (then) new idea of the loose-leaf book as a ledger would improve management information, e.g., debtors' accounts could be arranged so that a block of accounts related to the particular salesman who serviced them.

(4) A detailed monthly analysis of cash transactions could be extracted from a fully analysed cash book.

With the information which the system provided, Millar expected that the management would be in a better position to take decisions and, if observant, significant patterns might be detected, e.g.—

> " The sales in any month might correspond fairly with the cash received, one, two or three months hence. . . . If such a relationship were fairly established it would afford a basis for estimating what might be received . . . during the next month."

In other words the system would enable management to make crude cash forecasts.

Millar's work was distinguished from most other writers of the time by the fact that he stressed the now topical idea of accountants considering the users of accounting information. He saw that double-entry bookkeeping was not an end in itself but only the means towards achieving an end, i.e., satisfying " user needs ". In Millar's case only the manager or owner was considered as a user but the principle was applied.

A quote from a later work emphasises his view of double-entry bookkeeping:

> " If it is possible . . . to classify business fact minutely so as to give management information, and also in such a way as to enable final accounts to be prepared without considering double-entry, is it not reasonable to suggest that double-entry might occupy a subordinate place in the classification? Might one not more truly elevate the multiplication table into a phrase parallel to book-keeping by double-entry—thus, say, ' stock valuation by the multiplication table '."[6]

Millar died in 1946, at a time when his first publication[7] was still a recommended text for the Institute's examinations. The originality of his ideas is admirably illustrated by one of his audit docquets for the Stair Society's accounts. The docquet reads:

> " Heard, seen, considerit, calculat and allowit by the auditor.
> T. J. Millar."

[6] " Classification of Business Fact v. Double-Entry of Business Fact as the Main Consideration in Book-keeping ", THE ACCOUNTANTS' MAGAZINE, February 1916.
[7] References, Remits and Proofs in Scotland, 1896.

111

George Lisle, C.A., F.F.A. (1864-1940)

K. MacNeal, writing in 1939 (" Truth in Accounting ", *reprinted by Scholar's Book Co.*, Kansas, 1970), identifies three noteworthy British books which appeared at the beginning of the twentieth century; these were Dicksee's " Auditing ", Pixley's " Auditors and their Liabilities ", and Lisle's " Accounting in Theory and Practice ". Lisle taught at Heriot-Watt College from 1896 to 1903, and " Accounting in Theory and Practice " (first edition 1899) has now attained the status of a classic; it has recently been reprinted by *Arno Press*, New York.

The book is very modern in many ways. It discusses the economic view of profit (pp. 47-49) and capital (p. 68), and Lisle advocates that accountancy students should read Adam Smith's " Wealth of Nations ". It also points out that the correct valuation procedure to adopt is dependent on the purpose for which the valuation is required (p. 53). Loose-leaf systems and manufacturing and cost accounts are considered and there is an interesting discussion on the reasons for placing assets on the right-hand side of the Balance Sheet; this he dismisses as the English method in contrast to the correct " Continental or Scotch form " (pp. 70-74). He considers that the English method arose because of—

" . . . the influence of the forms given in Acts of Parliament, chiefly the Companies Act 1862, which must have been prepared by those unacquainted with the theory of accounts."

An earlier, smaller, book of Lisle's was " Elementary Bookkeeping " (published in 1894). This was referred to by Professor Hatfield (in his well known essay " An Historical Defense of Bookkeeping " [8]) as " one of the best elementary books ever written on the subject ". Lisle's exposition is based on the " ledger approach " advocated by Professor Augustus De Morgan,[9] which emphasised that the ledger account system was the basis of the double-entry method. Although the books of prime-entry are considered, they are not used to explain double-entry but as parts of a practical system which is introduced after the theory has been mastered via the ledger accounts. The ledger approach subsequently became popular but, before 1900, Jackson notes only two other writers who used this method of exposition.[10]

An interesting feature of this book is Lisle's apparent advocacy of the current cost method of valuing stock. He says:

" The Goods on hand should be valued at present cost price— that is, at such a price as you would now buy the goods for were you entering the market." (p. 26)

This point is not developed further, so that it is possible that too much is being read into it.

The work for which Lisle is to be most remembered is his monumental " Encyclopaedia of Accounting " (1903-1907), in 8 volumes and 4,076 pages. Professor R. H. Parker describes this as " the most ambitious accountancy publishing project ever attempted in Scotland ".[11] The encyclopaedia includes articles by Lisle himself; William Annan, who was later Professor of Accounting and Business Method at the University of Edinburgh; A. L. Bowley, the statistician;

[8] THE JOURNAL OF ACCOUNTANCY, April 1924, reprinted in Studies in Accounting Theory, edited by W. T. Baxter and S. Davidson, *Sweet and Maxwell*, 1962. The identification of Professor Hatfield's remark with Lisle is not definite, but it seems fairly clear that he was referring to Lisle.

[9] The Elements of Arithmetic, *Taylor and Walton* (5th edition) 1846, pp. 180-189.

[10] J. G. C. JACKSON, " The History of Methods of Exposition of Double Entry Bookkeeping in England ", Studies in the History of Accounting, edited by Littleton and Yamey, *Sweet and Maxwell*, 1956.

[11] Accounting in Scotland: A Historical Bibliography (2nd edition 1976), *The Institute of Chartered Accountants of Scotland.*

V. V. Branford, on the relationship between accounting and economics; Richard Brown, the accounting historian; L. L. Dicksee, who wrote on auditing and cost accounting (Dicksee was the first UK professor of accounting); Sir John Mann, giving the earliest UK discussion of the break-even chart; R. C. Millar, on decimal weights, measures and money; and F. W. Pixley, on company bookkeeping.

Lisle was in practice in Edinburgh and he included among his appointments the auditorship of the accounts of the City of Edinburgh. He was in partnership with William Middleton, who was also a Heriot-Watt lecturer, and in 1911 the partners collaborated in writing " Account-keeping in Principle and Practice ", *W. Green & Sons.*

George Lisle was proud of the fact that he had, in his younger days, been a friend of Robert Louis Stevenson and he would have agreed with Stevenson when he said:

" The problem of education is two fold: first to know, and then to utter. Everyone who lives any semblance of an inner life thinks more nobly and profoundly than he speaks."

With Robert Millar, Thomas Millar and George Lisle, Heriot-Watt College was fortunate in having the services of three lecturers whose knowledge of accounting was profound and who had the gift of being able to communicate this knowledge.

BOOKS AND ARTICLES ON ACCOUNTANCY AND RELATED TOPICS WRITTEN BY LECTURERS AT HERIOT-WATT COLLEGE 1885-1920

Robert Cockburn Millar

*Accountants' Handbook of Interest States, Decimal Calculations, Consignment and Joint Accounts, etc., *J. Menzies & Co.* 1889	1891
Notes on Money, Foreign Exchanges and Prices, *J. Menzies & Co.*	1891
*" The Metric System of Weights and Measures ", THE ACCOUNTANTS' MAGAZINE, August 1897	1897
*" The Taking of Excerpts from Books and Accounts ", THE ACCOUNTANTS' MAGAZINE, February 1898	1898
*" DuoDecimal Versus Decimal Notation ", THE ACCOUNTANTS' MAGAZINE, January 1918	1918

Thomas John Millar

*References, Remits and Proofs in Scotland, The Transactions of the CA Students' Society of Edinburgh, Volume VIII	1896
Building Society Finance and Statistics, *T. & T. Clark*	1905
*Note on the Principles of Book-keeping and Modern Methods applied to Lawyers' Transactions, *George Waterston & Sons*	1906
*Check Numbers and Other Aids to Balancing Books of Account, *George Waterston & Sons*	1907
*Methods of Stating Accounts with particular reference to Trust Accounts, *Gee & Co.*	1908
*Management Book-keeping, *Charles & Edwin Layton* (London) and *George Waterston & Sons* (Edinburgh)	1910
Arithmetic, A New View, *MacDonald & Evans*	1915
*Logarithms for Business Purposes, *MacDonald & Evans*	1915
*" Classification of Business Fact v. Double-Entry as the Main Consideration in Book-keeping ", THE ACCOUNTANTS' MAGAZINE, February 1916	1916
*" Materials—Stock-keeping, Stock Taking and Stock Checking, Etc.", THE ACCOUNTANTS' MAGAZINE, June 1919	1919
Manufacturing and Trading Stock Valuation, *MacDonald & Evans*	1921

George Lisle

*Deposit Receipt Interest Tables, *George Waterston & Sons*	1888
Local Government Scotland Act, 1889, *George Stewart & Co.*	1891
Examination Papers of the Chartered Accountants of Scotland General Examining Board 1893, *W. Green & Sons*	1894
Elementary Book-keeping, *W. & R. Chambers*	1894

Solicitors' Book-keeping—The Transactions of the CA
Students' Society of Edinburgh—Volume VII   1895
Income Tax Tables (Referred to in Elementary Book-
keeping)   No date given
*Accounting in Theory and Practice, *W. Green & Sons*
(reprinted by Arno Press, New York, 1976)   1899 1906 1909
*" On the Book-keeping for a Heritable Property Investment
Company Granting Loans Repayable by Instalments
Exemplified in a Model Set of Books, with Notes on the
Auditing of such Accounts ", THE ACCOUNTANTS' MAGA-
ZINE, November 1899   1899

*Encyclopaedia of Accounting (Editor), *W. Green & Sons* 1903
Forms & Precedents for the Use of Accountants (Editor),
W. Green & Sons   1906
*Account-Keeping in Principle and Practice (with Wm.
Middleton), *Wm. Green & Sons*   1911

* *In the Antiquarian Collection at the Edinburgh Library of The
Institute of Chartered Accountants of Scotland.*

© F. Mitchell, M. J. Mepham, 1976.

113

The Accounting Historians Journal
Vol. 10, No. 1
Spring 1983

T. A. Lee
UNIVERSITY OF EDINBURGH

THE EARLY DEBATE ON FINANCIAL AND PHYSICAL CAPITAL

Abstract: This paper evidences the contribution of leading writers in the early 1900s to the vexed problems associated with capital maintenance and periodic income determination. It reveals that the issues which were then being discussed (such as the treatment of holding gains) remain as unresolved problems for today's accountancy practitioners.

115

The concept of capital is central to the determination of periodic income, irrespective of whether the latter is based on the principles of economics or accounting. Without adequate and consistent definitions and computations of capital at succeeding points of time, there can be no credible income data. This has been well evidenced in the recent professional prescriptions of current cost accounting for external financial reporting purposes.[1] These pronouncements have focused attention on the need to understand the concept of capital which underlies each specific income proposal. In particular, they have identified the existence in practice of two alternative capital maintenance approaches—that is, maintenance based on capital defined in terms either of a specific monetary attribute such as the money unit or the purchasing power unit (hereafter termed *financial* capital); or a specific attribute of the reporting entity's physical asset structure such as its physical units or operating capacity (hereafter termed *physical* capital).

The distinction between the two concepts of capital (and their related maintenance functions) is not a new one. Sweeney (1933a), for example, presented one of the best analyses in this area, and his work should be required reading for interested students of capital definition and measurement. However, despite its antecedents, the distinction has provoked a debate in the late 1970s and early 1980s concerning the utility and relevance of the financial and physical approaches for purposes of external financial reporting. Indeed, a recent international symposium has been held on the sub-

---

This paper has benefited considerably from the comments of its reviewers.

ject.[2] Contributions to this meeting discussed the relative merits of financial capital and physical capital and, in so doing, identified significant problem areas for the producer of current cost accounting information which utilises a physical capital maintenance approach—for example, the needs of external report users, the accounting treatment of holding gains, coping with changing asset structures and technologies, accounting for price decreases as well as increases, the feasibility of using current values in financial reports, and alternatives to current cost accounting.

It should not be surprising to find these matters debated in the 1980s. After all, if current cost accounting contains these problems, it is only right and proper to discuss them with a view to the establishment of current cost accounting as a credible system of financial reporting. However, it is of some concern to find the discussion taking place *ex post* the prescription of current cost accounting. What is even more disturbing is the discovery that the same issues were identified and debated in the early 1900s. Indeed, in 1930,[3] a symposium on asset value appreciation covered much of the ground dealt with in the aforementioned one in 1981. And resolution of the issues identified at that time is no further forward despite the passage of 50 years of thought and experience.

Not only was the debate about financial capital and physical capital raised in the early 1900s, it was also fully documented in the relevant accountancy literature, and contributed to by some of the leading academics and practitioners of the day. It was largely of United States origin, considerably influenced by German thinking, and can be attributed to a major concern about the purpose and role of both appreciation and depreciation of fixed assets.[4] The lack of legal and accounting guidance in these matters in the last quarter of the nineteenth century and first quarter of the twentieth century were also catalysts for the debate. According to Brief (1976), revaluation of fixed assets was common, depreciation accounting was relatively undeveloped, the realisation principle was not fully recognised prior to World War I, and lawyers did not appear to wish to pronounce on business practices and thereby give guidance to accountants.

The interest in the United States debate petered out in the 1940s largely due to the impact of World War II; was resumed at a very modest level in the 1950s and 1960s (when relatively low rates of inflation prevailed); and burst into full prominence in the 1970s with double digit inflation. It has not diminished since despite the practical implementation of current cost accounting in several English-

116

speaking countries.[5] It therefore appears pertinent to go back in time to rediscover the early contributions to the debate—first, to acknowledge their significance in the development of financial reporting thought; secondly, to identify the main issues with which they were concerned and to compare them, where relevant, with the issues of today; and, thirdly, to speculate from such an analysis on the reasons why no apparent progress has been achieved in the United States and, to a lesser extent, in the United Kingdom in the resolution of the capital debate. In this way, it is hoped that lessons from the past may be learned in order to avoid lack of progress in the future.

Early Recognition of the Problem

It can be argued that the earliest accounting practitioners of the modern era recognised the need to maintain the physical asset structure of the reporting entity, and to implement methods of financial accounting which could aid this process. Brief (1976) provides a reminder that, prior to 1875, the practice of replacement accounting (that is, charging the cost of fixed asset replacement against sales revenue in arriving at periodic income) was fairly widespread, and was adopted in place of conventional depreciation policies. Income was therefore determined on a quasi-replacement cost basis with the balance sheet containing outdated and undepreciated historic costs. The replacement costs used for income purposes, however, were those occurring at the time of replacement rather than at the time of reporting. The practice was apparently limited to replaced fixed assets, and its use can be confirmed in the United States railway industry which was governed by the regulations of the Interstate Commerce Commission (which specified the use of replacement accounting).[6]

There was also evidence of revaluation of fixed assets prior to 1875, and an awareness of the danger of distributing any resulting unrealised holding gains.[7] But, gradually, a more conservative approach to accounting was adopted, and historical cost depreciation practices to maintain invested money capital were implemented.[8] Also, at about the same time, a further accounting practice was being advocated—that is, the *appropriation* of amounts from income to reserve (in excess of historical cost depreciation) in order to aid the funding of fixed asset replacements.[9]

Thus, although the conventional depreciation practices of the time may have been relatively primitive (that is, appropriations of income rather than cost allocations), there was an obvious aware-

117

ness by certain leading accountants of the day that adequate accounting could aid the function of *financing* the reporting entity's physical asset structure. However, a contrary view existed which, despite recognising the potential financial problem of inadequate depreciation to fund fixed asset replacement, preferred to depreciate historical costs and not to recognise value changes, either because of the danger of overvaluation when prices eventually fell after a period of rising[10] or because the entity was a going concern which was unaffected financially by the recognition of unrealised holding gains—these ultimately being realised at some future date.[11]

118

The latter historical cost school of thought appeared to prefer the financial capital approach of maintaining the original invested capital. The alternative approaches of replacement accounting and reserve accounting indicated a movement towards physical capital maintenance without abandoning the traditional historical cost system. In addition, a further school of thought was to develop in the early 1920s—balance sheet revaluations being encouraged (usually based on replacement costs) to provide more realistic descriptions of entity financial position, but with the income statement recommended to continue on a historical cost basis, thus not reflecting a maintenance of the revalued position.[12] In this way, realised holding gains were included in the income statement and unrealised holding gains were put to reserve. By contrast, replacement accounting and reserve accounting effectively excluded a certain proportion of realised holding gains from income, and historical cost accounting failed to recognise unrealised holding gains.

These different contributions mark a useful starting point for the debate on capital and capital maintenance—particularly in the 1920s and 1930s.[13] They reveal the first major problem facing accountants in this area—that is, the difficulty of separating the *managerial* need to fund the replacement of assets underlying invested capital from the *accounting* need to maintain that capital. This particular problem was first made explicit in the literature by Saliers (1913) but is also to be found in the work of others throughout the 1920s and 1930s—including Jackson (1921); Scott (1929); Paton (1934); and Crandell (1935). At times, it is somewhat difficult to distinguish the two functions in the recommendations of these writers, and this is perhaps best evidenced in the words of the accountants concerned.

Bauer produced the following major statement of the problem:[14]

> The question therefore arises, is the purpose of management merely to maintain investment in terms of dollars, and to show current costs and profits accordingly, or is it really

to keep up the plant and equipment and to maintain the physical productivity of the property?

He obviously identified the managerial task of asset replacement, and linked it with the accounting process of capital maintenance. He therefore appeared to see no need to separate the two functions, and was quite clear in his accounting answer to the managerial question posed—the expected cost of replacement and not historical cost should be matched against sales revenue. He went even further than modern theorists in this respect, appearing to advocate the use of *future* rather than current replacements costs.

Jackson asked the same question in a much briefer manner:[15]

> Is the purpose of the depreciation charge to maintain the capital investment or is it to replace the physical plant?

It should be noted that the question was asked solely in connection with fixed asset replacement, and this appeared to be the major preoccupation of these early accounting theorists (working capital being usually ignored). Jackson argued that historical cost was the true cost for accounting purposes (without defining the term "true"), and advocated financial capital maintenance based on historical costs. However, as the above quotation reveals, accounting and managing are completely merged in the question asked.

Rorem was much less confused but arguably no less confusing, fully recognising the alternative physical capital basis for accounting:[16]

> The purpose of writing the appreciated value into the cost of manufacturing is entirely independent of any accounting procedure for insuring the maintenance of physical capital. It is true, that physical capital must be maintained if an enterprise is to continue business operations. It is true, however, that an enterprise must be considered unprofitable unless its accounts are so handled as to deduct provision for capital maintenance as a cost of business operations. The charge for depreciation is a writing off of values which have already appeared; it is in no sense a provision for expenses which are yet to be incurred.

Rorem then argued for the use of replacement costs for depreciation purposes, criticising the alternative policy of transfers from income to reserve in addition to historical cost depreciation. He undoubtedly regarded replacement cost accounting as a means of determining the profitability of the entity (the primary aim) while maintaining physical capital (the secondary aim). His paper clearly and logically makes the case for accounting for the physical structure of the entity, separate from the issue of financially managing asset replacements.

The then radical proposals of Rorem contrasted with the continuing support of leading accountants for historical cost accounting supplemented with income appropriations to reserve. Thomas (1916) had suggested the latter approach to preserve the financial solvency of the entity; Rastall (1920) preferred to reserve prudently to avoid overdepreciation; Jackson (1920) believed the use of historical cost depreciation reflected the "privilege" of using low cost equipment in higher cost times, but thought that additional amounts should be reserved from income; and other similar contributions come from Martin (1927), Scott (1929) and Daniels (1933). Each of these writers appeared to support a financial capital-based approach to income accounting, capital being measured in terms of aggregations of money units comprising historical costs. Some recognised the need also to provide separately for a funding of asset replacement at higher costs by reserve accounting. This approach was well described by Martin:[17]

> Such a reserve has the advantage of keeping the attention of the management and the stockholders centered on the real significance of increases in asset values. If they are to continue the business with the physical capital intact they must provide sufficient net earnings to make possible an increase in the money statement of net worth equal to the difference between original cost and replacement cost.

The above quotation is a useful way of summarising the somewhat confused state of thinking about income accounting and capital maintenance in the 1920s particularly. Financial capital recognition (for example, the money statement of net worth) was a popular approach, coupled with a growing awareness of the need to fund asset replacement and aid this by some form of accounting (for example, transfers to reserve). Managing and preserving the physical structure of the reporting entity was therefore a fairly well-known idea; accounting for its maintenance tended to be relatively crude. Also, it must be noted that the physical structure was normally interpreted in a limited way to nonmonetary fixed assets — inventory and other assets typically being ignored.

Thus, there appeared to be some confusion in the minds of writers between the financial mangement function of replacing entity assets, and the financial accounting function of reporting on entity profitability and financial position.[18] It would therefore seem relevant to pursue further the early arguments for accounting to aid management or preserve the physical assets and capital of the entity. To do so, may provide clues as to why the writers concerned had difficulty distinguishing between asset management and capital accounting. To do so is important, for the common cry nowadays from companies is—why do we need current cost accounting when we manage effectively with regard to price changes? As the chairman of one United Kingdom company has put it:[19]

> From a management point of view we have all the information we require in our monthly accounting statements to ensure that the full effects of inflation are taken into account in arriving at management decisions and . . . the attached accounts do not provide our management with any additional useful information. . . .

121

The present United Kingdom current cost accounting provision[20] confuses internal and external accounting needs in its statement of aims, and provides no answer to the above statement.

Managerial Needs and Capital Maintenance

The replacement of assets appeared to be regarded at the end of the nineteenth century as essentially a matter for good management rather than formal accounting procedures.[21] According to Brief (1976), for example, the question of whether or not to provide for fixed asset depreciation was left very much in the hands of management and the internal rules and regulations of the reporting entity— courts of law gave little or no guidance and the accountancy profession was in its infancy. Thus, the accounting emphasis for income determination purposes arguably included some notion of financial capital maintenance in a great many cases, depreciation procedures being largely ignored and revaluations being fairly common.

This picture of self-regulation undoubtedly must have influenced writers in the 1920s and 1930s who were concerned to ensure that management had sufficient relevant information with which to make adequate funding arrangements for fixed asset replacements. Not unexpectedly, writings occasionally merged the separate issues of internal management information systems with external financial reporting.[22] It is therefore important to read them with care.

The use of replacement accounting and reserve accounting procedures appear to have been devices for reflecting the funding of fixed asset replacements (particularly) without interfering with the then traditional practices of accounting based on historical cost measurements and financial capital maintenance (of original invested capital). However, in the first decades of the twentieth century, a number of writers began to advocate the use of replacement costs for internal management information purposes. Paton (1918), for example, argued that managers (and shareholders) needed replacement cost data—to aid the making of management decisions (presumably including asset replacement), and to let shareholders know their rights (presumably referring to the need to disclose total income, including unrealised holding gains).

122

By 1920, however, Paton (1920) was arguing for the use of replacement cost accounting for management only in order to aid it in preserving physical assets and productive capacity. Canning (1929), while not recommending the use of replacement costs generally for external reporting, believed they might be useful to management for purposes of deciding which goods to buy in the future, and for determining selling prices. Scott (1929), Schmidt (1930), and Wasserman (1931) held relatively similar views on the managerial relevance of replacement costs.

Each of these contributors to the United States literature therefore appears to have had a clear idea of the utility of replacement cost accounting for management purposes, particularly as an aid to funding asset replacement. Some of them also supported its use for external financial reporting, but to a far lesser extent. Occasionally, their recommendations were unclear as to the distinction between internal and external reporting. But it can be concluded that they were reasonably of a single mind with regard to one matter—they did not believe it was essential to account formally for the maintenance of physical capital in order to preserve the physical asset structure of the reporting entity. Instead, they felt that the latter could be aided by reserve transfers of financial capital-based income; and also by an adequate determination of selling prices to be charged to customers. In addition, it should be noted that replacement cost accounting was originally devised as a system of internal management accounting—particular by Paton (1920).

The above comments contrast sharply with the ideas of the Dutch theorist, Limperg (1964). Throughout the 1920s and 1930s, he argued for the use of replacement value-based accounting to aid management in the buying and selling activities associated with its products. He defined replacement value as a measure of the sacrifice by the producer when selling his products or using his assets (Limperg's replacement value referred only to replaceable assets, and was the cost at the time of sale or use of what was technically necessary and economically unavoidable to replace the asset concerned). In addition, he argued for the use of replacement value to determine selling prices. However, he did appear to have a firm view regarding physical capital maintenance (without specifically defining or using the term). His definition of income was essentially a physical capital-based one—holding gains being taken to reserve, and holding losses being treated in the same way until the reserve containing aggregate holding gains was exhausted. Any holding losses thereafter were to be written off against income.

This concept of preserving what Limperg described as the "source of income" was something which he saw as being useful both for internal *and* external reporting purposes—to aid the analysis of business operations, provide sufficient funds to finance asset replacements, and to prevent over-consumption. He felt that, by such a process of capital maintenance, income could be determined "without ambiguity and with certitude"—presumably for all its users. Nevertheless, as with that of Paton in the United States, Limperg's system was devised essentially as one of management accounting—although, undoubtedly, he also felt that external interests such as investors could benefit considerably from the reporting of such management-orientated information. Continuing evidence of this belief is provided by the limited but important use of replacement valuing accounting for external reporting by certain Dutch companies.

123

Replacement Costs and Selling Prices

Several writers in the 1920s and 1930s made strong statements on the place of replacement costs in the managerial determination of selling prices of goods and services to customers. Paton (1922), in an all too rare paper on accounting for current assets, claimed that replacement cost was the only price relevant to management as it governed the selling price of a good or service in the long-term. Rorem (1929), too, argued that replacement cost accounting was relevant to management because it represented the minimum value established by competition and to be paid when looking forward to the eventual resale of the good or service concerned. For this reason, Rorem went on to argue for the use of replacement costs in external reports because he regarded the difference between replacement cost and historical cost as the provision for capital maintenance which should be treated as a *cost* of business operations. Daniels (1933) also felt that the customer should be paying for the replacement cost of goods in the long-run (in this case, fixed assets), and thus concluded that the entity's pricing policy should result in income which was sufficient to replace fixed assets at higher costs.[23] He believed the function of depreciation, however, was not to provide for physical capital maintenance (recommending instead the funding of replacement by prudent reserving).

The idea of funding asset replacement by passing on increasing costs to the entity's customers, and thereby hopefully preserving its physical structure, was not universally accepted by the writers of the day. Jackson (1920) thought it unfair to ask customers to pay for anything other than the original cost of fixed assets in the case of public utilities, but thought it fair to charge replacement cost to private enterprise customers (so long as the realised difference between replacement cost and historical cost was taken to reserve). The 1930 Symposium on Appreciation[24] produced an even stronger position. It was argued that only historical costs should be passed on to the consumer because of the danger of being priced out of a competitive market, and that what was really needed in this area was good management rather than amendments to traditional accounting. Littleton (1936) argued along similar lines.

Thus, from these writings, it can be concluded that there was a recognition that management had to make decisions concerning the entity's asset structure, and that financial information was needed for this purpose. Some writers argued for using replacement costs, and others for historical costs. But it was also apparent that there was no general consensus that the use of the former data in external financial reports could provide a more informed way of describing how the physical structure of the entity had been maintained by management. In other words, there appeared to be a growing awareness in the 1920s and 1930s of the need to use replacement costs (*ex ante*) for management decisions, and the possibility of using them (*ex post*) for external reporting—in both cases, the aim being to reflect the need to maintain the physical asset structure of the entity; the first to demonstrate how to provide sufficient funds to finance replacement and the second to report on the maintenance of the capital representing the replaced and replaceable assets. The common factor in all this seemed to be the physical assets of the entity, and this brought into question the purposes of external financial reporting—what was to be reported and to whom was it to be reported?

Aims and Uses

The previous two sections have attempted to show that the early accounting theorists were concerned with asset replacement and the management of financial funds to do so. This inevitably raised the question of whether or not these matters should be the subject of a formal accounting in external financial reports. In other words, should external reports reflect such matters as the maintenance of the physical capital of the entity?

Views varied from one extreme to another. Paton (1918) stated that the physical nature of an asset was only important in terms of its influence on value. Bauer (1919) argued that external accounting should reflect the maintenance of the physical productivity of the assets. Jackson (1921) believed that maintenance of original invested costs was essential. Sweeney (1927 and 1930) complained that maintenance of physical capital did not maintain the general purchasing power of capital which gave the entity command over goods and services. And Daniels (1933) and Littleton (1936) felt that the job of accounting was to allocate past costs and not to value. Therefore, some were for financial capital maintenance (in money value or purchasing power terms) and others favoured physical capital maintenance. Few statements were made by these writers as to why these approaches should be the preferred ones from the point of view of the report users. 125

Daines (1929), for example, wrote of the objectives of accounting (and of current values) mainly in relation to the dividend decision. However, he also felt that users other than investors should be recognised—but made little effort to specify who these users were. Krebs (1930), too, wrote of unspecified users in relation to accounting for asset appreciation but without amplifying the matter. Littleton (1936) preferred to concentrate on uses rather than users, even arguing against the use of financial accounting data for dividends, taxation, and selling price determination.

Other writers clearly identified investors as the main external user group to which income and capital issues could be related—Paton (1920), when arguing for physical capital maintenance, sympathised with reporting on this for management decision purposes only, and not for investors (holding gains not being treated as distributable income); Schmidt (1930) made a similar argument, and defined distributable income as that remaining after maintaining business assets; and in a later paper, Schmidt (1931) identified distributable income more directly as current operating profit (that is, after full provision for the replacement cost of assets consumed). The Dutch position, too, as expressed by Limperg (1964), despite its management accounting basis, also appeared to concentrate on the owner/investor as the main external user—replacement value arguments being related to the determination of income for consumption or dividend decisions. All in all, however, the coverage of report users and uses by writers advocating change to traditional practice was poor, and resulted in a significant gap in the financial versus physical capital debate. It was at least partly bridged by proponents of the traditional historical cost school of thought.

The Need for Historical Cost Accounting

Although the aims of financial reporting in the 1920s and 1930s may have been poorly covered in the literature, several writers were adamant in their view of the nature of the process—that is, it was an attempt to reflect what had actually happened in the reporting entity rather than to hypothesise about what might have occurred under different circumstances and transactions. Canning (1929), for example, argued strongly along these lines—that historical costs were needed to calculate income on past transactions; costs are history and nothing can be done to change them; and fictitious data should not be introduced into accounting. Gower (1919) pleaded for the maintenance of invested capital and the use of historical costs, so long as a going concern could be assumed for the reporting entity. Jackson (1920) pointed out that historical costs had actually been transacted, and that replacement costs depended on some as yet nonexistent event. Prudence was given as the main reason for historical cost usage by Mather (1928). Littleton (1928 and 1929) believed income only existed when a sale transaction took place, and that it could not therefore be recognised in the form merely of unrealised asset value changes.

Each of these writers argued against the use of replacement costs, and their main reason appeared to be the need to attempt to reflect in financial reports the income which had been realised through sale transactions. They seemed to regard asset value appreciation as purely fictitious data so long as sale or exchange had not taken place. As previously mentioned, the emphasis was on what had happened. But these arguments were made in relation to external financial reports; several of these writers were at pains to point out the utility of replacement cost accounting for purposes of internal management decisions. In addition, they pinpointed a major problem in income and capital accounting which remains a

126

contemporary issue—that is, whether or not holding gains are income or capital adjustments.

The Nature of Holding Gains

The early accounting theorists in the income and capital debate were fully aware of the nature and possible existence of holding gains and the problems of accounting for them. Initially termed asset appreciation, the holding gain arose as a reporting issue from the 1920s debate concerning asset values, and gained practical importance because of the possibility of distributing unrealised asset value increases as well as realised gains. However, as a result of the debate concerning the maintenance of physical capital generally, and replacement cost depreciation particularly, the holding gain question was extended to include both realised and unrealised elements. It thus reached a status in the early literature akin to that given to it today.

127

Paton (1918) was one of the earliest writers on holding gains. He called for their inclusion in income (whether realised or unrealised) in order to let shareholders "know their rights," while preventing balance sheets from being understated (he did not expand on these advocations). However, Paton (1920) soon changed his mind regarding the treatment of holding gains as income—he later argued that they were capital adjustments, thus supporting the physical capital approach and treating holding gains as nondistributable. He gave no reasons for this change of viewpoint.

Jackson (1920) also adopted Paton's latter stance—holding gains in his opinion being funds of the entity belonging to future investors, and thus not to be accounted for until realised. Several years went by following this contribution, until Martin (1927) wrote a paper which relied heavily on the earlier work of Paton. He agreed that holding gains should be recognised and treated as capital adjustments in order to keep managers and investors aware of the historical cost profits required to be retained in order to fund the increased cost of replacing assets.

Two years later, Rorem (1929) produced a major paper arguing for the inclusion of at least realised holding gains in income measurements, although he would have required them to be separately disclosed in the income statement. However, he was very unclear as to his views on the distributability of holding gains—he was fully aware of the need to calculate cost of sales and depreciation on a replacement cost basis in order to provide for the maintenance of physical capital. But he also believed customers should pay for asset replacement increases through increased selling prices. He made no specific comment on distributable income.

Schmidt (1930 and 1931) was more certain in his approach—holding gains are not income; they cannot be distributed because they may not be realised. In this way, he appeared to support physical capital maintenance, although his argument for the use of replacement costs was for management purposes only in the first paper, but appeared to extend to external reports in the second.

Sweeney (1932) also supported the view that holding gains should not be treated as income, being capital adjustments. However, after making general purchasing power adjustments to the holding gain to eliminate the inflationary element, he further advocated the inclusion of real holding gains in the income statement once they had been realised (thus, presumably making them available for distributions).

The Dutch view on the treatment of holdings is evidenced in the writings of Limperg (1964) in the 1920s and 1930s. Consistently, he argued that holding gains were not income and should be taken to a nondistributable reserve. This is compatible with a physical capital maintenance approach. Holding losses were also recommended to be charged against the aforementioned reserve so long as there were gains at its credit to cover them. Thereafter, when the reserve was exhausted, Limperg suggested holding losses should reduce income, thereby implying a switch to financial capital maintenance. No particular reason seems to have been forthcoming to explain this apparent inconsistency in his accounting arguments.

In summary, it can therefore be seen that the problem of the treatment of holding gains was well recognised in the early 1900s, and usually debated within the context of writings on income and capital involving aspects of physical capital maintenance. The consensus appeared to be for the recognition of holding gains, usually not as income (generally) or distributable income (particularly). The main reason for this approach appeared to be the need to ensure the maintenance of physical capital by retaining funds to aid the replacement of assets at higher costs. However, the recognition and accounting treatment of holding gains within the context of capital maintenance raises questions concerning the changing structure of the capital to be maintained. The latter problem was recognised by the early accounting theorists, although not necessarily to the extent of providing a feasible solution.

Changing Asset Structures and Technologies

Several writers on income and capital matters indicated their awareness of the problem of maintaining capital in physical terms when the nature of the underlying asset structure was changing due to related changes in operating activities and/or technologies. Bauer (1919), for example, when discussing the specific example of accounting for the renewal cost of street cars, wrote of the difficulty of doing so when there was a constantly changing structure of physical assets. He presented this as a problem to be faced by accountants without advocating any particular solution. Martin (1927) also recognised the problem—but merely as one which caused instability in asset valuations, thus making accounting for fixed assets a somewhat more hazardous function than would be the case with a situation of stability. But, again, no solution was prescribed or recommended. Limperg (1964), too, offered no answers, merely suggesting (without definition) that the accounting should allow for "economic replacement"—implying non-identical replacement. This is confirmed by his definition of replacement value as the technically necessary and economically unavoidable cost of the asset concerned at the time of its sale or use.

129

Sweeney (1927) was far more forthright in his comments on the matter. Because he recognised there would be a decline in the business need for certain assets as others became more desirable resources for the reporting entity, he disagreed with accounting for physical capital and its maintenance. Instead, he (then) favoured the alternative financial capital approach of applying general price-level adjustments to historical cost data to "preserve economic power over goods and services." In other words, he presumably felt that the difficulties associated with changing asset structures were such that the reporting accountant should focus his attention on the more easily identified financial features of capital.

Rorem (1929), on the other hand, took a contrary stance—akin to the one associated with contemporary systems of current cost accounting.[25] Totally committed to the idea of reporting in replacement cost terms, he recognised the problem of technological change, and the problem of obtaining replacement costs for accounting in such circumstances. He therefore suggested that the replacement cost used to value a fixed asset should be adjusted to represent equivalent services to those obtained from the existing asset—that is, similar to the contemporary concept of the modern equivalent asset.[26]

This approach would have been wholeheartedly condemned by Canning (1929). A consistent critic of replacement cost accounting because of its reliance on "fictitious data" and "imponderables," he had this to say of asset structure changes:[27]

> Outlay cost is a real thing—a fact. So, too, will replacement cost *become* a real thing when it is incurred. But because prices of equipment fluctuate, because there are always many alternative ways of getting service, that is, many kinds of serving agents that will do a given kind of work, and because the amount and kind of service needed in an enterprise change with its selling, as well as with its buying, opportunities—because of all these extremely elusive matters it requires a good deal of positive evidence to show on which side of experienced cost per unit of service a future unit cost is likely to lie.

> We do not often see old establishments duplicated in new ones. Cost of reproduction new less an allowance for depreciation may be a good working rule in damage suits; it is absurd as a sole rule of going-concern valuation.

Not surprisingly, Canning preferred to account for capital in financial terms—ideally, those of present value, but practically in terms of a mixture of historical costs and net realisable values (when these could be obtained directly). He was not alone in this respect. Paton (1934) was by then arguing against the use of replacement costs, admitting that historical cost accounting could be the best basis for mainstream accounting purposes, with replacement costs only being reported as supplementary data. One of his reasons for this radical change of heart was the specialist complexity of fixed assets which meant that replacement in the same form as the original asset was impossible.

Thus, the problem of continually changing asset structures was not unknown in the 1920s and 1930s, although its discussion was limited (mainly to fixed assets), and usually avoided by advocacy of the adoption of some form of financial capital approach for reporting purposes. The support for the latter can be best evidenced by those writings which discussed the need to maintain capital in general purchasing power terms.

General Purchasing Power Accounting

Financial capital maintenance using general purchasing power techniques gained considerable support during the 1920s and 1930s.

130

Middleditch (1918) provided the impetus for historical cost adjusted data, but paid little direct attention to ideas of capital maintenance (he suggested losses on monetary items—including inventory as such—should be taken to reserve, and implied that purchasing power gains on liabilities should be treated as income). Paton (1918), on the other hand, argued that information ought to reflect specific price changes rather than changes in the general price level.

By 1920, however, Paton's views on general purchasing power accounting were changing.[28] Although favouring replacement cost accounting, he did recognise the difficulty of comparing data at different points of time for income purposes when the general price level was changing. Thus he argued that replacement cost figures should only be used for management purposes. The idea of general purchasing power accounting, however, was not developed further until the work of Sweeney was published in the late 1920s. Indeed, Canning (1929) stated that, although accountants would prefer such a system of accounting, they did not use it because of the lack of data available in time to make the adjustments (that is, presumably general price indices took a considerable time to prepare and publish at that time).

131

Nevertheless, the work of Sweeney had a considerable influence on income measurement—even if this was not immediate. He did not agree with the maintenance of physical capital in replacement cost accounting and, instead, preferred the maintenance of real capital in order to preserve the reporting entity's economic power over goods and services.[29] In this way, he would adjust historical costs for the general movement in prices, maintaining the outward form of capital (general command over goods) rather than the inner substance (physical assets).[30] By 1931, however, although still roundly condemning the use of pure historical cost and replacement cost systems, he argued at least that the latter was better than the former.[31]

In 1932, his views regarding replacement costs had changed somewhat.[32] Although his main system was based on general purchasing power, he also recommended the introduction of replacement cost changes in the balance sheet on top of the general price level-adjusted data—the total holding gains being taken to reserve until realised when the real element was transferred to income. Thus, he preferred to use a replacement cost system which, when combined with general price-level changes, effectively maintained financial capital—only allowing holding gains to be treated as income when realised, and only to the extent of real price changes. This combined approach was also favoured by Schmidt (1931), although he only regarded speculative holding gains as income.

By 1933, Sweeney (1933b) regarded all realised and unrealised gains as income, advocating their separation in the income statement. These ideas were developed within the context of a combined replacement cost and general price-level system. Monetary gains and losses appeared in the income statement [a point disagreed with by Jones (1935)], but no calculation was made of liability gains or losses of purchasing power. Fixed asset depreciation was measured in general purchasing power terms, thus emphasizing the financial capital approach. A summation of his ideas appeared in two further papers.[33]

132

The work of Sweeney in the 1920s and 1930s did much to establish a case for adopting an accounting approach which depended on financial capital maintenance. Indeed, he revealed clearly that it was perfectly possible to do this *and* to use replacement costs—that is, financial capital maintenance and replacement cost accounting are not incompatible.[34] This last point is something which remains a matter of confusion for contemporary accountants (for example, the attempt to maintain physical capital and financial capital in the provisions of the most recent current cost accounting recommendations).[35]

Little Support for Sale Values

Sweeney's relatively lone effort in the 1920s and 1930s to promote a financial capital maintenance approach (using general price changes) indicates a possible reluctance to move away from the traditional historical cost-based model. There was also a reluctance to adopt an alternative financial capital strategy which has been consistently and vigorously advocated in more recent times[36]—that is, the use of allocation-free sale values. This reluctance was a deep-seated one, reflecting an unwillingness to account for income before it was realised and a contrary support for the eventual accounting for income as and when it is realised by the entity as a going concern.[37] Paton (1918) was against the use of sale values, believing that to do so was to anticipate income (in a way which he also believed replacement costs did not do—a point which confirms that he regarded holding gains from replacement costs as potential income at that time).

By 1929, however, there were signs of some support for the idea of using sale values for external financial reporting—but only in limited circumstances. Rorem (1929) advocated the use of replacement costs but, following a "value to the business" rule akin to that seen in most contemporary systems of current cost accounting, suggested the use of net realisable value in circumstances when the latter had fallen below replacement cost. Daines (1929), on the other hand, indicated sale values might be of use in financial reports, but only to creditors interested in liquidity matters. And Canning (1929) advocated the use of sale values for reporting on assets where valuations could be applied directly to the objects concerned —for example, as in inventory for resale [as did MacNeal (1970)]. In fact, so far as these direct valuations were concerned, he indicated merit in reporting historical costs, replacement costs and sale values. His reasons for this approach were less than clear.

Limperg (1964), on the other hand, advocated the occasional use of net realisable values for reporting purposes. His valuation rule was the lower of replacement value and net realisable value, thereby reflecting the sacrifice of the owner of the assets concerned when he sold or used the latter. In addition, he argued that net realisable value, when compared with replacement value, should be the higher of the immediate liquidation value and the sale value on an orderly liquidation. Limperg therefore represented one of the few writers on accounting in the 1920s and 1930s who attempted to use sale values within a mixed value system—somewhat similar to that evidenced in present-day current cost accounting systems.[38]

The above brief commentary reflects a limited attention paid to net realisable value accounting in 1920s and 1930s, a situation not unlike that of today. It meant that the capital debate centered around historical costs, replacement costs and purchasing power units.

Dealing with Price Decreases

A further problem created by replacement cost accounting and physical capital maintenance is the treatment of price decreases. To treat them in a similar way to price increases results in increasing operating income and decreasing financial capital (due to the setting off of holding losses against reserves).[39] Arguably, this problem can be resolved by reverting to a financial capital system when prices are falling[40] but this does not cater for a situation in which some prices are rising and some falling. Brief (1970), when reviewing late nineteenth century contributions to the income and capital debate, indicated that these early writers were aware of the problem of falling prices, and this is clear from the writings of Best (1885)

133

and Cooper (1888)—capital losses being written off against income for dividend purposes. This awareness was also to be seen in the work of later writers.

Knight (1908), for example, advocated depreciation based on original cost because of the danger of fixed asset values falling. Rastall (1920) pointed out the danger of overstating income by underdepreciating when prices fell. And Sweeney (1930) complained that, if a physical capital maintenance approach were adopted when prices were falling, then the reporting entity's general command over goods would not be maintained (that is, its financial capital in terms of generalised purchasing power would diminish) and, if prices continued to fall, would reduce capital towards zero. This would be no problem so long as the reporting entity continued to invest in and replace assets subject to price decreases. But, as Sweeney indicated, it creates a problem when the entity wishes to diversify into assets subject to different price movements. On the other hand, Daniels (1933) took a pragmatic stance by suggesting that historical cost depreciation policies should be applied in order to allow for both replacement cost increases and decreases. McCowen (1937) felt that a physical capital system, using replacement costs, should be applied irrespective of prices increasing or decreasing—replacement cost accounting reflecting, in his view, how much the reporting entity's selling prices must be adjusted upwards or downwards. Schmidt (1931) also took this approach of consistently accounting for replacement costs, recommending that operating income be distributable (that is, before deduction of holding losses) on the grounds that the entity did not need such income in order to maintain its operations.[41]

Thus, the 1920s and 1930s witnessed three alternative treatments for falling prices: (1) either revert from a physical capital to a financial capital approach; (2) continue to use original costs as a financial capital basis; or (3) consistently apply physical capital accounting irrespective of the direction of price movements. As the problem has not been specifically covered in the United Kingdom current cost accounting provisions,[42] it can be reasonably stated that the early writings were sensitive to a problem which remains today.

Summary and Conclusions

There are many more topics which were debated in the 1920s and 1930s, and which could be analysed in this paper. For example, Sweeney (1931) recommended that all expenses deducted in arriving at income should be in replacement cost terms if such account-

134

ing was adopted; several writers[43] commented on the problem of using current or future replacement costs for assets yet to be replaced; and the feasibility of finding suitable replacement costs was commented on by at least one writer.[44] Space prevents such issues being discussed further, but the following general conclusions can be drawn from the previous sections: first, the early writers were fully aware of the distinction between financial and physical capital and capital maintenance (some favouring one or the other); secondly, much of the discussion centered around the possible use of replacement costs as an alternative to historical cost accounting, although general purchasing power accounting and net realisable value accounting were discussed also; thirdly, there was a confusion in the minds of early writers about the role of external financial reporting, many of the proposals inadequately distinguishing external reporting from internal reporting and asset management; fourthly, the previous point may have arisen because of the relative brevity and lack of detail in external financial reports of the time; fifthly, replacement cost accounting was viewed not merely as a means of maintaining physical capital but also as a means of adequately determining selling prices in times of changing input prices; sixthly, a considerable amount of the debate in the 1920s and 1930s concerned the aims and uses of financial reports; seventhly, the need for historical cost accounting was debated rather than swept aside; and, finally, some of the problems of replacement cost accounting were not only revealed but analysed in detail—for example, holding gains, changing asset structures and technologies, and price decreases.

135

It would be wrong to suggest that the early writers on income and capital cited in this paper either adequately recognised and analysed the problems or presented credible solutions. Certainly, there appeared to be little general acceptance by professional accountants and accountancy bodies of the ideas proposed. However, it is disturbing to find the same problems being, at best, debated and, at worst, ignored today in the various alternatives to historical cost accounting. Accountants thus appear to perpetuate problems rather than resolve them, and it is interesting to hypothesise some reasons for this, using the foregoing commentary as a basis:

1. The issue of income and capital measurement is a complex one, involving many problems, and reflecting numerous schools of thought. If a particular system is to be recommended to accountancy practitioners, it is essential that there is an adequate and prior discussion of all relevant matters. The present-day debate over cur-

rent cost accounting has been fragmented, hasty, and lacking in sustained debate involving all interested parties (including users and preparers).

2. The early contributions to the debate reveal, in the complexities of the various arguments, the need to present the major viewpoint in full in order that accountants, businessmen and others are fully apprised of all the issues involved. Current cost accounting proposals have failed to do this, concentrating solely on a limited argument to support them.

3. The reasons for the benefits of a particular reporting system must be fully explained and understood if it is to succeed. The early writers tended to concentrate more on technical matters and less on aims and purposes, and thus major confusions arose over the recommendations. Current cost accounting has suffered a similar fate today.

136

4. Changing circumstances can alter viewpoints and stances, and the early writers (particularly Paton) were prepared to adapt. This is difficult to handle in a complex area but systems such as current cost accounting must be allowed to change as circumstances dictate. Changing views must never be used as reasons for not changing or for unnecessary doubt regarding the credibility of the system concerned.

5. Finally, given all the problems of attempting to account and report on physical capital, it is of concern to see no attempt made in the early 1900s (or today) to discuss whether or not these problems outweigh the benefits to be gained from an accounting system based on the maintenance of physical capital. The difficulties of defining physical capital, and its changing nature over time, make it a concept with considerable practical problems regarding implementation. The early debate, and the present unrest with it in countries such as the United Kingdom, indicate it may remain a matter of conceptual rather than practical significance.

FOOTNOTES

[1]For example, Accounting Standards Committee, 1980a. Australian Society of Accountants and The Institute of Chartered Accountants in Australia, 1976, 1978. Financial Accounting Standards Board, 1979.

[2]Lemke and Sterling, 1982.

[3]Symposium, 1930.

[4]There was also at the same time a considerable Dutch contribution based on the work of Limperg, 1964. However, because of its inaccessibility, and isolation from the English-speaking literature, it is difficult to integrate it in this paper beyond making relevant mention of Límperg's theory at particular points. The sources for these comments have been Mey, 1966 and Burgert, 1972.

[5]It is interesting to note that the accounting theory of Limperg, 1964, which was developed in the 1920s and 1930s, influenced his students sufficiently to go beyond the debating stage, and to implement a system of accounting containing several features of present-day current cost practice—see, for example, Goudeket, 1960, and Burgert, 1972.

[6]Stockwell, 1909.

[7]Brief, 1976.

[8]Brief, 1976.

[9]Dickinson, 1904. Cole, 1908. Sells, 1908.

[10]Knight, 1908.

[11]Gower, 1919.

[12]Paton, 1920, 1922. Rastall, 1920. Moss, 1923.

[13]By contrast the Dutch debate commenced at about the same time for a somewhat different reason. Limperg, 1964, was concerned about changes in thinking about the economic approach to valuation (particularly regarding business decisions based on marginal utility), and preferred an accounting system for management based on the producer. Thus, economic arguments to aid management accounting practice were the basis for the Dutch debate, rather than the more pragmatic accounting issue of how best to account for fixed assets in practice.

[14]Bauer, 1919, p. 414.

[15]Jackson, 1921, p. 83.

[16]Rorem, 1929, pp. 172-173.

[17]Martin, 1927, p. 123.

[18]This was not the case with Limperg, 1964. His writings make it quite clear that he saw his system of accounting based on replacement values (using a valuation rule of the lower of replacement value and net realisable value) as being primarily for management accounting purposes but also of considerable use for financial accounting. He did not appear to regard it as essential to separate the two functions.

[19]Wedgewood, 1981, p. 3.

[20]Accounting Standards Committee, 1980a.

[21]Litherland, 1951.

[22]This is specially true of the work of Limperg. 1964.

[23]It should be noted that these views are compatible with those of Limperg, 1964, who believed that, on average, the use of replacement costs to determine selling prices would generate sufficient cash to fund asset replacements.

[24]Symposium, 1930.

[25]Accounting Standards Committee, 1980a.

[26]Accounting Standards Committee, 1980b.

[27]Canning, 1929, pp. 254-255.

[28]Paton, 1920.

[29]Sweeney, 1927.

[30]Sweeney, 1930.

[31]Sweeney, 1931.

[32]Sweeney, 1932.

[33]Sweeney, 1934, 1935.

[34]But his was a lone view—arguably one of the leading replacement cost advocates of the time, Limperg, 1964, made no attempt to account for general price-level changes.

[35]Accounting Standards Committee, 1980a.

[36]Chambers, 1966. Sterling, 1970.

[37]Guthrie, 1883. Best, 1885.

137

[38]For example, Accounting Standards Committee, 1980a.
[39]See Sterling, 1982.
[40]See Lee, 1980. Attention should also be paid to the work of Limperg, 1964, in this respect. He recommended holding losses should be written off against income when they exceeded aggregate holding gains taken to reserve.
[41]Note should be taken, however, of the aforementioned objection of Sweeney.
[42]Accounting Standards Committee, 1980a.
[43]Bauer, 1919. Scott, 1929. Paton, 1932. Crandell, 1935.
[44]Rorem, 1929.

BIBLIOGRAPHY

Accounting Standards Committee. "Current Cost Accounting." *Statement of Standard Accounting Practice 16,* Accounting Standards Committee, London, 1980a.

Accounting Standards Committee. *Guidance Notes on SSAP 16 Current Cost Accounting.* Accounting Standards Committee, London, 1980b.

Australian Society of Accountants and The Institute of Chartered Accountants in Australia. "Current Cost Accounting." *Statement of Provisional Accounting Standards 1.1,* Australian Society of Accountants and The Institute of Chartered Accountants in Australia, Melbourne, 1976; 1978.

Bauer J. "Renewal Costs and Business Profits in Relation to Rising Prices." *Journal of Accountancy* (December 1919), pp. 413-419.

Best J. W. "Payment of Dividend Out of Capital." *The Accountant* (December 5, 1885), pp. 7-10,

Brief R. P. "The Late Nineteenth Century Debate Over Depreciation, Capital and Income." *The Accountant* (November 26, 1970), pp. 737-739.

—————————. *Nineteenth Century Capital Accounting and Business Investment.* New York: Arno Press, 1976.

Burgert R. "Reservations about 'Replacement Value' Accounting in The Netherlands." *Abacus* (December 1972), pp. 111-126.

Canning J. B. *The Economics of Accountancy: A Critical Analysis of Accounting Theory.* New York: Ronald Press, 1929.

Chambers R. J. *Accounting, Evaluation and Economic Behaviour.* Englewood Cliffs, N.J.: Prentice-Hall, 1966.

Cole W. M. *Accounts: Their Construction and Interpretation.* Boston: Houghton Mifflin, 1908.

Cooper E. "What is Profit of a Company?" *The Accountant* (November 10, 1888), pp. 740-746.

Crandell W. T. "Income and Its Measurement." *Accounting Review* (December 1935), pp. 380-400.

Daines H. C. "The Changing Objectives of Accounting." *Accounting Review* (June 1929), pp. 94-110.

Daniels M. B. "The Valuation of Fixed Assets." *Accounting Review* (December 1933), pp. 302-316.

Dickinson A. L. "Profits of a Corporation." *The Financial Record, Lawyers' and Accountants' Manual* (November 2, 1904), pp. 38-43.

Financial Accounting Standards Board. "Financial Reporting and Changing Prices." *Statement of Financial Accounting Standards 33,* Stamford, Conn.: Financial Accounting Standards Board, 1979.

Goudeket A. "An Application of Replacement Value Theory." *Journal of Accountancy* (July 1960), pp. 37-47.

Gower W. B. "Depreciation and Depletion in Relation to Invested Capital." *Journal of Accountancy* (November 1919), pp. 353-368.

Guthrie E. "Depreciation and Sinking Funds." *The Accountant* (April 21, 1883), pp. 6-10.

Jackson J. H. "Depreciation Policy and True Cost." *Journal of Accountancy* (June 1920), pp. 452-455.

_____. "Some Problems in Depreciation." *Journal of Accountancy* (February 1921), pp. 81-102.

Jones R. C. "Financial Statements and the Uncertain Dollar." *Journal of Accountancy* (September 1935), pp. 171-197.

Knight A. "Depreciation and Other Reserves." *Journal of Accountancy* (January 1908), pp. 189-200.

Krebs W. S. "Asset Appreciation—Its Economic and Accounting Significance." *Accounting Review* (March 1930), pp. 60-69.

Lee T. A. "Current Cost Accounting and Physical Capital." In Lemke K. W. and Sterling R. R., eds. *Maintenance of Capital—Financial Versus Physical.* Houston, Tex.: Scholars Book Co., 1982, (forthcoming).

Lemke K. W. and Sterling R. R., eds. *Maintenance of Capital—Financial Versus Physical.* Houston, Tex.: Scholars Book Co., 1982, (forthcoming).

Limperg, Th. *Industrial Economy.* Amsterdam: Collected Works, 1964. This is the best available reference to the work of Limperg, and is cited by Burgert.

Litherland D. A. "Fixed Asset Replacement a Half Century Ago." *Accounting Review* (October 1951), pp. 475-480.

Littleton A. C. "What is Profit?" *Accounting Review* (September 1928), pp. 278-288.

_____. "Value and Price in Accounting." *Accounting Review* (September 1929), pp. 147-154.

_____. "Contrasting Theories of Profit." *Accounting Review* (March 1936), pp. 10-15.

McCowen G. B. "Replacement Cost of Goods Sold." *Accounting Review* (September 1937), pp. 270-277.

MacNeal K. *Truth in Accounting.* Houston, Tex.: Scholars Book Co., 1970.

Martin O. R. "Surplus Arising Through Revaluation." *Accounting Review* (June 1927), pp. 111-123.

Mather C. E. "Depreciation and Appreciation of Fixed Assets." *Journal of Accountancy* (March 1928), pp. 185-190.

Mey A. "Theodore Limperg and His Theory of Values and Costs." *Abacus* (September 1966), pp. 3-24.

Middleditch L. "Should Accounts Reflect the Changing Value of the Dollar?" *Journal of Accountancy* (February 1918), pp. 114-120.

Moss A. G. "Treatment of Appreciation of Fixed Assets." *Journal of Accountancy* (September 1923), pp. 161-179.

Paton W. A. "The Significance and Treatment of Appreciation in the Accounts," in Coons, G. H., ed. *Twentieth Annual Report of the Michigan Academy of Science,* 1918, pp. 35-49.

_____. "Depreciation, Appreciation and Productive Capacity." *Journal of Accountancy* (July 1920), pp. 1-11.

_____. "Valuation of Inventories." *Journal of Accountancy* (December 1922), pp. 432-450.

_____. "Aspects of Asset Valuations." *Accounting Review* (June 1934), pp. 122-129.

Rastall E. S. "Depreciation Reserves and Rising Prices." *Journal of Accountancy* (February 1920), pp. 123-126.

139

Rorem C. R. "Replacement Cost in Accounting Valuation." *Accounting Review* (September 1929), pp. 167-174.

Saliers E. A. "Depreciation Reserves Versus Depreciation Funds." *Journal of Accountancy* (November 1913), pp. 358-365.

Schmidt F. "The Importance of Replacement Value." *Accounting Review* (September 1930), pp. 235-242.

——————————. "Is Appreciation Profit?" *Accounting Review* (December 1931), pp. 289-293.

Scott DR. "Valuation for Depreciation and the Financing of Replacement." *Accounting Review* (December 1929), pp. 221-226.

Sells E. W. *Corporate Management Compared with Government Control.* New York: Press of Safety, 1908.

Sterling R. R. *Theory of the Measurement of Enterprise Income.* Kansas: University of Kansas Press, 1970.

——————————. "Limitations of Physical Capital," in Lemke K. W. and Sterling R. R., eds. *Maintenance of Capital—Financial Versus Physical.* Houston, Tex.: Scholars Book Co., 1982, (forthcoming).

Stockwell H. G. "Depreciation, Renewal and Replacement Accounts." *Journal of Accountancy* (December 1909), pp. 89-103.

Sweeney H. W. "Effects of Inflation on German Accounting." *Journal of Accountancy* (March 1927), pp. 180-191.

——————————. "The Maintenance of Capital." *Accounting Review* (December 1930), pp. 277-287.

——————————. "Stabilised Depreciation." *Accounting Review* (September 1931), pp. 165-178.

——————————. "Stabilised Appreciation." *Accounting Review* (June 1932), pp. 115-121.

——————————. "Capital." *Accounting Review* (September 1933a), pp. 185-199.

——————————. "Income." *Accounting Review* (December 1933b), pp. 323-335.

——————————. "How Inflation Affects Balance Sheets." *Accounting Review* (December 1934), pp. 275-299.

——————————. "The Technique of Stabilised Accounting." *Accounting Review* (June 1935), pp. 185-205.

Symposium, "What is Appreciation?" *Accounting Review* (March 1930), pp. 1-9.

Thomas J. L. "Depreciation and Valuation." *Journal of Accountancy* (January 1916), pp. 24-33.

Wasserman M. J. "Accounting Practice in France During the Period of Monetary Inflation (1919-1927)." *Accounting Review* (March 1931), pp. 1-32.

Wedgewood Ltd. *Annual Report 1981,* 1981.

140

Overview

The Evolution and Revolution of
Financial Accounting: a Review Article

T. A. Lee

142

The upheaval of recent events in financial accounting may have persuaded many accountants that these are uniquely critical times for their profession. However, to do so would be to view the present too narrowly and without a relevant context. The problems of accounting must be placed within a wider perspective, otherwise they may appear to be more troublesome than they deserve.

The most relevant context appears to be the historical one, in which the problems of today can be seen also to have been the problems of yesterday. In other words, they are long-lasting problems, and may not lend themselves to permanent solutions. The aim of this review article is to attempt to provide at least part of such a historical context by utilising material published in four texts from the second Arno Press collection.[1] It is largely concerned with events and activities at the end of the last and the beginning of this century, a period which, surprisingly, has been neglected by accounting historians despite its apparent importance in the development of contemporary financial accounting.

The texts of Chatfield and Hein will be used to describe some of the main problems facing the accountancy profession during the last two decades of the nineteenth century. This will provide the background to the material in Brief's text which reflects the state of accounting at the beginning of the twentieth century. Yang's more detailed text concentrates on a particularly long-lasting accounting problem and, together with the later material in Hein, provides evidence of developments from the earlier foundation. Each text will therefore not be reviewed in the conventional way but, instead, will provide witness to the longevity of financial accounting problems.

[1] M. Chatfield, *The English View of Accountants' Duties and Responsibilities 1881-1902*, Arno Press, 1978; L. W. Hein, *The British Companies Acts and the Practice of Accountancy 1844-1962*, Arno Press, 1978; R. P. Brief, ed., *Selections from Encyclopaedia of Accounting*, 1903, Arno Press, 1978; and J. M. Yang, *Goodwill and Other Intangibles*, Arno Press, 1978.

Present-day problems of financial accounting

The 1970s have seen accountants grappling with a number of seemingly vital issues. Arguably the most important of these is the establishment of acceptable accounting standards to improve the quality of reported financial accounting information by reducing the number of alternative practices and improving the relevance of accounting data. These include the vital measurement problems associated with accounting for changing prices and price-levels. A second significant issue has centred on the need for a conceptual framework for financial reporting—a matter strongly related to the accounting standards programme. Auditing standards (both technical and ethical) have constituted yet another important area of concern. And, finally, the qualifications of accountants (pre- and post-qualifying) have also been the subject of serious scrutiny and debate in the 1970s.

No doubt such a brief list could be enlarged and expanded. To do so, however, would be largely an irrelevance in relation to this paper. Suffice to say that major elements of each of these problem areas are to be seen in the writings being reviewed and, despite their age, appear to be as unresolved as ever. Of course the problems have become somewhat more sophisticated and complex but, nevertheless, they remain as 'critical' today as they were in the late 1800s and early 1900s. There is an evolution as well as a revolution in accounting matters which ought to be noted by those that currently seek speedy solutions.

Professional responsibility in the 1880s and 1890s

The writings reproduced in Chatfield are all excellent pieces which reflect the mood and attitudes of the times. They were written by the most eminent accountants of the day (many of whom founded

the accountancy profession in its modern form)—
for example, Cooper, Pixley, Whinney, Dicksee,
Harmood-Banner and Crewdson. Their approach
to accounting and auditing problems was consistent and reflects the newness of the profession at
that time—that is, be optimistic yet realistic about
the problems yet to be discovered let alone
resolved. They were proud men, full of the self-
confidence of the Victorian age, and splendid in
their belief in their personal honesty and integrity.
They were also noticeably worried about the lack
of precedent and experience in matters relating to
their professional responsibilities and of lack of
public credibility in their work. For example,
Crewdson commented in 1902:[2]

> In plain English, while I believe there is today
> no profession the members of which believe
> more thoroughly in themselves and in the im-
> portance of their duties, or who as a whole
> do their work with a more elaborate conscien-
> tiousness, those who have the best opportuni-
> ties of judging will admit that the public do
> not as yet greatly believe in us; and, on the
> other hand, in the effort to prove that our ser-
> vices are valuable, writers have sought to
> extend as far as possible the field of our oper-
> ations, without regard to the liabilities which
> were thereby imposed upon us.

Given the 'youth' of the profession at that time,
this position is not surprising. What is, however,
is the just-as-evident present-day concern of accountants about the precise nature of their responsibilities (particularly those in the area of
auditing), thus reflecting the almost continuous
and unplanned chain reaction in UK accounting
life of legal decision to accepted professional practice to legal decision; and the failure to resolve
these matters on a long-term basis.

The problem of professional responsibility is as
old as the accountancy profession itself, and will
probably never be far from the thoughts of its
members. Each of the writers represented in Chatfield acknowledged the difficulties associated with
defining professional responsibilities, particularly
when a profession is in its infancy. But, and this
is evidenced by the amount of statutory control
over accounting and auditing in the UK as compared with the US, there appears to have been
a strange reluctance in the profession to regulate
these matters internally. For example, it was not

until the 1970s that a programme of accounting
and auditing standards was initiated—despite an
almost continuous commentary on these matters
in the literature from 1880 onwards, and despite
the existence of numerous court decisions and
Companies Acts related to them.

This lack of authority on the part of the UK
accountancy profession, coupled with an inevitable reliance on statutory control and court decisions, is hard to explain. Certainly, many writers
appeared to be concerned to limit the responsibilities of accountants to factual matters. Anything
to do with opinions and valuations was frowned
upon. Thus, they may not have felt that such
work required formal standardisation so long as
they dealt only with 'facts'. The early importance
of fraud and error detection in auditing is one
example of this rather narrow approach to 'factual' work. Whitehill described it in 1897 in the
following manner:[3]

> A certificate in its simplest form may be de-
> scribed as a written declaration of some fact
> or facts. Accountants' certificates are usually
> written declarations made upon accounts
> which accountants are called upon to examine
> into and verify. They are as important in rela-
> tion to what they may be made to omit to
> disclose, as they are in relation to what they
> are made to purport to reveal. What, clearly,
> they are required to make known is truth;
> what to omit, falsity.

This rather 'black and white' view of accounting
and auditing is typical of most of the earliest writings being reviewed. It does not, however, provide
an explanation of why the members of the accountancy profession of that time were largely left
to judge their responsibilities individually and
personally. It may have been because these early
practitioners were fiercely independent and
wished to prove to the world at large that they
could manage their own affairs in a competent
manner. It may also have been because of a high
regard for the rule of law although some, such as
Dicksee, felt that the law in relation to accountancy matters was in need of considerable improvement.[4] On the other hand, it may simply
have been because of the newness and fragmented
nature of the profession—a co-ordinated voice

143

---

[2]E. Crewdson, 'Codification of an Audit,' in Chatfield, *op cit*,
pp. 143-4.

[3]R. Whitehill, 'Some Notes on the Responsibilities of Chartered Accountants With Regard to Their Certificates,' in Chatfield, *op cit*, p. 93.
[4]L. R. Dicksee, 'The Liabilities of Auditors Under the Companies Acts,' in Chatfield, *op cit*, pp. 106-17.

thus not being available (such as that which now exists in bodies such as the Accounting Standards Committee and the Consultative Committee of Accountancy Bodies).

No firm or convincing explanation of the ill-defined nature of professional responsibility at the turn of the century can therefore be given. Because of a great deal of pressure for accounting and auditing change from non-accounting sources (for example, from various Chambers of Commerce), and despite obvious resistance to such change from professional accountants (and firms), UK accounting and auditing developments largely stemmed from company statutes.[5] Early accountants therefore appeared to be exceedingly reluctant to initiate change through their professional bodies, and it should not be surprising to witness the current muddle over inflation accounting in the UK—the early slowness to recognise the need for radical, long-term solutions despite external criticism to this effect; the stepping in by government in the form of the Sandilands Committee as a prelude to possible legislation; and the almost indecent haste of the professional bodies to produce a solution before such an event took place. In other words, as Hein demonstrates, there was an understandable reluctance in both the UK and US to be regulated by legislation, but an inexplicable unwillingness and inexperience in the UK to self-regulate.[6] In the US, self-regulation is a well-developed process in the accountancy profession.

Uncertainty in profit measurement

Brief is quite clear in his opinion that the major accounting problem from the 1880s to the present day has been the degree of uncertainty inherent in the measurement of profit—that is, the amount of subjective judgment with which reporting accountants and auditors have to cope:[7]

> The last two decades of the nineteenth century were a 'golden age' in accounting and most of the major issues connected with the subject of the accountant's responsibility were brought out in the period. Questions concerning full disclosure, alternative techniques, scope of audit and the meaning of the audit certificate were widely discussed in the first few years after the profession was formally established.

However, nineteenth century accountants did not 'solve' most of the problems which they debated. One explanation for the perennial nature of controversy is the accountant's early attitude to uncertainty. During the last century, the profession began to emphasise the historical nature of accounting calculations even though many theorists recognised that forecasts and estimates were inherent in most problems.

From a review of the evidence in Chatfield and Hein, it is apparent that accounting practitioners were fully aware of what has come to be described as the issue of accounting standards. Despite the origins of the profession in legally-oriented matters such as bankruptcies, liquidations, executorships and arbitration, the accountants of the 1880s and 1890s were concerned with the difficulties of accounting practice—for example, in relation to stock valuations, depreciation of fixed assets, foreign exchange transactions, etc. The writings of practitioners such as Murray, Cooper, Pixley, Harvey and Dickinson testify to this.[8] However, a reading of each of these authors indicates that the emphasis was on the 'tidiness' of allocation procedures for matching purposes rather than in their relevance and suitability to the circumstances. Murray, for example, mainly discussed the relative merits of straight-line and reducing-balance methods of depreciation;[9] and Harvey made no definition of cost in relation to stock valuation whilst emphasising the need to ensure arithmetic correctness in the stock sheets.[10]

The general lack of emphasis in the late 1880s and early 1900s on the measurement of profit must have contributed to the profession's relative lack of attention to accounting standards. A reading of the evidence in Hein reveals that there was a generally accepted attitude in the accountancy profession and the business community against the disclosure of measured profits—an activity which was regarded as potentially harmful to business and, in any case, being the private concern of management.[11] The lack of compulsory auditing provisions in the Companies Acts from 1856 to 1900, and the emergence for the first time

---

[5]See Hein, op cit, passim.
[6]Hein, op cit, pp. 11–86.
[7]R. P. Brief, 'The Accountant's Responsibility in Historical Perspective,' in Chatfield, op cit, p. 13.

[8]All in Chatfield, op cit.
[9]A. Murray, 'On the Progress of Accountancy and the Duties Which Come Within the Scope of an Accountant's Practice,' in Chatfield, op cit, p. 18.
[10]B. S. Harvey, 'The Limits Which a Chartered Accountant Should Place on His Duties and Responsibilities as an Auditor,' in Chatfield, op cit, p. 103.
[11]Hein, op cit, pp. 244–71.

of compulsory profit reporting in the Companies Act 1929, further confirm the early efforts not to disclose profits. It is therefore not surprising that a formal accounting standards programme was not introduced in the UK until the early 1970s. Nor is it surprising that, to date, no Companies Act has contained specific provisions relating to measurement standards. Instead, the role of the Companies Acts has been to prescribe levels of accounting disclosure only.

The ability of accountants and managers to manipulate profits and balance sheet positions is at the basis of any contemporary accounting standards programme. It was also a problem not unknown to the early accounting practitioners. For example, Harvey had this to say of it:[12]

As regards capital and revenue it is the duty of the auditor to discriminate between them. The natural tendency of companies will be to overcharge capital and reduce the charge to revenue; and, equally, the duties of the auditor will lie the other way, since a charge on revenue will mean a decrease of the profit available for dividend.

The role of the auditor to reduce profits for dividend purposes is perhaps a curious one, but reflects the inherent conservatism of accountants typified and formalised today by the prescription of accounting policies such as realisation and prudence.[13] In addition, it should be noted that Harvey's attention to profit measurement for dividend purposes is one of the most recurrent themes in the history of financial accounting. It is seen in most of the writings being reviewed, and is most evident in the considerable case law which was built up in the late 1880s and early 1900s—for example, in cases dealing with depreciation and distributable profits (such as *Lee v. Neuchatel Asphalte Co. Ltd.* (1889 41 Ch. 1); *Bolton v. Natal Land and Colonisation Co. Ltd.* (1892 2 Ch. 124); and *Wilmer v. McNamara & Co. Ltd.*, (1895 2 Ch. 245)). It is equally evident, however, in the most recent of financial accounting proposals. For example, the Sandilands Committee introduced current cost accounting in terms of a definition of profit related to distribution. Using and adapting the well-known Hicksian definition of 'well-offness', profit was defined by it as:[14]

... the maximum value which the company can distribute during the year, and still expect to be as well off at the end of the year as it was at the beginning.

Despite a warning that the current cost profit does not necessarily equate with the distributable profit, the emphasis of the adjustments in the recently published Exposure Draft 24 on current cost accounting is similarly inclined—for example, the computation of current cost profit after allowing for the current cost of sales, depreciation and working capital (each abated by a suitable gearing adjustment), and the recommended transfer to a capital maintenance reserve of all realised and unrealised holding gains (again abated where relevant).[15] The erosion of the operating capability of the business by over-distribution was stated to be a primary consideration in this respect.

Thus, little has changed in the major aims of financial accounting. The earliest writings reproduced in Chatfield, together with the research of Hein, reveal that the function at the turn of the century was orientated almost exclusively to proprietors (generally) and shareholders (particularly). This proprietary approach to accounting was further emphasised in the statutory control of companies and in the decisions of the courts. It should not therefore be surprising to see it appearing in many contemporary accounting proposals and practices. It is, however, of concern that such a narrow view of financial accounting and reporting has persisted so long, thus excluding the more neutral enterprise approach to the accounting entity concept, which allows for a wider, more liberal approach to accounting disclosures and the satisfaction of report user needs.[16]

Who are accountants?

The early years of any profession are obviously testing for it, if for no other reason than it has to establish its credibility (and that of its members). It is evident from a review of these early writings that accountants believed they were not highly regarded in the community, and were concerned to improve their image and their knowledge—for example, Murray advocated the attendance by

---

[12]Harvey, *op cit*, p. 103.
[13]See 'Disclosure of Accounting Policies,' *Statement of Standard Accounting Practice 2*, 1979.
[14]*Report of the Inflation Accounting Committee*, HMSO Cmnd. 6225, p. 29.

[15]'Current Cost Accounting,' *Exposure Draft 24*, Accounting Standards Committee, 1979.
[16]See T. A. Lee, 'The Accounting Entity Concept, Accounting Standards, and Inflation Accounting,' *Accounting and Business Research*, forthcoming.

practitioners at university law classes in order to improve their knowledge of the legal matters related to the work of the accountant;[17] Griffiths urged the need to ensure that the public was aware of what were the accountant's duties, as well as the requirement that accountants use clear, simple and understandable language in their financial reports;[18] an editorial in *The Accountant* outlined the problem of identifying who could properly be described as accountants;[19] Cooper described the first essential quality of an auditor as his independence;[20] Mather complained of the over-charging of fees for work done, and of the blatant touting for business which was taking place at the time;[21] and Crewdson suggested the codifying of audit practices in order to safeguard the client and provide a proper basis for the audit fee.[22]

Most of these matters have a relevance today, as they relate to issues which have yet to be resolved, and which therefore remain under current consideration in the accountancy profession. The need for compulsory post-qualifying education is being considered in order to ensure a proper maintenance of technical standards amongst all practitioners; the need to produce accounting information in a comprehensible way is a major problem which is currently being researched;[23] the exclusion of unqualified persons from professional bodies does not prevent them describing themselves as 'accountants'; the question of independence is a long-standing one and is a major part of recent UK ethical statements;[24] advertising is under consideration and the subject of fees is a matter which causes accountancy firms great concern in relation to establishing proper systems (including adequate audit working papers) to ensure valid fee computations. In other words, there are many matters which currently concern the profession and which will continue to concern it and its members. The past is an adequate witness to that.

[17]Murray, *op cit*, p. 21.
[18]J. G. Griffiths, 'Accountants and the Public,' in Chatfield, *op cit*, p. 28.
[19] "Accountants" and Accountants,' in Chatfield, *op cit*, p. 24.
[20]E. Cooper, 'Chartered Accountants as Auditors of Companies,' in Chatfield, *op cit*, p. 33.
[21]J. Mather, 'The Ethics of Accountancy,' in Chatfield, *op cit*, p. 47.
[22]Crewdson, *op cit*, pp. 142–7.
[23]See, for example, T. A. Lee and D. P. Tweedie, *The Private Shareholder and the Corporate Report*, The Institute of Chartered Accountants in England and Wales, 1976.
[24]Ethical Guide for Members of the Institute of Chartered Accountants of Scotland', *Statements of Professional Conduct 1*, 1975, p. 5; and 1979, pp. 9–10.

The state of the 'art' in 1903

What the previous sections have attempted to do is to reflect some of the main features and problems influencing accounting at the end of the nineteenth and beginning of the twentieth centuries—particularly as seen by practitioner writers of the times. The next section deals with a selection of writings (edited by Brief) which describe matters of importance in the accountancy profession in the first years of the twentieth century. Because they are commissioned writings on a variety of topics, however, they portray not only the practices and attitudes of the early 1900s but also pinpoint the problem areas then yet to be examined and resolved by practitioners over the next decades. As in the other collection of readings, the writers are, in the main, well known—for example, Richard Brown on 'Accountants' (reflecting the Scottish influence on world accountancy); Th. Limperg on accounting in Holland (Dutch accountants in 1900 apparently required a working knowledge of three languages other than Dutch!); Branford on the relationship of accounting to economics (particularly the theory of value so crucial to present-day debates on accounting measurements); Dicksee on 'Auditing' (and the relationship of accounting and auditing); Lisle on 'Balance Sheets'; Guthrie on 'Depreciation'; and Mann on 'Oncost' (reflecting again the influence of economics on accounting).

The writings in this volume of essays were largely ahead of their time. In them are seen the beginnings of issues of much concern to accountants today. They fall mainly into the area of accounting measurements based on arbitrary allocations. However, the then conventional view was expressed by Lisle in his description of a balance sheet:[25]

A balance sheet is a concise statement compiled from the books of a concern which have been kept by double entry, showing on the one side all the assets and on the other side all the liabilities of the concern at a particular moment of time.

Lisle emphasised the concern of accountants at the time with accounting classification (that is, where to place data in financial statements rather than how to allocate or value it). This he did despite stating that assets should be described at their 'fair value'. He did not define the latter term

[25]G. Lisle, 'Balance Sheets,' in Brief, *op cit*, p. 203.

(a situation to be evidenced consistently in the history of UK financial reporting, with the use of undefined phrases such as 'full and fair', 'true and correct' and 'true and fair' in disclosure legislation). A contrary and much more contemporary approach to accounting problems was evidenced in the work of Branford who regarded accounting as a system dealing with values:[26]

The system of accounting is historically the means which experience has devised for comparing anticipated with actual valuations. Accounting from this broad point of view is to be regarded as that specialised form of activity to which the private individual, the man of business, the family group, or the state government all have recourse in the record and computation of values.

Profit, according to Branford, was the increase in the value of the proprietor's wealth. Values were identified as market prices (both buying and selling). The valuation approach to accounting, obviously rooted in economic theory, has only recently been recognised by accounting practitioners as being relevant to financial accounting practice (that is, as part of the resolution of the inflation accounting problem). It was therefore far ahead of its time in 1903.

The 'middle ground' between the classification approach of Lisle and the valuation approach of Branford is represented in the writings of several other contributors to the volume. For example, Dicksee, when identifying the need to relate accounting and auditing matters, was adamant in his view that balance sheets were not statements of fact (rather they were statements of opinion), and that the problem of cost allocation was crucial to the work of the auditor concerned with verifying the distributability of profits (a view which appears to be compatible with the present-day accounting standards programme).[27] Guthrie, too, expressed identical sentiments in relation to accounting for depreciation, regarding it as the crucial link between profit and capital.[28] He, like Dicksee, viewed the capital-revenue classification of expenditure as a most crucial matter in this respect.

Thus, by the early 1900s, the evidence from these writings shows growing attention being paid to cost allocations, although the major emphasis

was more on cost classification and applying generally accepted allocation formulae than on the fundamental relevance of the information derived from such procedures. Mann, for example, went into great detail about the need to classify and document factory costs.[29] Much the same approach can be attributed to Mackenzie[30]— such writers evidencing the beginnings of contemporary cost and management accounting. An early attention to the topic of satisfying user needs is seen in a statement of Mackenzie (sadly not to be found elsewhere in writings specifically concerned with financial accounting):[31]

The principal consideration in framing factory or workshop accounts is, what does the owner require to know?

One final matter of contemporary relevance in these writings relates to the vexed question of reserve accounting. This has always been a problem to accountants (particularly in relation to the practice of accounting for so-called secret reserves). It has become more of an explicit issue in recent times due to the introduction of current cost accounting in the UK, with its emphasis on maintaining operating capacity and thereby requiring elements of gain to be 'reserved' rather than treated as profit (as was the case formerly under the conventions of historic cost accounting).

Dawson contributed an article of 'Reserves and Reserve Funds'.[32] In it, he established the main question as the decision as to what is or is not a reserve. He preferred to treat all relevant gains or transfers as surpluses, and to identify as reserves those with assets set aside to cover them—in other words, a reserve only existed (in his view) if an equivalent asset could be identified. This is what he described as:[33]

An asset held as a hostage for contingencies.

Such an approach reflects the conservatism of the accounting of the time, and goes well beyond the present approach to reserves (where assets are not identified in such a deliberate way). Nevertheless, in current cost accounting (as per Exposure Draft

147

[26]V. V. Branford, 'Accounting in Its Relation to Economics,' in Brief, *op cit*, p. 27.
[27]L. R. Dicksee, 'Auditing,' in Brief, *op cit*, p. 167.
[28]E. Guthrie, 'Depreciation,' in Brief, *op cit*, pp. 357–8.

[29]J. Mann, 'Cost Records or Factory Accounting,' in Brief, *op cit*, pp. 260–99.
[30]C. Mackenzie, 'Factory Organisation and Costing Arrangements,' in Brief, *op. cit*, pp. 464–79.
[31]Ibid, p. 465.
[32]S. S. Dawson, 'Reserves and Reserve Funds,' in Brief, *op cit*, pp. 482–8.
[33]Ibid, p. 485.

148

24, for example), the transfer of 'realised' holding gains for stock (cost of sales), fixed assets (depreciation), and monetary working capital to a capital maintenance reserve would indirectly identify assets being held in the business for particular purposes other than for distribution to its owners. However, Dawson appears to have gone further, regarding reserve assets as being available only to meet contingencies:[34]

> A given concern may have a very large surplus of assets over its paid-up capital and liabilities, and yet have none of that surplus in such a form that it can be relied upon as a reserve asset to meet a contingency.

This almost suggests that reserves can only exist if there are equivalent assets in a realisable form. This is far from the modern approach to reserve accounting, but is entirely compatible with published balance sheets of the times which contained large amounts of liquid or near-liquid assets existing to 'cover' reserves.[35]

The problem of goodwill

The work of Yang in 1927 reflects well on the growing maturity of the accountancy profession in the 1880s and 1890s.[36] His topic was goodwill accounting, and much of what he writes about is just as relevant today as it was in the late 1920s. Goodwill constitutes what is arguably one of the least resolved of accounting issues, mainly because it relates to matters of considerable importance in accounting but over which there is little agreement as to how to account.

Yang emphasises these difficulties by isolating the main characteristics of goodwill and other intangibles—that is, their lack of substance; their unrealisability; and the difficulty of separating them from the more tangible features of a business enterprise. He also explains them in terms of their psychological attributes:[37]

> Goodwill is that aspect of our thinking which lends itself to a favourable judgement or choice toward a person or thing.

as well as their economic characteristics:[38]

Goodwill represents the present worth or capitalised value of the estimated future earnings of an established enterprise in excess of the normal results that it might be reasonably assumed, would be realised by a similar undertaking established anew.

In this way, he strongly linked goodwill to prices and their profits, although he was exceedingly careful to point out the possible contributors to its existence—these including workers and management, consumers, location, and financial and credit agencies. The difficulties of isolating 'superior earnings' in order to capitalise the value of intangibles were also evident in this text, to such an extent that Yang condemned the procedure altogether:[39]

> Such a procedure would tend to destroy the essential purpose of accounting as a barometer of business efficiency.

Instead, he preferred to ignore the possibility of accounting for such 'created' goodwill and other intangibles, and to account for it in accordance with the conservatism which, by that time, was a well established part of accounting practice. Indeed, he advocated the use of a form of realisation:[40]

> The values of intangibles must come through the door of income. Until it is realised through income, an intangible value is usually but an unrealisable, indefinite, and incommensurable potentiality—an estimated earning power.

In a sense he continued this policy of prudence in his analysis and recognition of purchased goodwill—that is, he recommended it be accounted for by treating it as an asset to be written off over its estimated useful lifetime. How the latter was to be estimated was vague and unclear in the text and, as such, provided a clue as to why the problem of accounting for goodwill remains to this day. Nevertheless, the work of Yang is a good example of the advances that were being made in the 1920s in accounting thinking (if not in practice) as a result of the foundations laid down at the turn of the century.

Conclusions

All four texts covered in this review article reveal clearly a relative lack of progress in financial accounting thought and practice over the last one

---

[34]Ibid, p. 486.
[35]See T. A. Lee, 'Company Financial Statements: An Essay in Business History 1830-1950,' in *Business and Businessmen*, S. Marriner, ed., Liverpool University Press, 1978, pp. 235-62.
[36]Yang, *op cit*.
[37]Ibid, p. 21.
[38]Ibid, p. 88.

[39]Ibid, p. 136.
[40]Ibid, p. 139.

hundred years or so. Most of the problems identified by practitioners at the beginning of this period are still problems to the practitioners of today. Accounting is gradually maturing as a profession and a discipline. As such its theory and practice are evolving over the years. On the evidence briefly presented in this review, however, they are also revolving—as if on a spinning wheel. Perhaps this more than any other comment should be of most concern to today's accounting policymakers. For how many of these same problems will remain unresolved at the end of the next one hundred years? Finally, the books reviewed evidence the considerable impact on accounting matters of the leaders of the profession at the turn of century. They provided leadership in both thought and practice, and were obviously the academics of their day. It is therefore tempting to ask where this intellectual leadership is today amongst practitioners for, if it has disappeared, then the future development of accounting must be viewed with some concern.

149

For Product Safety Concerns and Information please contact our EU
representative GPSR@taylorandfrancis.com
Taylor & Francis Verlag GmbH, Kaufingerstraße 24, 80331 München, Germany